A YUMCHA STUDIOS GRA

# DIM SUM WARRIORS™
# 点心侠

## VOLUME 2
## FEAST OF FURY

Created and Written by
**COLIN GOH & YEN YEN WOO**

Illustrated by
**SOO LEE**

Colored by
**MIKE LUCKAS**

YUMCHA STUDIOS
饮茶工作室

This volume contains Dim Sum Warriors
episodes 7 through 11 in their entirety

Story by
Colin Goh & Yen Yen Woo

Illustrations by
Soo Lee

Colors by
Mike Luckas

Lettering by Colin Goh

Cover Illustration by
Colin Goh (pencils), Soo Lee (inks)
& Mike Luckas (colors)

Edited by
Yen Yen Woo & Colin Goh

Published by
Yen Yen Woo

© 2014 Yumcha Studios LLC
Dim Sum Warriors 点心侠 and all characters, their
distinctive likenesses and related indicia are trademarks
of Yumcha Studios LLC. All rights reserved. No
unauthorized reproduction allowed.  The stories,
characters and incidents featured in this publication are
entirely fictional.

Published by
YUMCHA STUDIOS
33-59 Farrington St
2nd Floor
Flushing, NY 11354
www.dimsumwarriors.com
Email: info@dimsumwarriors.com

ISBN-10: 0988189925
ISBN-13: 978-0-9881899-2-8
Printed in Singapore - 1st Printing

# Table of Contents

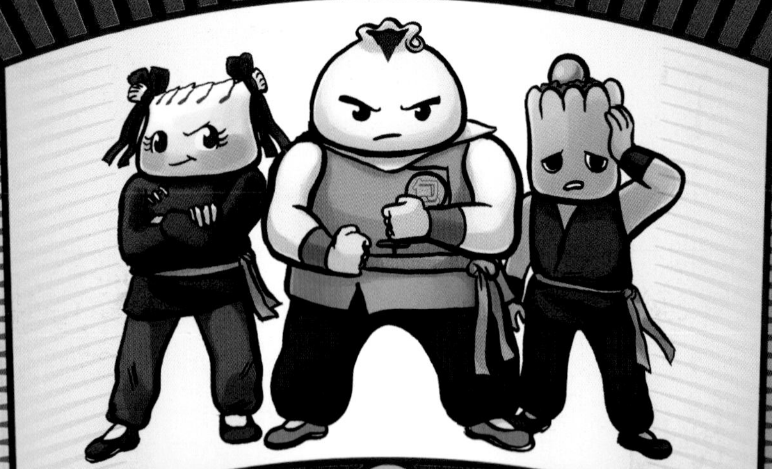

For all our
perfect little dumplings

Creators & Writers
**Colin GOH**
**& Yen Yen WOO**

Pencil & Ink Artwork
**Soo LEE**

Colors
**Mike LUCKAS**

Thumbnails
**Colin GOH**

Cover Art
**Colin GOH, Soo LEE**
**& Mike LUCKAS**

Letters
**Colin GOH**

Graphic Design
**Rory MYERS**

Art Assistant
**Dion SANDY**

Layout
**Christine TSENG**

Martial Arts Consultant
**Suo LIU**

Editors
**Yen Yen WOO**
**& Colin GOH**

Publisher
**Yen Yen WOO**

Printer
**Tien Wah Press**

Inspiration
**Kai Kai**

Inspiration's Nanny
(without whom this
or any work would be
impossible)
**Min LI**

Very Special
Thanks To:
**Our families, Julian Kwek, Desmond Wee, Chade-Meng Tan, Shee Tse Koon, Teo Hiang Long, Steven Lo, Jason Lou, Ferry Djongianto, Edmund Baey, Eddie Ng, Daniel Long, Lieng Seng Wee, Judy Lee, Min Min Jiang, Simon Siah, Rob Salkowitz, Nick Sousanis, Calvin Reid, John Choe, our fabulous community in Flushing in New York City's borough of Queens, and our Kickstarter and non-Kickstarter supporters and friends for believing in the project and everything we do.**

MORE DIM SUM WARRIORS AT WWW.DIMSUMWARRIORS.COM

# MEET THE DIM SUM WARRIORS!

What happens when you mix delicious Chinese delicacies (点心 dim sum, or diǎnxīn) with sensational Chinese martial arts adventures (武侠 wǔxiá)? **YOU GET THE DIĂN XĪN XIÁ OR DIM SUM WARRIORS, OF COURSE!**

## About Dim Sum

The Chinese words 点心 ('diǎn xīn' in Mandarin, and 'dim sum' in Cantonese) literally mean 'a little bit of heart', and refer to a meal consisting mostly of small servings of delicately-crafted morsels, typically accompanied by pots of steaming tea. For more about the long history of dim sum and the different kinds available, visit www.DimSumWarriors.com

| Character | SOME OF OUR FLAVOURFUL FIGHTERS | Inspiration |
|---|---|---|
| 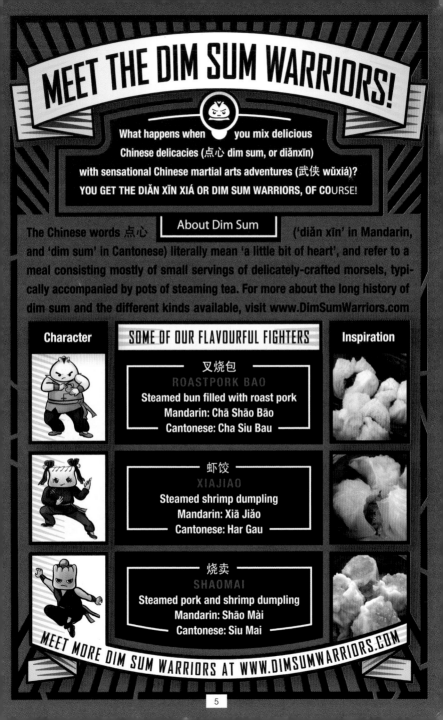 | **叉烧包**<br>ROASTPORK BAO<br>**Steamed bun filled with roast pork**<br>**Mandarin: Chā Shāo Bāo**<br>**Cantonese: Cha Siu Bau** | |
| | **虾饺**<br>XIAJIAO<br>**Steamed shrimp dumpling**<br>**Mandarin: Xiā Jiǎo**<br>**Cantonese: Har Gau** | |
| | **烧卖**<br>SHAOMAI<br>**Steamed pork and shrimp dumpling**<br>**Mandarin: Shāo Mài**<br>**Cantonese: Siu Mai** | |

MEET MORE DIM SUM WARRIORS AT WWW.DIMSUMWARRIORS.COM

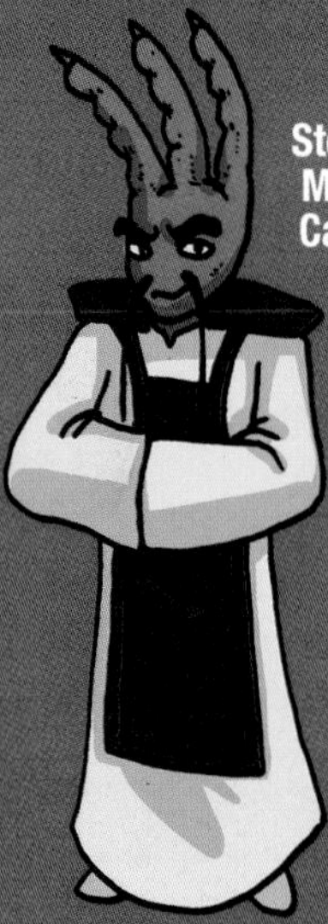

凤爪
**PHOENIX CLAW**
Steamed Chicken Feet
Mandarin: Fèng Zhuǎ
Cantonese: Fung Jow

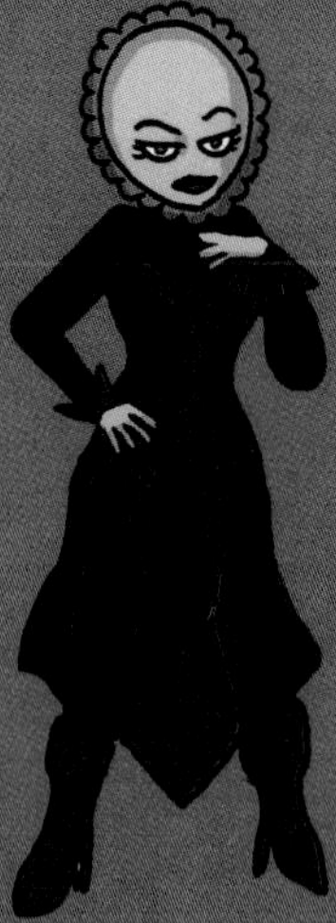

蛋挞
**EGG TART**
Baked Egg Custard Tart
Mandarin: Dàn Ta
Cantonese: Daan Tat

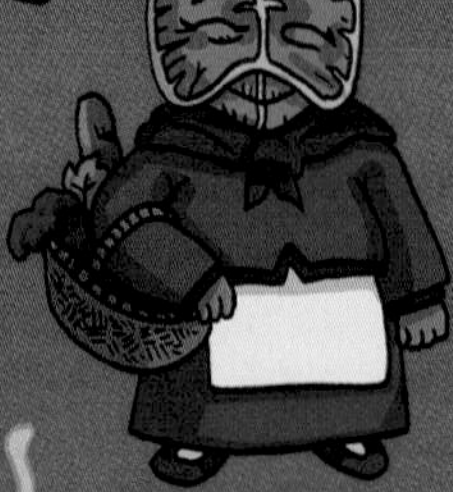

糯米鸡
**LOTUS LEAF STICKY RICE**
Glutinous Rice and Chicken Steamed in Lotus Leaves
Mandarin: Nuò Mǐ Jī
Cantonese: Lo Mai Gai

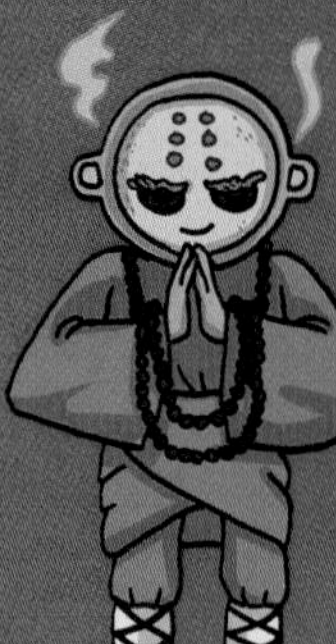

皮蛋粥
**CENTURY EGG CONGEE**
Rice Porridge with Preserved Eggs
Mandarin: Pí Dàn Zhōu
Cantonese: Pei Daan Chok

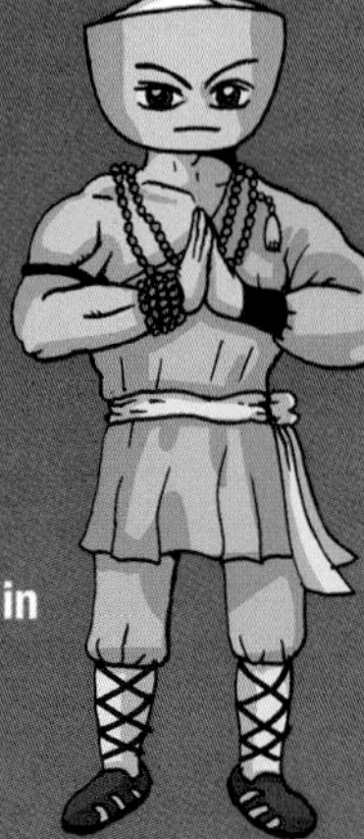

豆花
**SOYBEAN CUSTARD**
Soy Bean Curd Custard in Sweet Ginger Syrup
Mandarin: Dòu Huā
Cantonese: Dau Fu Fa

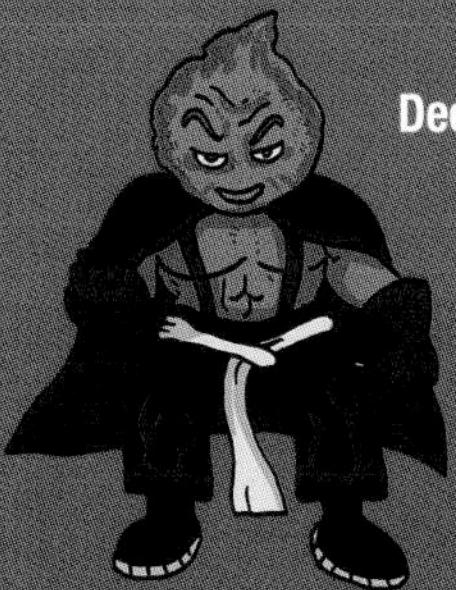

芋角
**TARO BALL**
Deep Fried Taro Dumplings
with Minced Pork
Mandarin: Yù Jiǎo
Cantonese: Woo Kok

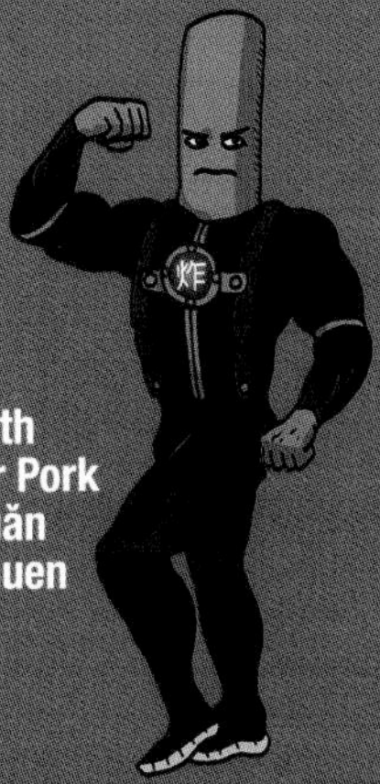
炸

春卷
**SPRING ROLL**
Deep Fried Roll with
Vegetables, Shrimp or Pork
Mandarin: Chūn Juǎn
Cantonese: Chuen Guen

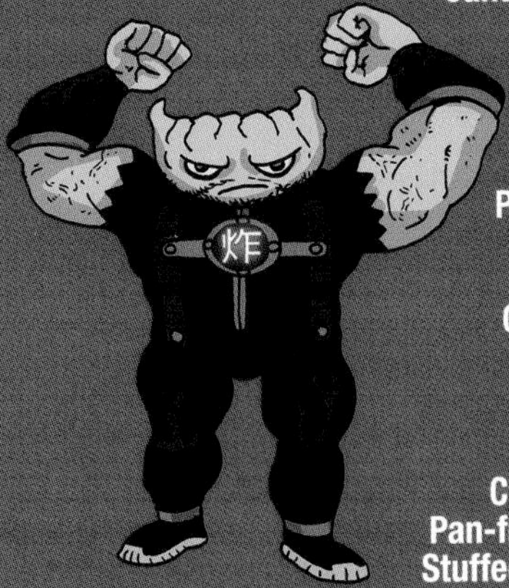
炸

锅贴
**POTSTICKER**
Pan-Fried Dumpling
with Pork
Mandarin: Guō Tiē
Cantonese: Wor Tip

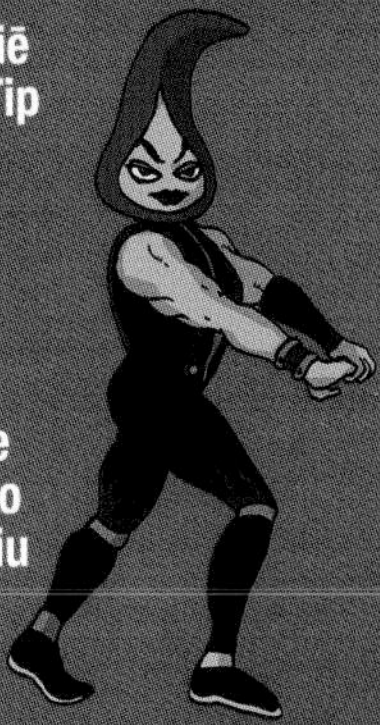

酿辣椒
**CHILI PEPPER**
Pan-fried Chili Pepper
Stuffed with Fish Paste
Mandarin: Niàng Là Jiāo
Cantonese: Yeung Lat Jiu

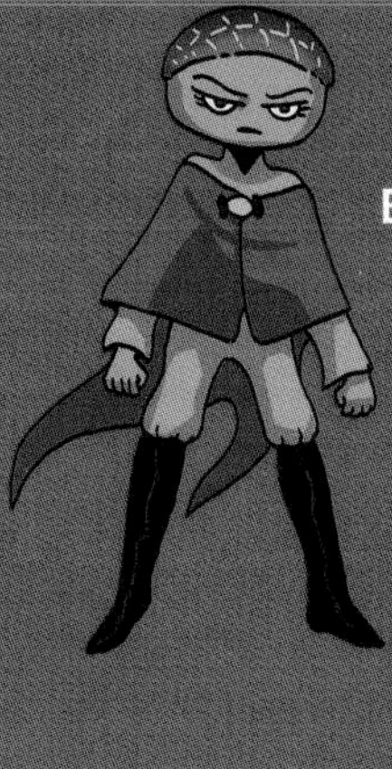

菠蘿包
**BOLUO BUN**
Baked Custard Bun with
a Pineapple-like Crust
Mandarin: Bō Luó Bāo
Cantonese: Bo Lo Bau

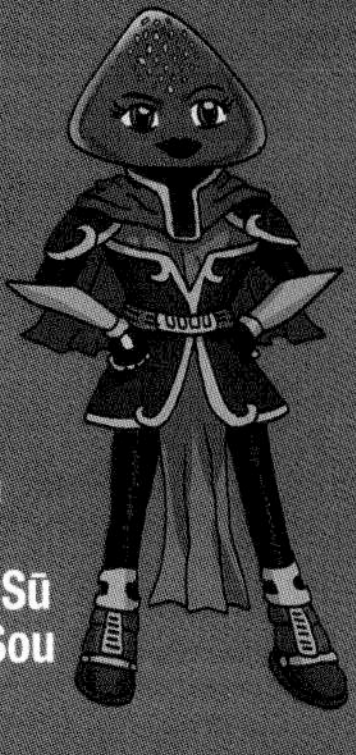

叉烧酥
**PORK PUFF**
Baked Pastry with
Barbecued Pork
Mandarin: Chā Shāo Sū
Cantonese: Cha Siu Sou

# PREVIOUSLY
## in Dim Sum Warriors Vol. 1 - Enter the Dumpling

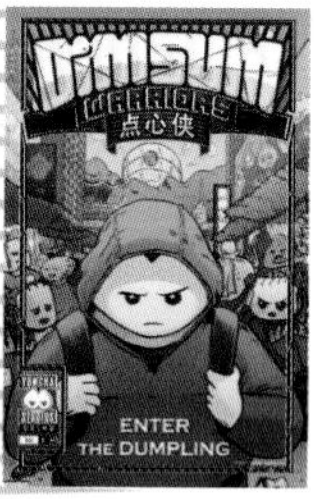
DIM SUM
WARRIORS
点心侠
ENTER
THE DUMPLING

Welcome to Dim Sum City - capital of the Xiaochi Empire, which is ruled by the grumpy Emperor Redbean Bao and the dotty Empress Custard Bao. The Empire is also home to the Dim Sum Warriors, legendary fighters who come from four ancient orders: the Fried Kung Academy, the Baked Kung Sisterhood, the Boiled Kung Temple and the School of Steam Kung.

It hasn't been a good day for the heir to the throne, Prince Roastpork "Porky" Bao. First, while wandering the street market in disguise, he gets into a scrap with two peddlers, Xiajiao and Shaomai.

Then, an innocent family from the nomadic H'otp'ot tribe gets beaten up by the thuggish members of the Fried Kung Academy when they arrive to drag Porky back to the Palace for his mother's birthday party.

Porky is shocked when Xiajiao and Shaomai turn up again at the party - they're actually disciples of the School of Steam Kung, a Dim Sum Warrior institution which has lost its lofty reputation under its current Principal, the slimy Master Phoenix Claw.

Later, a brazen attack on the party by H'otp'ot terrorists is single-handedly foiled by Colonel Quickynoodle, an enigmatic businessman who has gained fame for selling InnerStrength, a magical beverage that instantly gives its drinkers beautiful physiques and great strength. When Porky voices doubts about the Colonel's intentions, Quickynoodle suggests to the Emperor and Empress that they enroll their doughy little boy in the Fried Kung Academy for some toughening up.

Emperor Redbean Bao likes the idea, but doesn't want to seem biased, so he makes all four Dim Sum Warrior schools compete in a tournament for Porky's enrollment. The contest is brutal, with Xiajiao and Shaomai nearly being killed.

After some very rough play, the Fried Kung Academy wins. But before they can welcome their newest disciple, they find that Porky has gone missing... Where can he be?

# CHAPTER 7
# LOST & FOUND

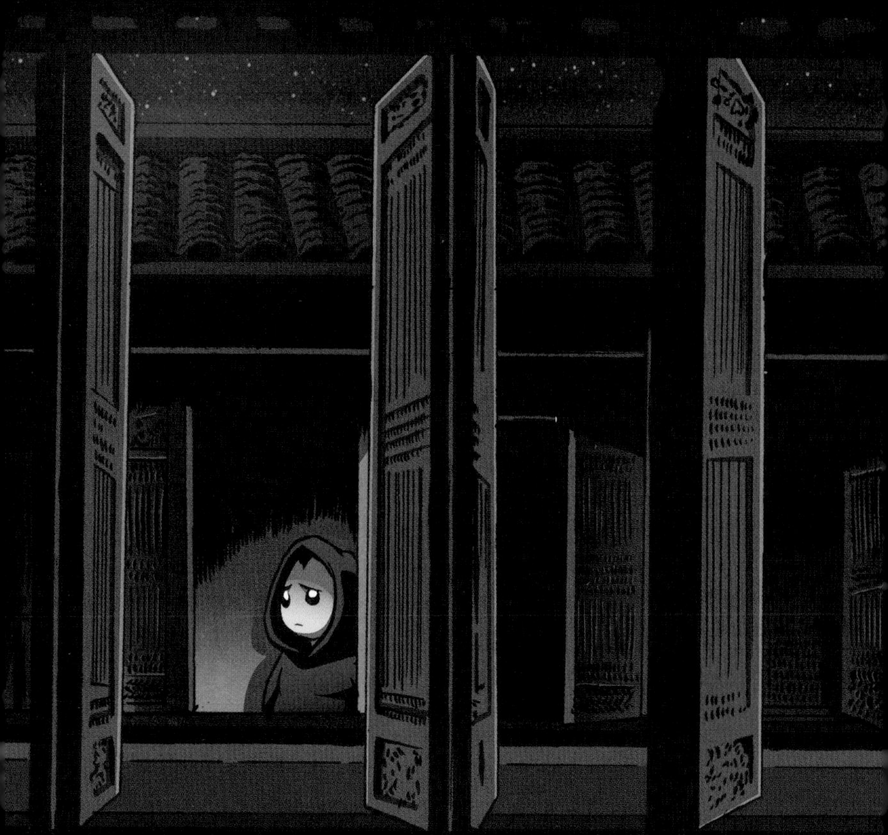

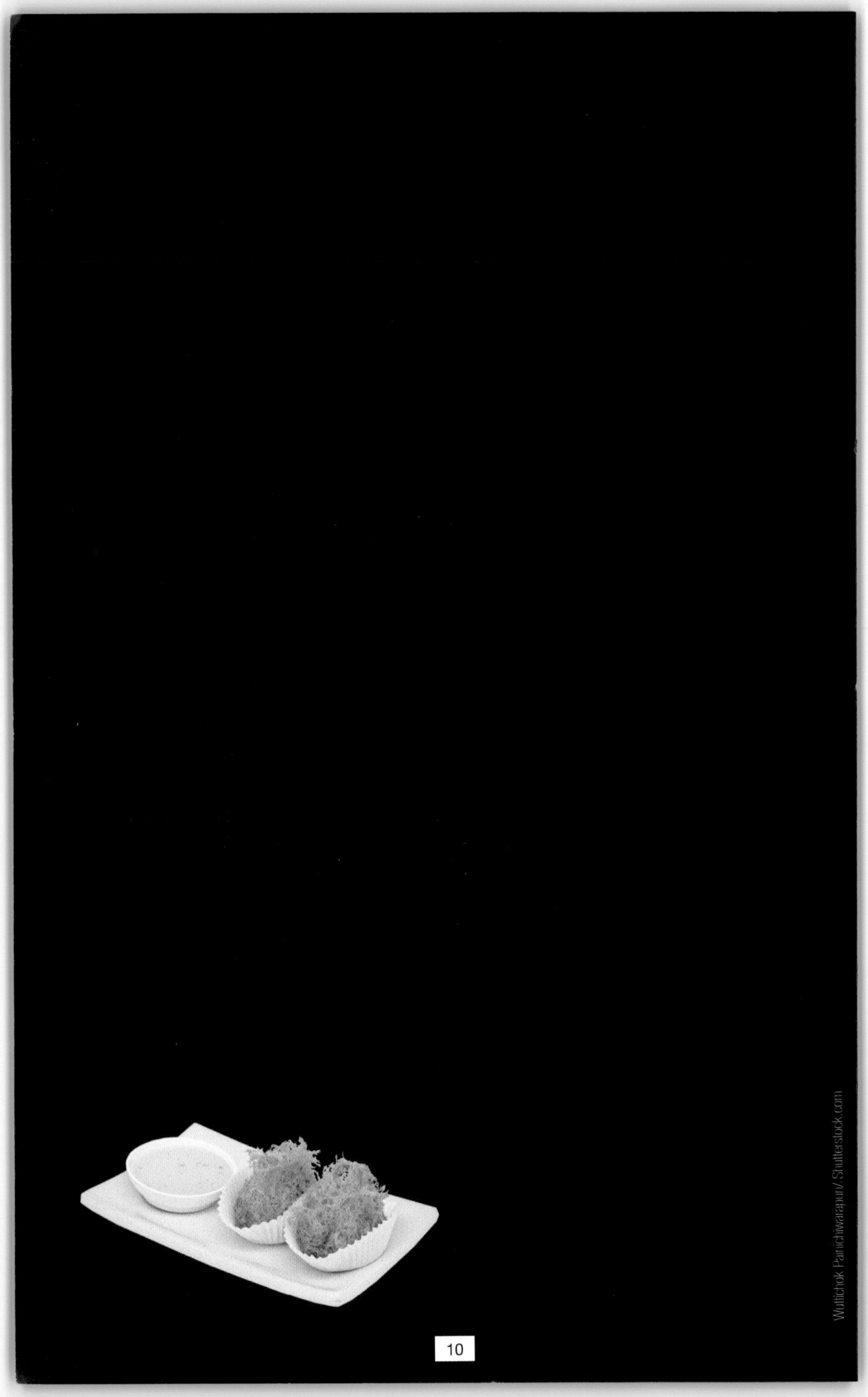

Wuttichok Painichiwarapun/ Shutterstock.com

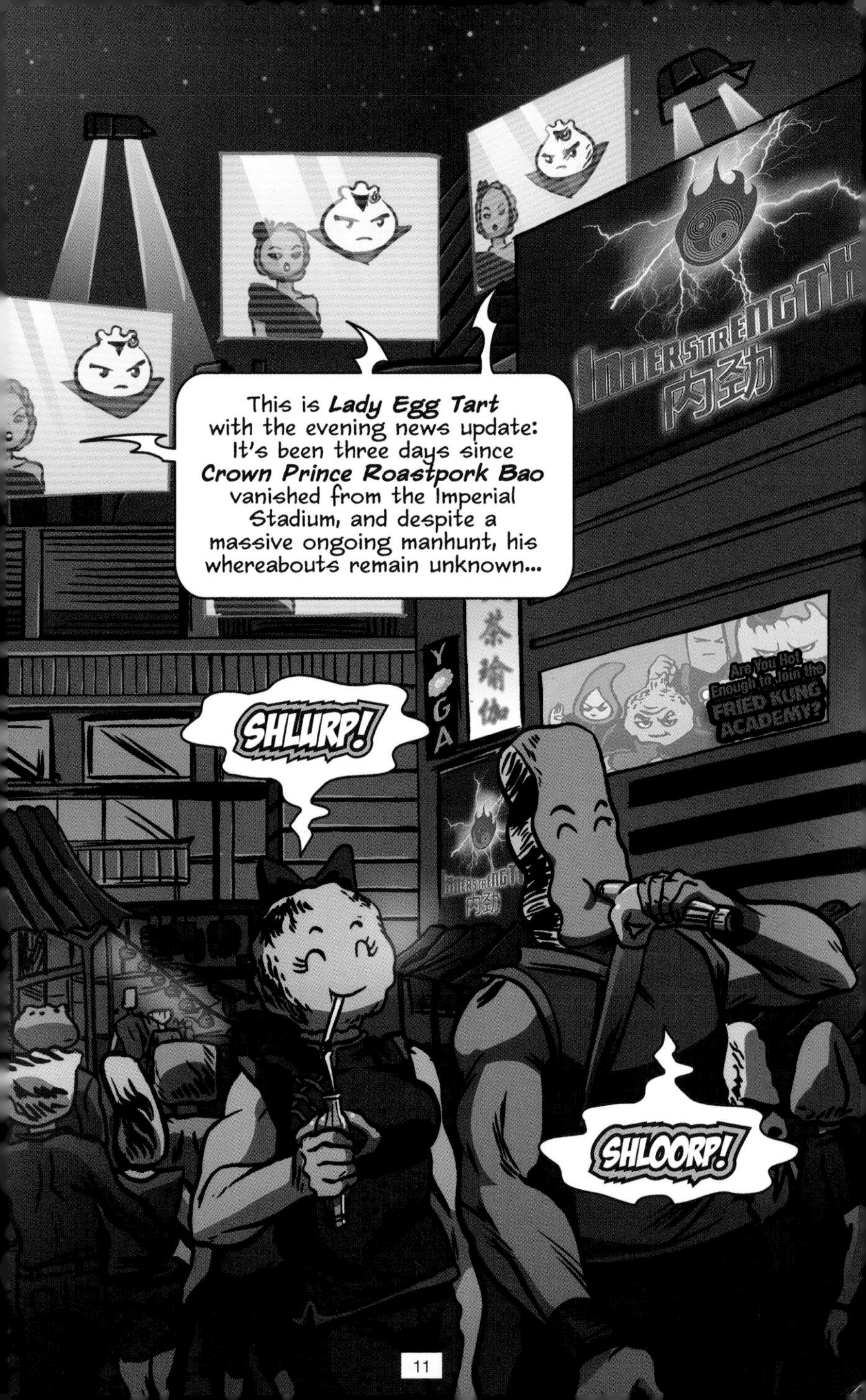
INNERSTRENGTH
内劲
This is *Lady Egg Tart* with the evening news update: It's been three days since **Crown Prince Roastpork Bao** vanished from the Imperial Stadium, and despite a massive ongoing manhunt, his whereabouts remain unknown...
YOGA
茶瑜伽
Are You Hot Enough to Join the FRIED KUNG ACADEMY?
SHLURP!
INNERSTRENGTH
内劲
SHLOORP!

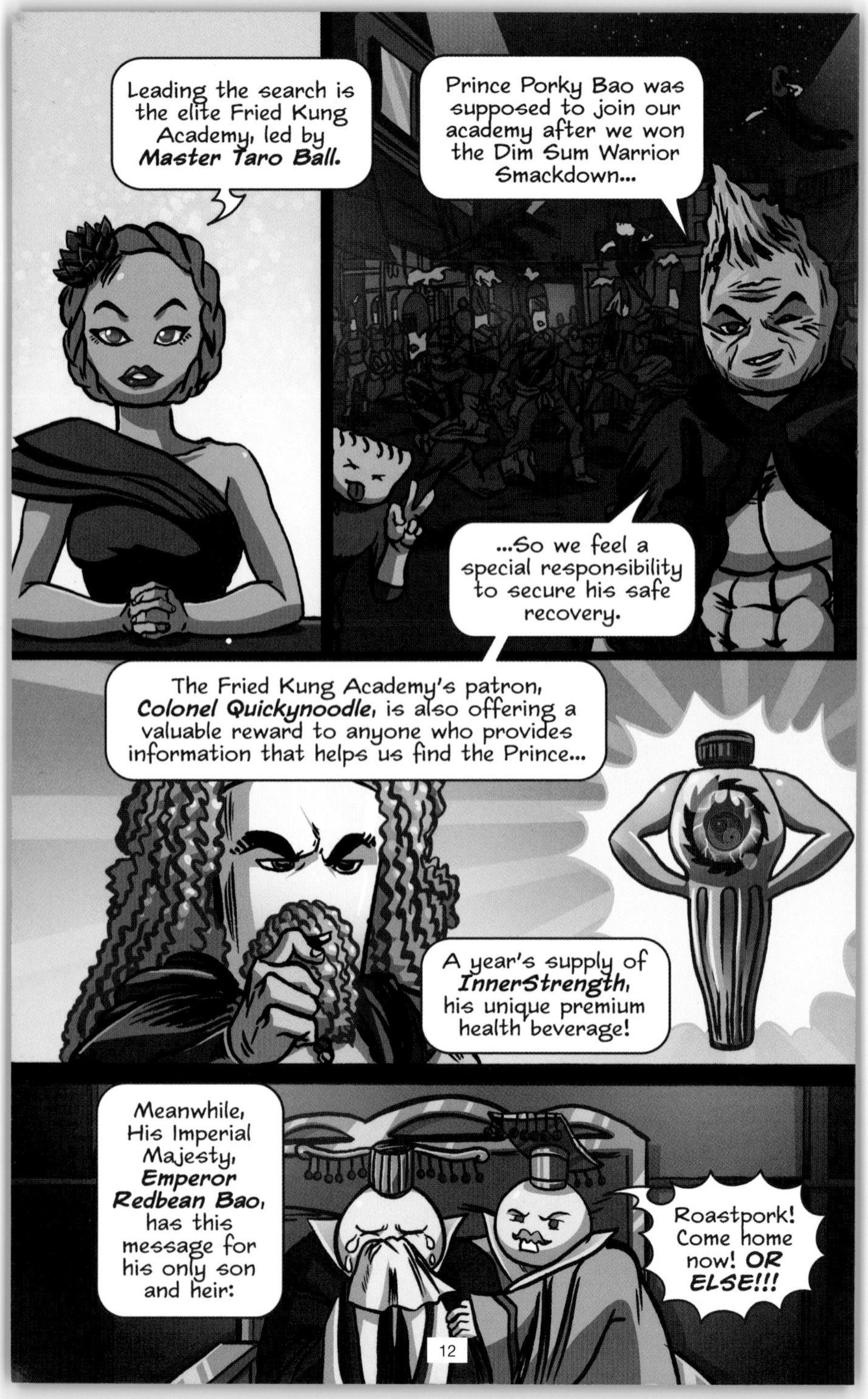
Leading the search is the elite Fried Kung Academy, led by **Master Taro Ball.**
Prince Porky Bao was supposed to join our academy after we won the Dim Sum Warrior Smackdown...
...So we feel a special responsibility to secure his safe recovery.
The Fried Kung Academy's patron, **Colonel Quickynoodle**, is also offering a valuable reward to anyone who provides information that helps us find the Prince...
A year's supply of **InnerStrength**, his unique premium health beverage!
Meanwhile, His Imperial Majesty, **Emperor Redbean Bao**, has this message for his only son and heir:
Roastpork! Come home now! **OR ELSE!!!**

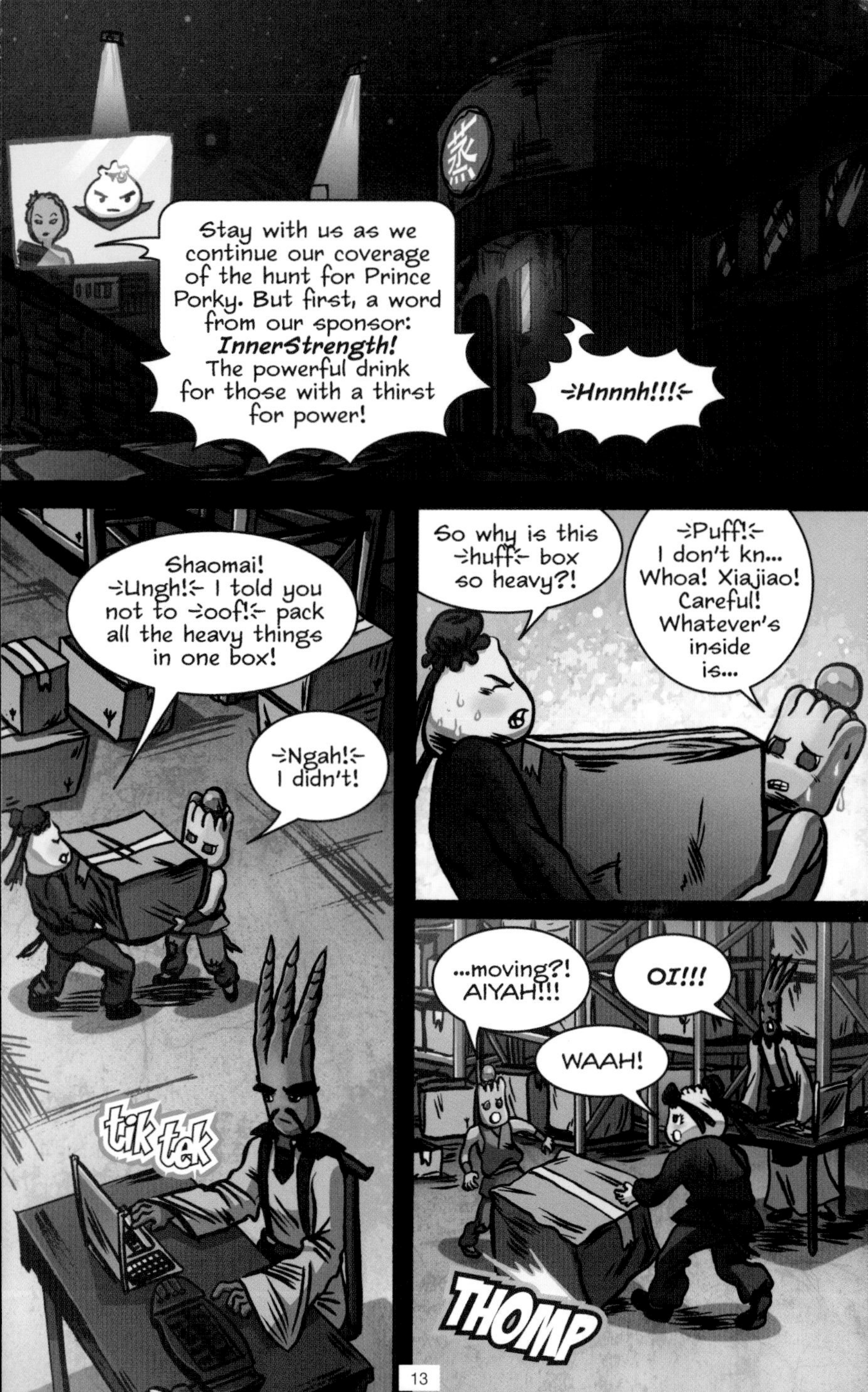

Stay with us as we continue our coverage of the hunt for Prince Porky. But first, a word from our sponsor: *InnerStrength!* The powerful drink for those with a thirst for power!
⇛*Hnnnh!!!*⇚
Shaomai! ⇛Ungh!⇚ I told you not to ⇛oof!⇚ pack all the heavy things in one box!
⇛Ngah!⇚ I didn't!
tik tek
So why is this ⇛huff⇚ box so heavy?!
⇛Puff!⇚ I don't kn... Whoa! Xiajiao! Careful! Whatever's inside is...
...moving?! AIYAH!!!
OI!!!
WAAH!
THOMP

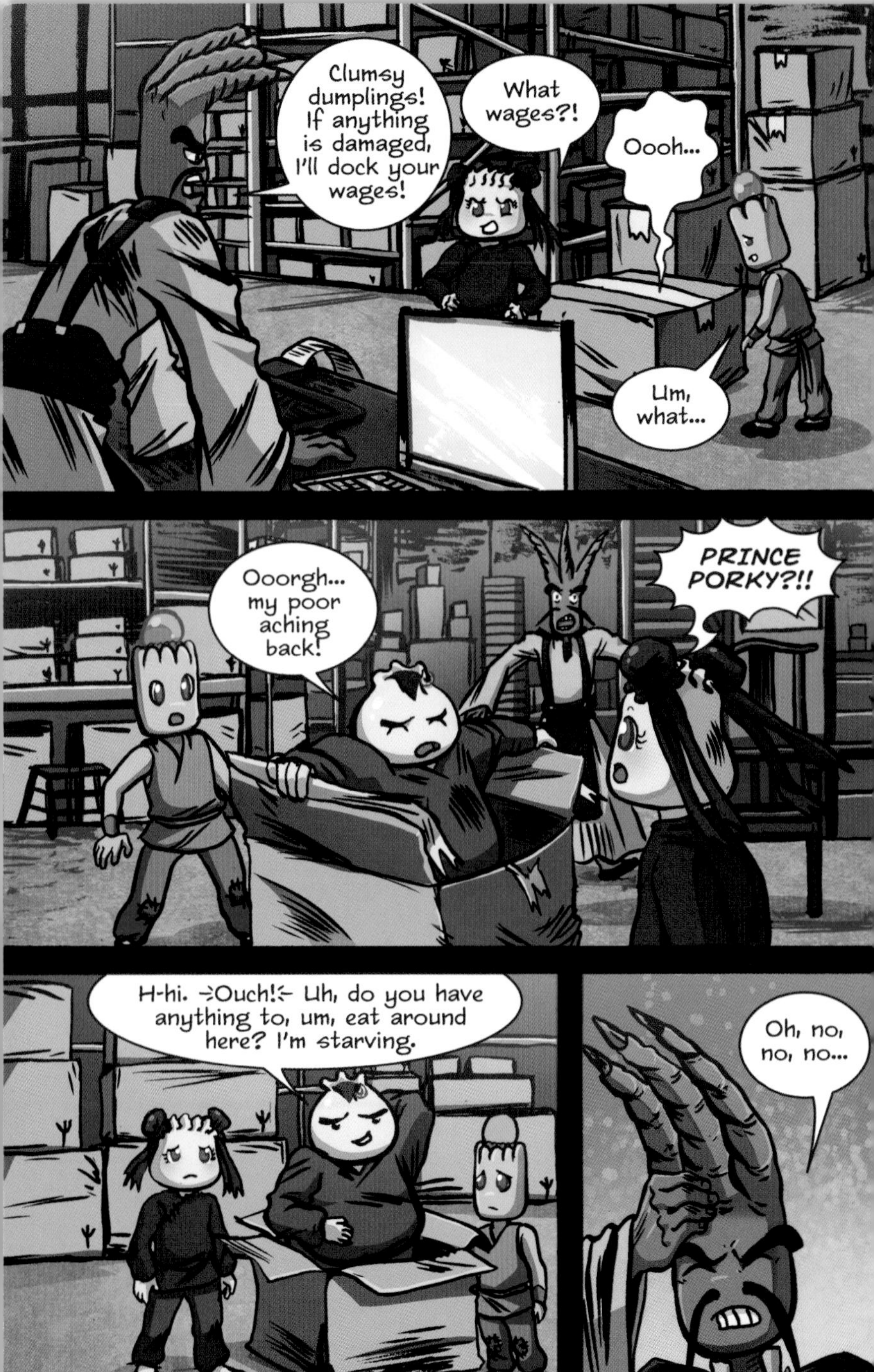
Clumsy dumplings! If anything is damaged, I'll dock your wages!
What wages?!
Oooh...
Um, what...
Ooorgh... my poor aching back!
PRINCE PORKY?!!
H-hi. ⇒Ouch!⇐ Uh, do you have anything to, um, eat around here? I'm starving.
Oh, no, no, no...

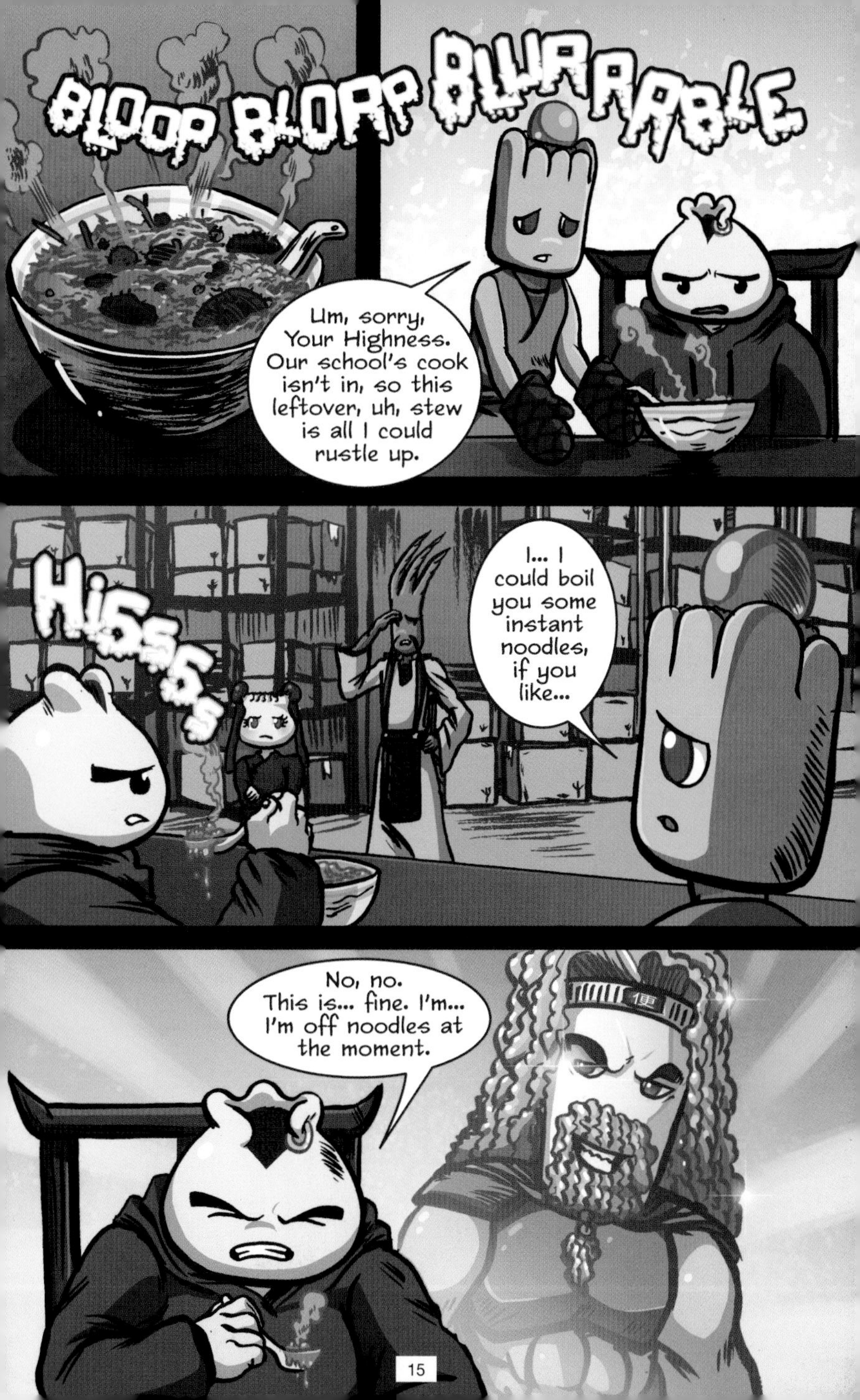
BLOOP BLORP BLURRRBLE
Um, sorry, Your Highness. Our school's cook isn't in, so this leftover, uh, stew is all I could rustle up.
HISSSSS
I... I could boil you some instant noodles, if you like...
No, no. This is... fine. I'm... I'm off noodles at the moment.

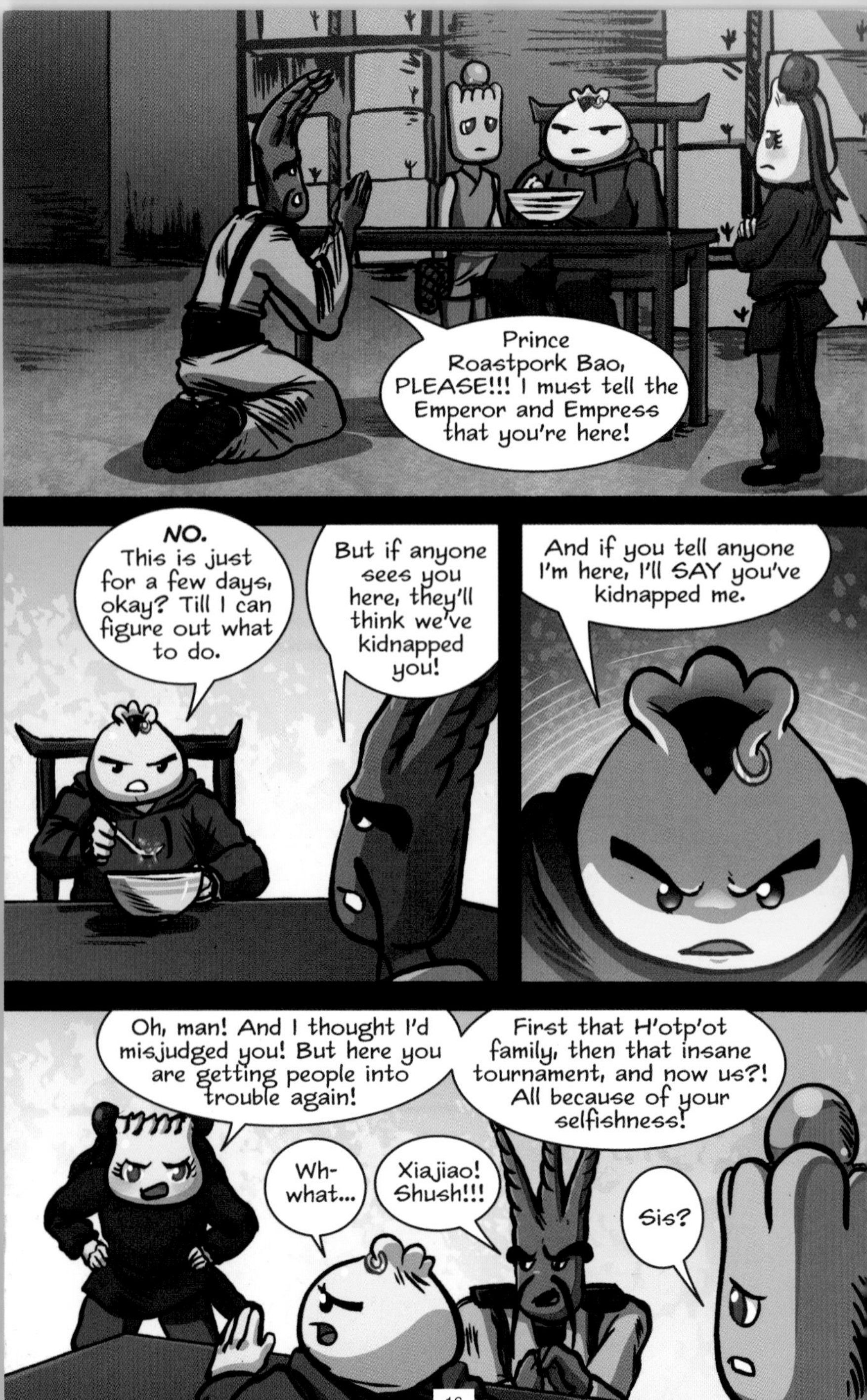

Prince Roastpork Bao, PLEASE!!! I must tell the Emperor and Empress that you're here!
NO. This is just for a few days, okay? Till I can figure out what to do.
But if anyone sees you here, they'll think we've kidnapped you!
And if you tell anyone I'm here, I'll SAY you've kidnapped me.
Oh, man! And I thought I'd misjudged you! But here you are getting people into trouble again!
First that H'otp'ot family, then that insane tournament, and now us?! All because of your selfishness!
Wh- what...
Xiajiao! Shush!!!
Sis?

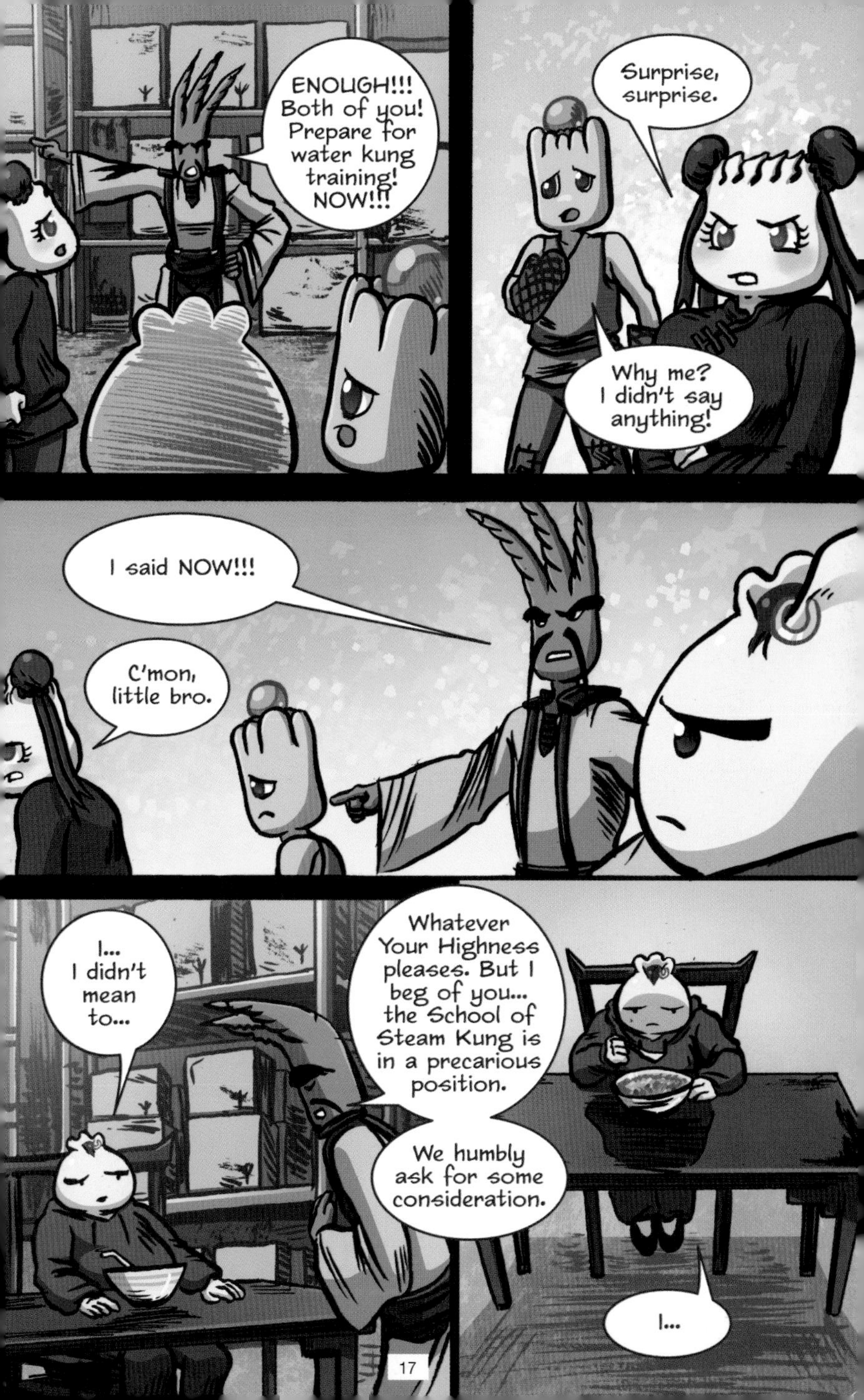
ENOUGH!!! Both of you! Prepare for water kung training! NOW!!!
Surprise, surprise.
Why me? I didn't say anything!
I said NOW!!!
C'mon, little bro.
I... I didn't mean to...
Whatever Your Highness pleases. But I beg of you... the School of Steam Kung is in a precarious position.
We humbly ask for some consideration.
I...

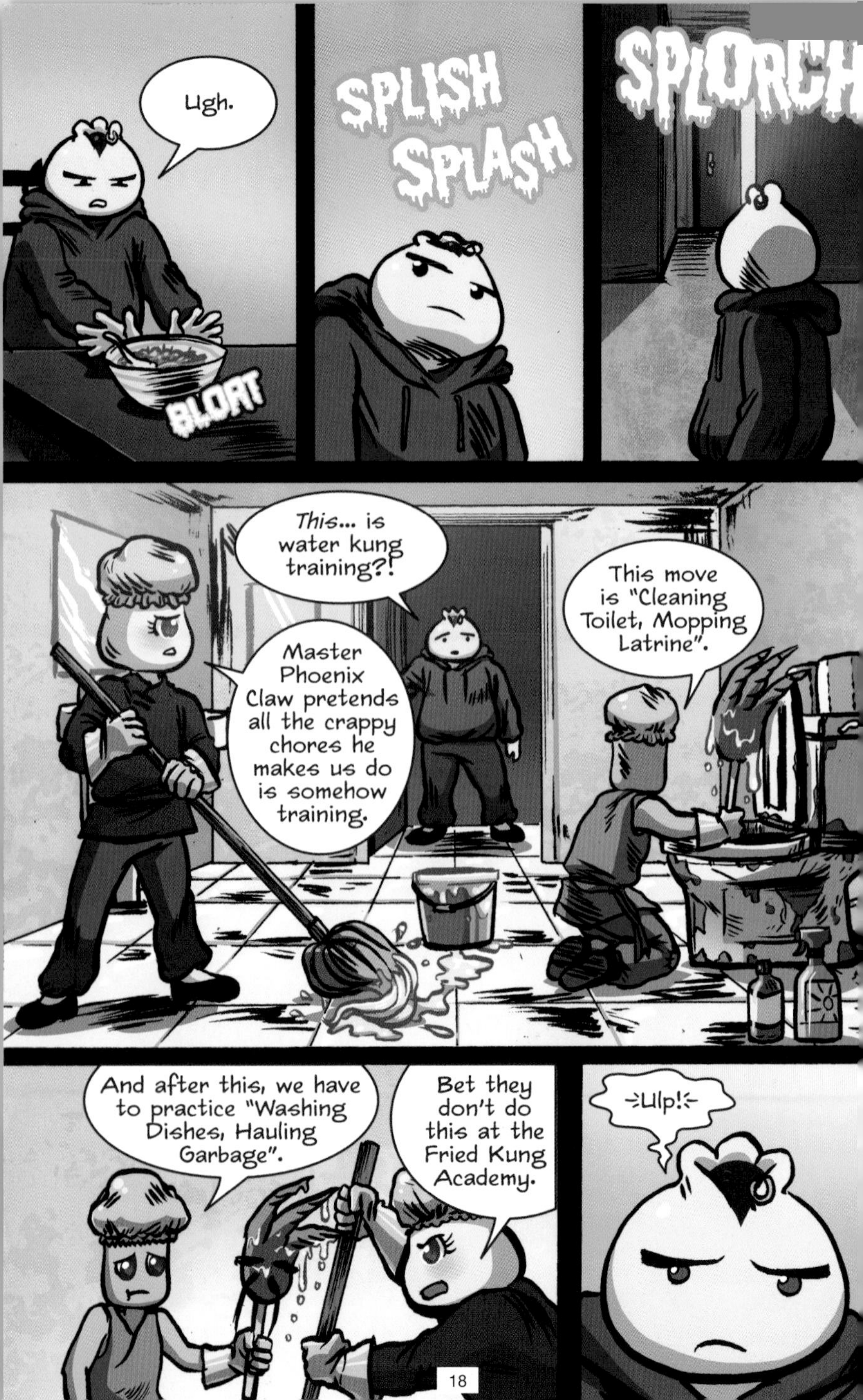
Ugh.
BLORT
SPLISH SPLASH
SPLORCH
This... is water kung training?!
Master Phoenix Claw pretends all the crappy chores he makes us do is somehow training.
This move is "Cleaning Toilet, Mopping Latrine".
And after this, we have to practice "Washing Dishes, Hauling Garbage".
Bet they don't do this at the Fried Kung Academy.
Ulp!

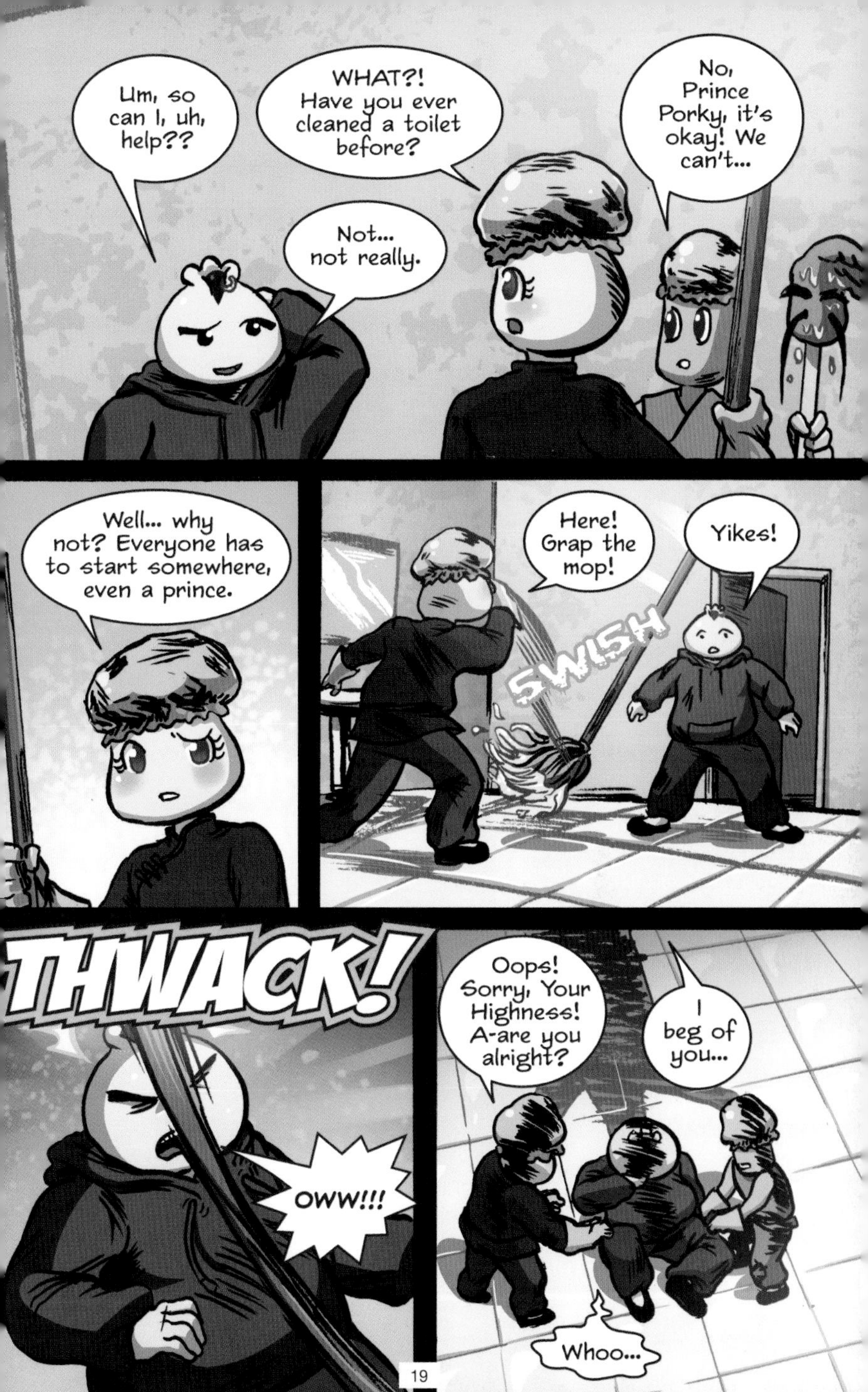

Um, so can I, uh, help??
WHAT?! Have you ever cleaned a toilet before?
Not... not really.
No, Prince Porky, it's okay! We can't...
Well... why not? Everyone has to start somewhere, even a prince.
Here! Grap the mop!
Yikes!
SWISH
THWACK!
OWW!!!
Oops! Sorry, Your Highness! A-are you alright?
I beg of you...
Whoo...

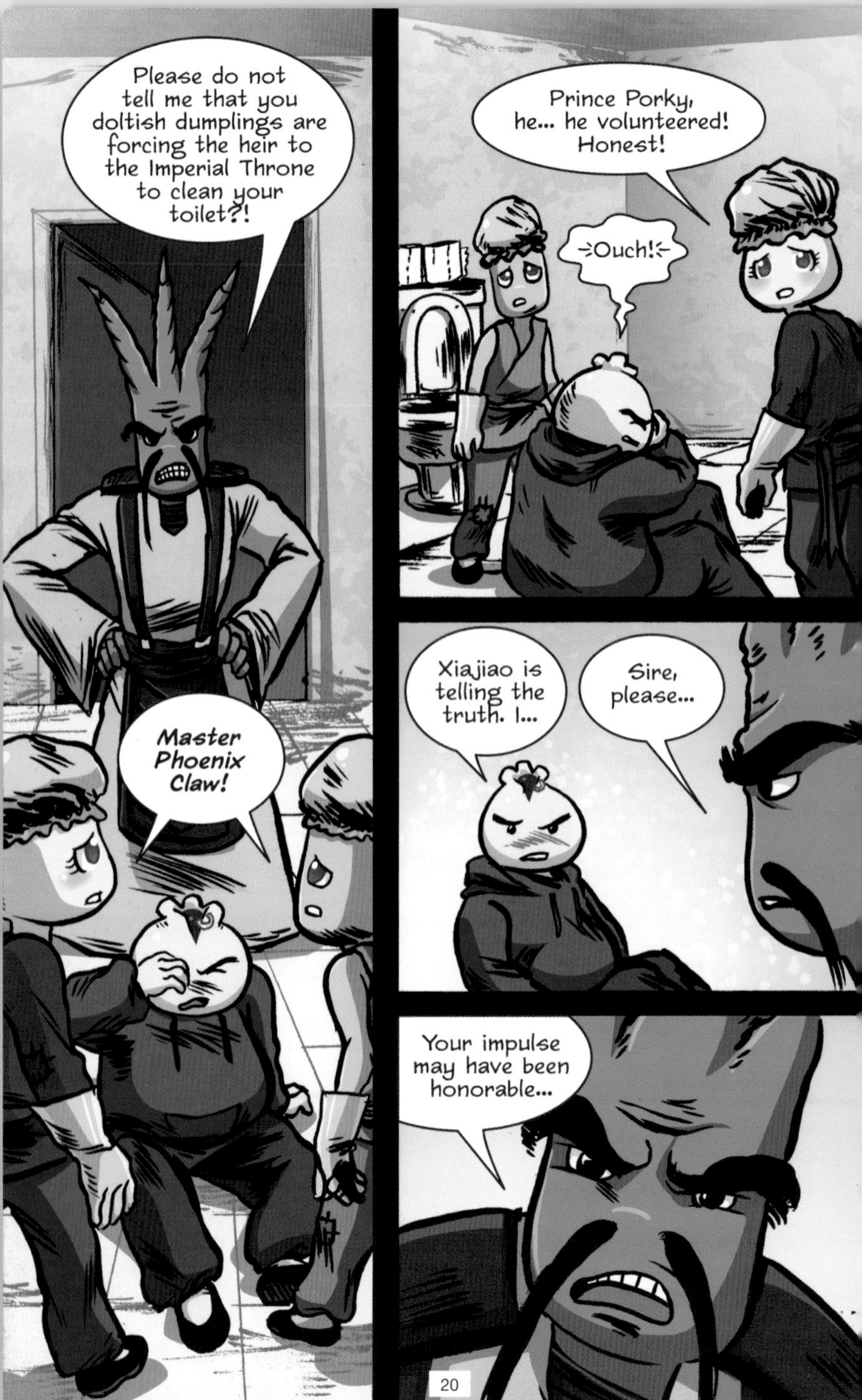
Please do not tell me that you doltish dumplings are forcing the heir to the Imperial Throne to clean your toilet?!
Master Phoenix Claw!
Prince Porky, he... he volunteered! Honest!
Ouch!
Xiajiao is telling the truth. I...
Sire, please...
Your impulse may have been honorable...

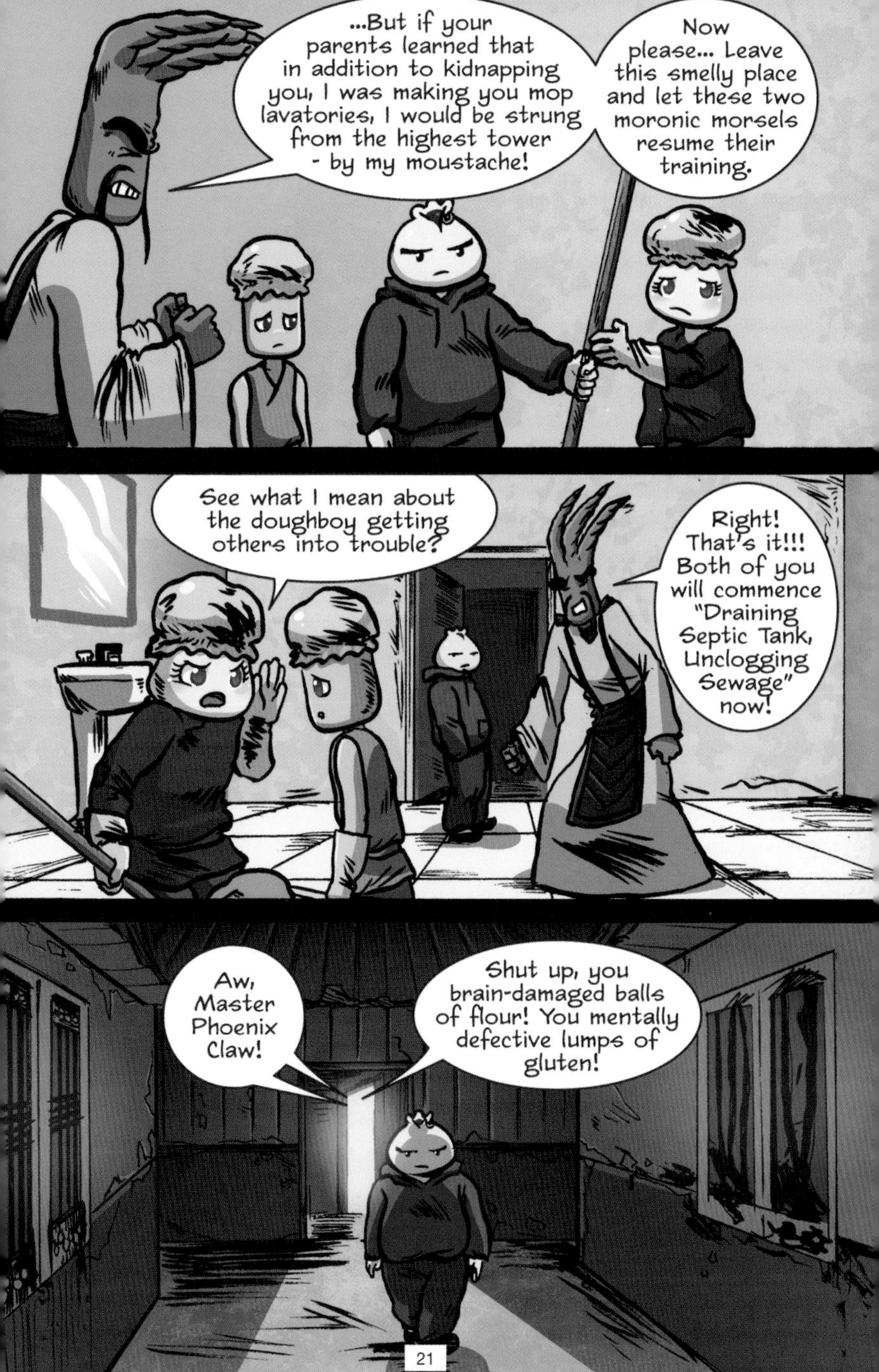
...But if your parents learned that in addition to kidnapping you, I was making you mop lavatories, I would be strung from the highest tower - by my moustache!
Now please... Leave this smelly place and let these two moronic morsels resume their training.
See what I mean about the doughboy getting others into trouble?
Right! That's it!!! Both of you will commence "Draining Septic Tank, Unclogging Sewage" now!
Aw, Master Phoenix Claw!
Shut up, you brain-damaged balls of flour! You mentally defective lumps of gluten!

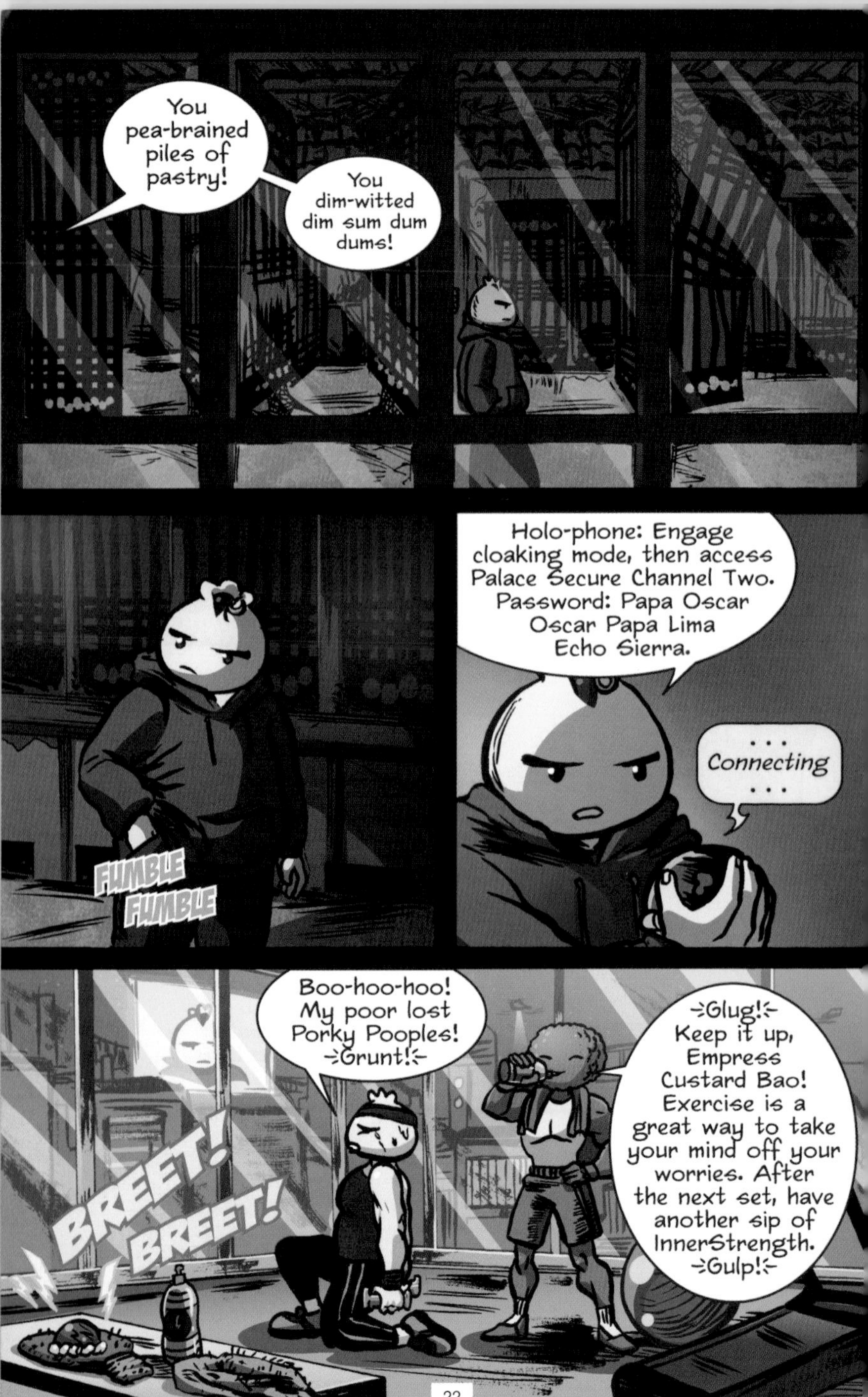
You pea-brained piles of pastry!
You dim-witted dim sum dum dums!
FUMBLE FUMBLE
Holo-phone: Engage cloaking mode, then access Palace Secure Channel Two. Password: Papa Oscar Oscar Papa Lima Echo Sierra.
... Connecting ...
Boo-hoo-hoo! My poor lost Porky Pooples! Grunt!
Glug! Keep it up, Empress Custard Bao! Exercise is a great way to take your mind off your worries. After the next set, have another sip of InnerStrength. Gulp!
BREET! BREET!

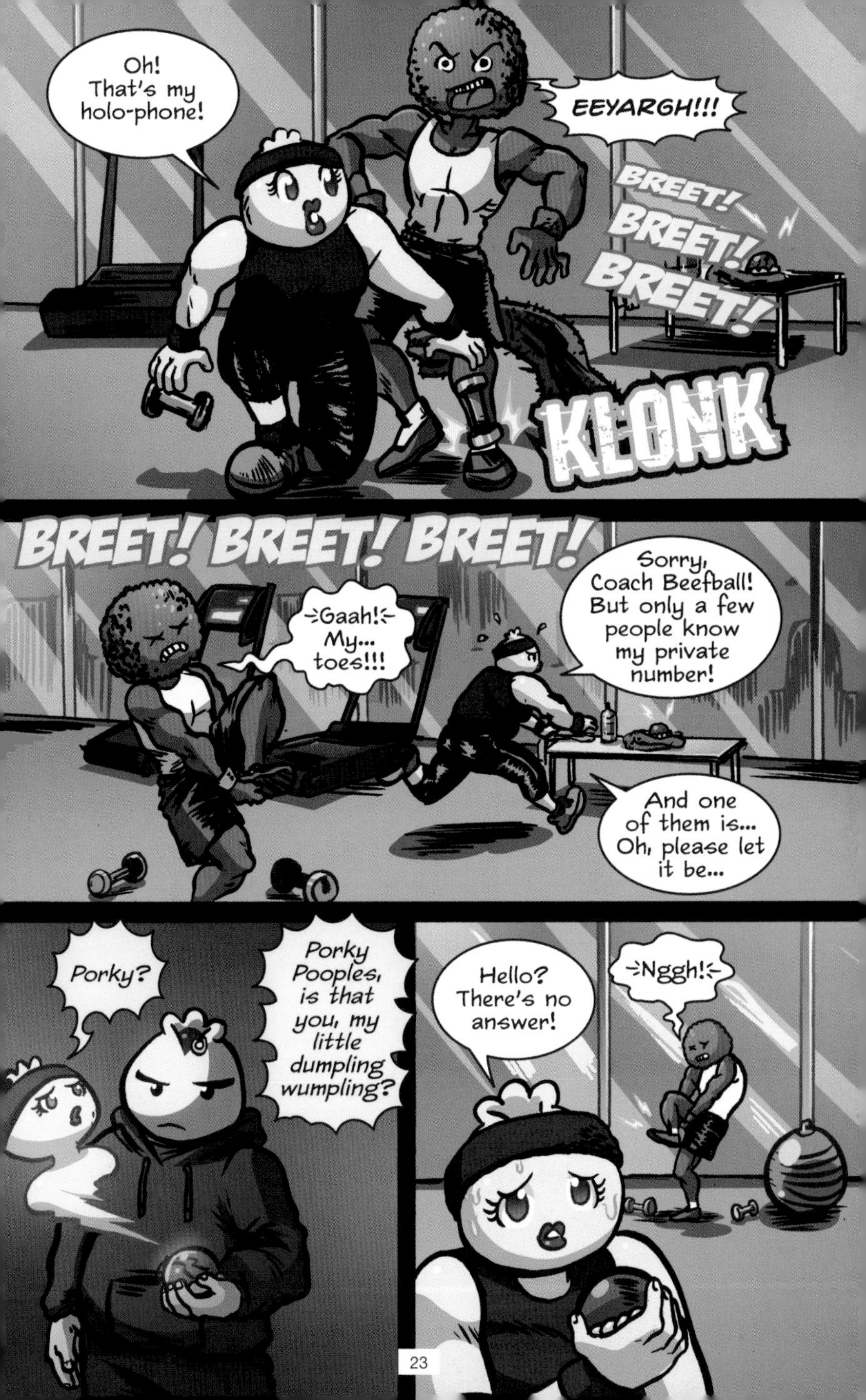

Oh! That's my holo-phone!
EEYARGH!!!
BREET! BREET! BREET!
KLONK
BREET! BREET! BREET!
Gaah! My... toes!!!
Sorry, Coach Beefball! But only a few people know my private number!
And one of them is... Oh, please let it be...
Porky?
Porky Pooples, is that you, my little dumpling wumpling?
Hello? There's no answer!
Nggh!

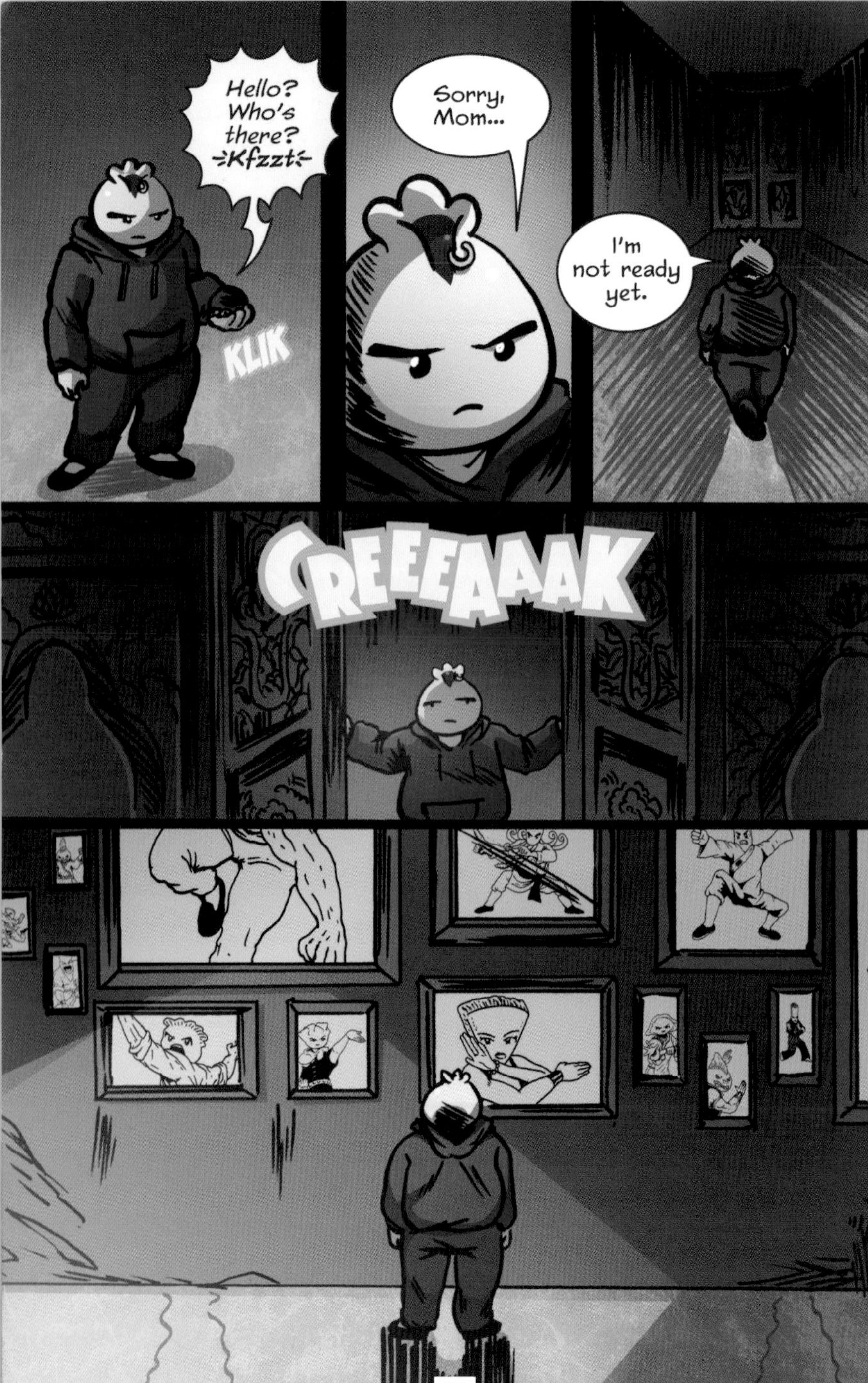
Hello? Who's there? -Kfzzt-
KLIK
Sorry, Mom...
I'm not ready yet.
CREEEAAAK

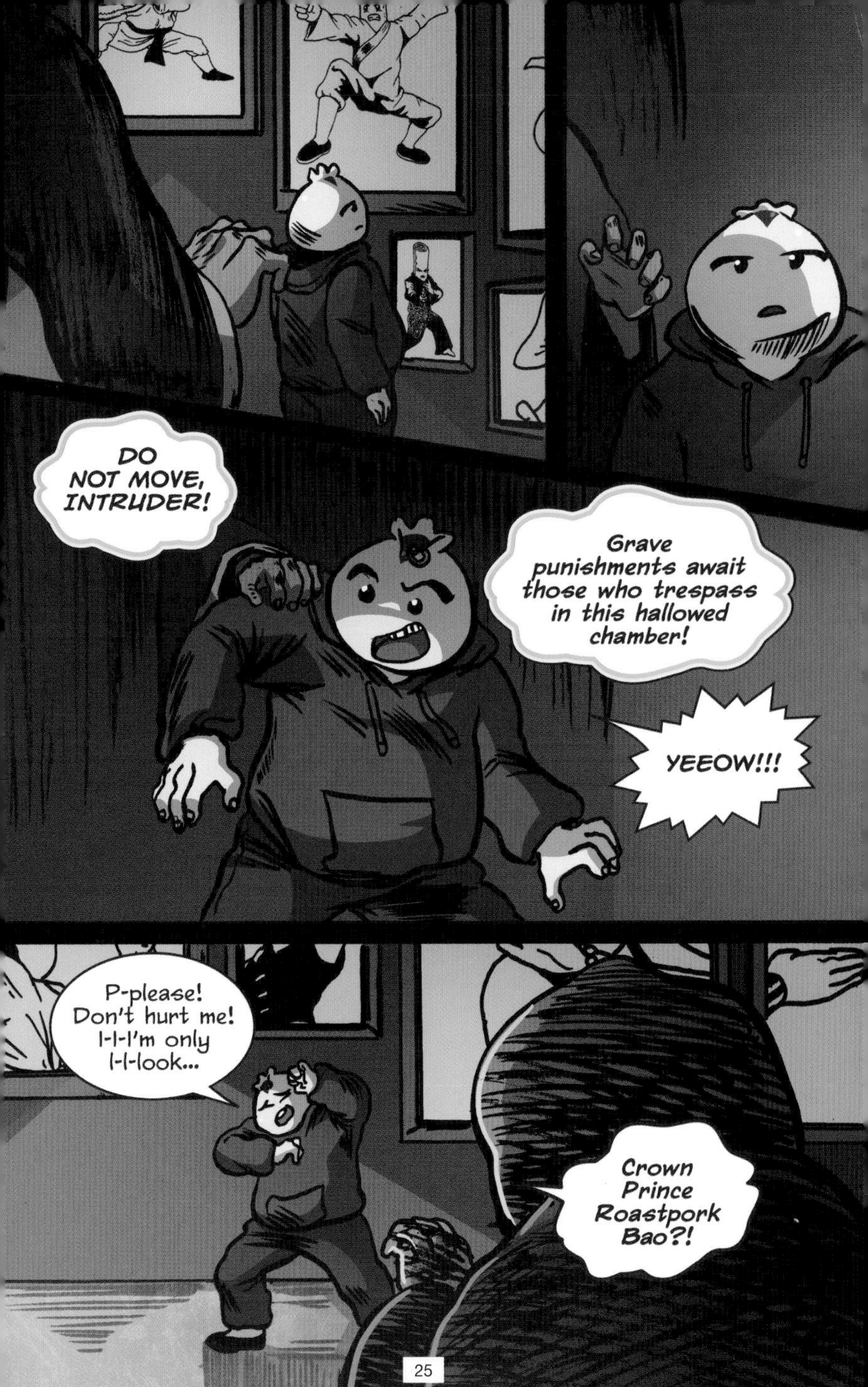
DO NOT MOVE, INTRUDER!
Grave punishments await those who trespass in this hallowed chamber!
YEEOW!!!
P-please! Don't hurt me! I-I-I'm only l-l-look...
Crown Prince Roastpork Bao?!

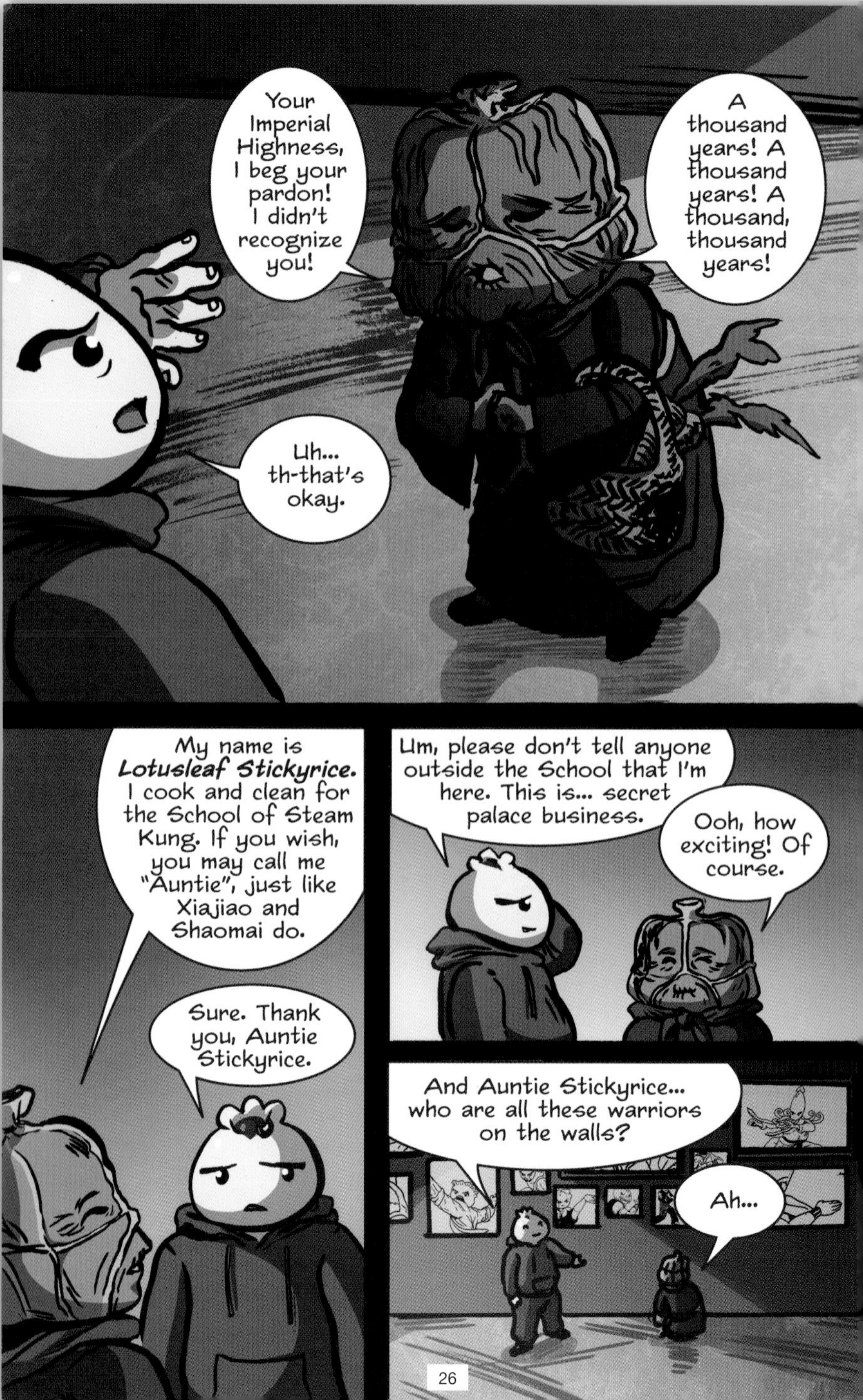
Your Imperial Highness, I beg your pardon! I didn't recognize you!
A thousand years! A thousand years! A thousand, thousand years!
Uh... th-that's okay.
My name is **Lotusleaf Stickyrice.** I cook and clean for the School of Steam Kung. If you wish, you may call me "Auntie", just like Xiajiao and Shaomai do.
Sure. Thank you, Auntie Stickyrice.
Um, please don't tell anyone outside the School that I'm here. This is... secret palace business.
Ooh, how exciting! Of course.
And Auntie Stickyrice... who are all these warriors on the walls?
Ah...

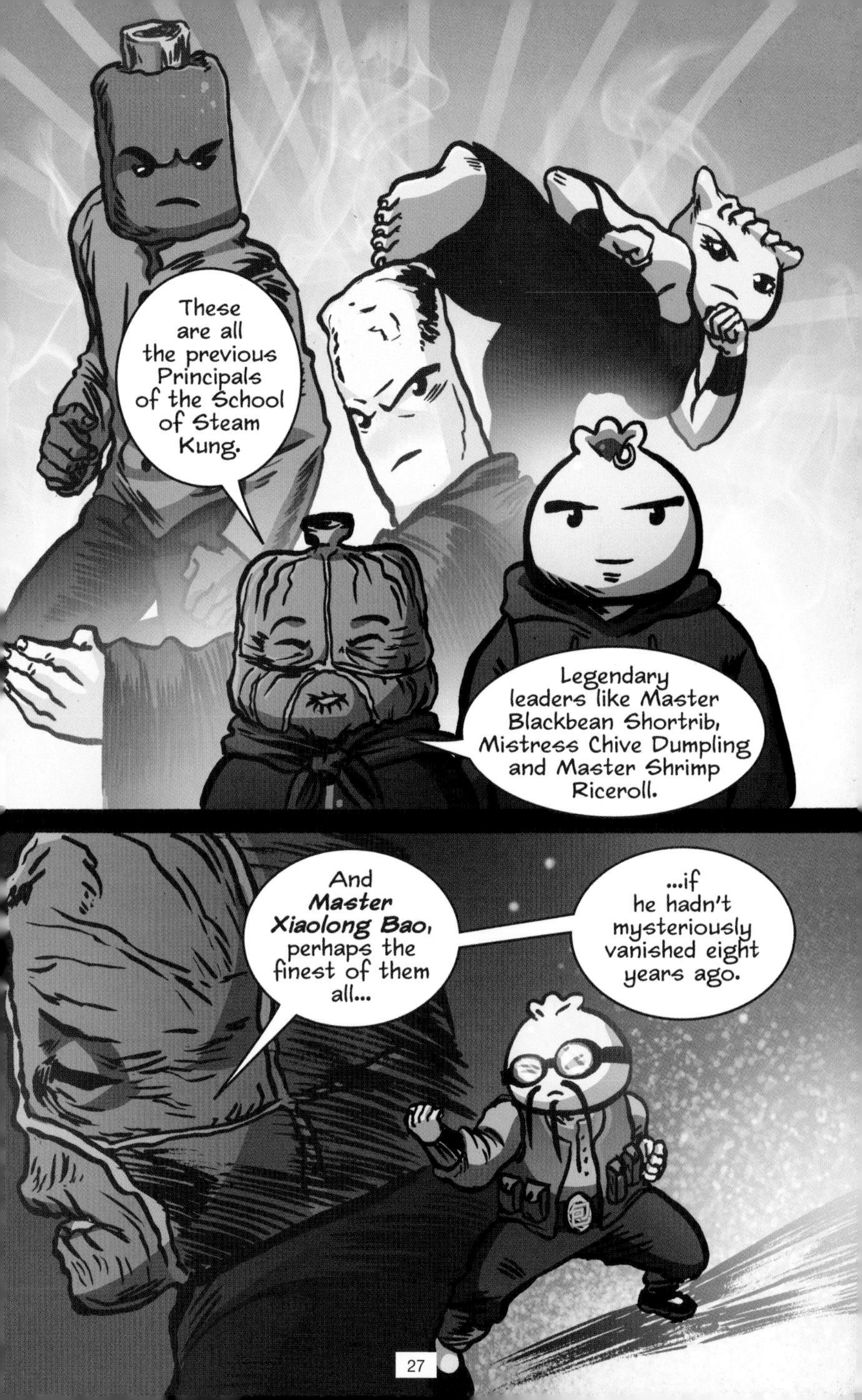
These are all the previous Principals of the School of Steam Kung.
Legendary leaders like Master Blackbean Shortrib, Mistress Chive Dumpling and Master Shrimp Riceroll.
And **Master Xiaolong Bao**, perhaps the finest of them all...
...if he hadn't mysteriously vanished eight years ago.

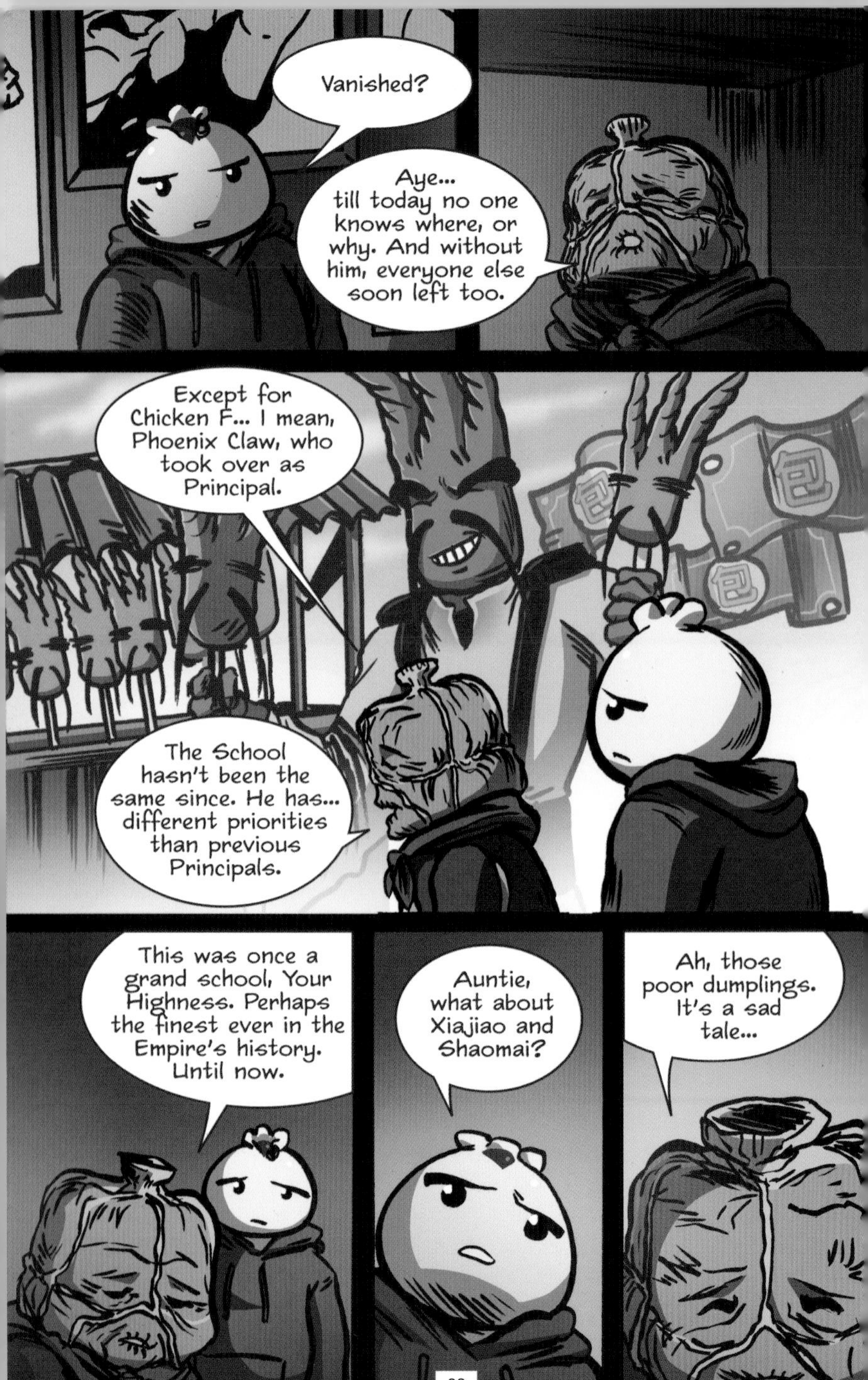
Vanished?
Aye... till today no one knows where, or why. And without him, everyone else soon left too.
Except for Chicken F... I mean, Phoenix Claw, who took over as Principal.
The School hasn't been the same since. He has... different priorities than previous Principals.
This was once a grand school, Your Highness. Perhaps the finest ever in the Empire's history. Until now.
Auntie, what about Xiajiao and Shaomai?
Ah, those poor dumplings. It's a sad tale...

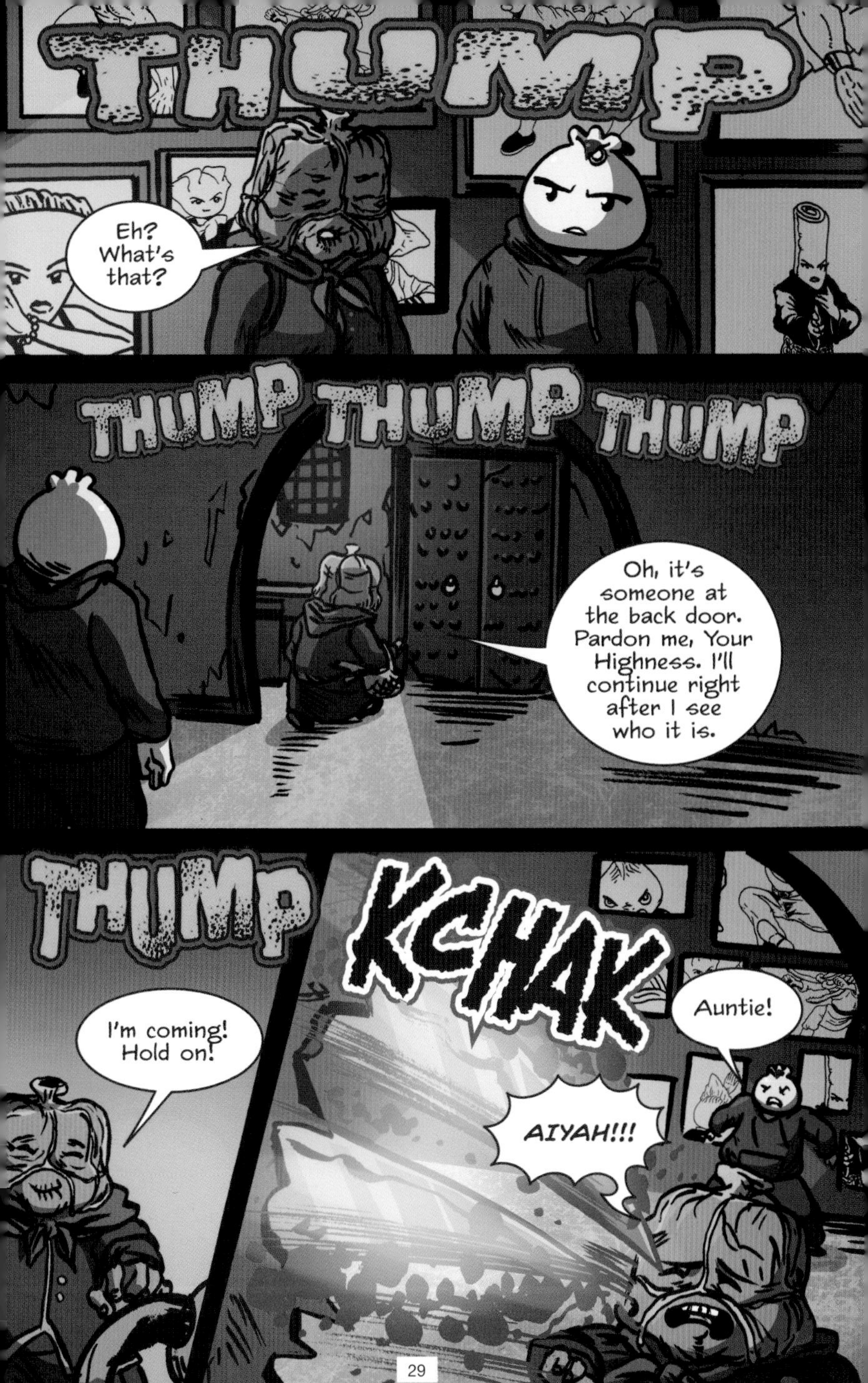
THUMP
Eh? What's that?
THUMP THUMP THUMP
Oh, it's someone at the back door. Pardon me, Your Highness. I'll continue right after I see who it is.
THUMP
I'm coming! Hold on!
KCHAK
Auntie!
AIYAH!!!

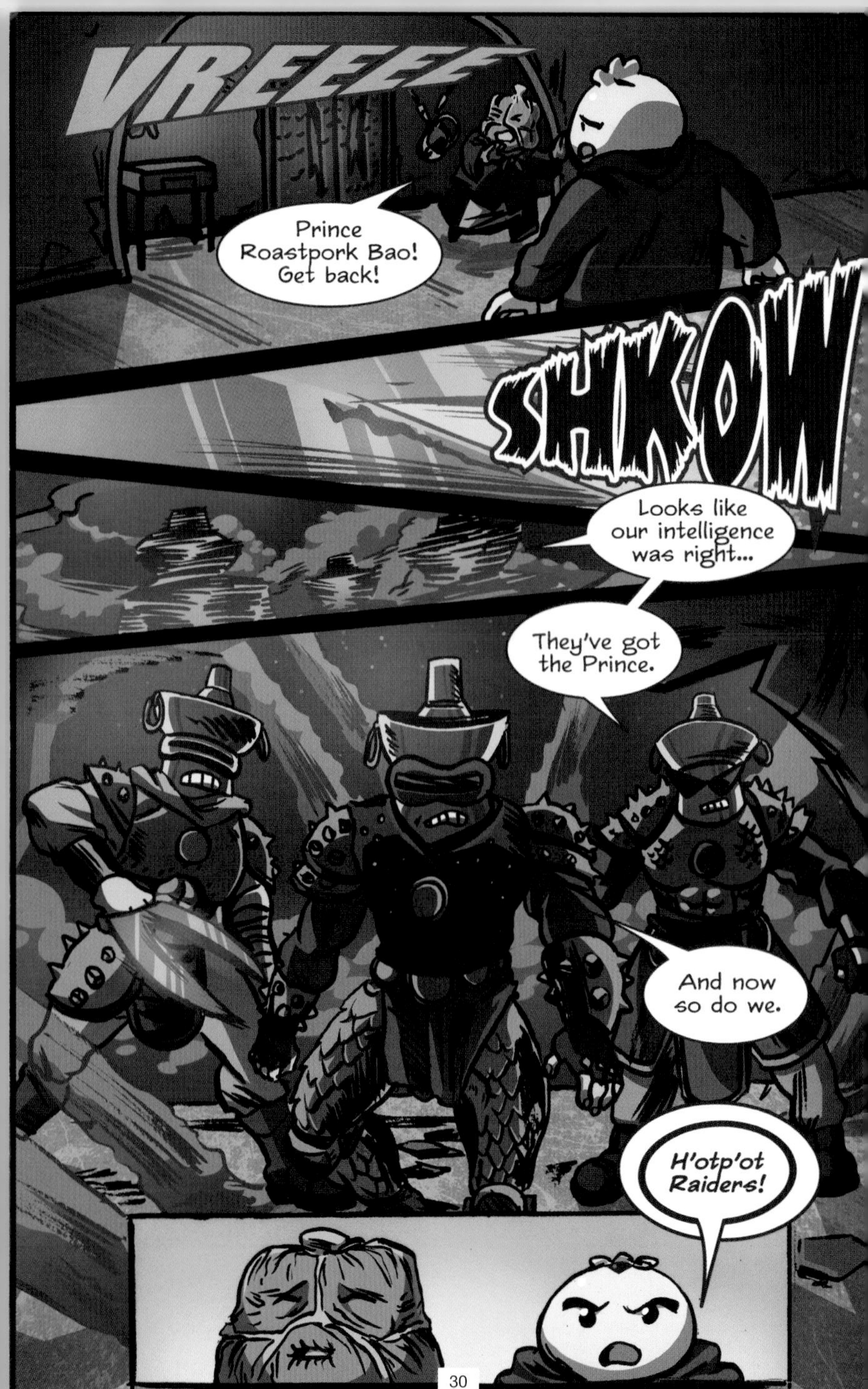
VREEEE
Prince Roastpork Bao! Get back!
SHKOW
Looks like our intelligence was right...
They've got the Prince.
And now so do we.
H'otp'ot Raiders!

# Chapter 8
# Turning Up the Heat

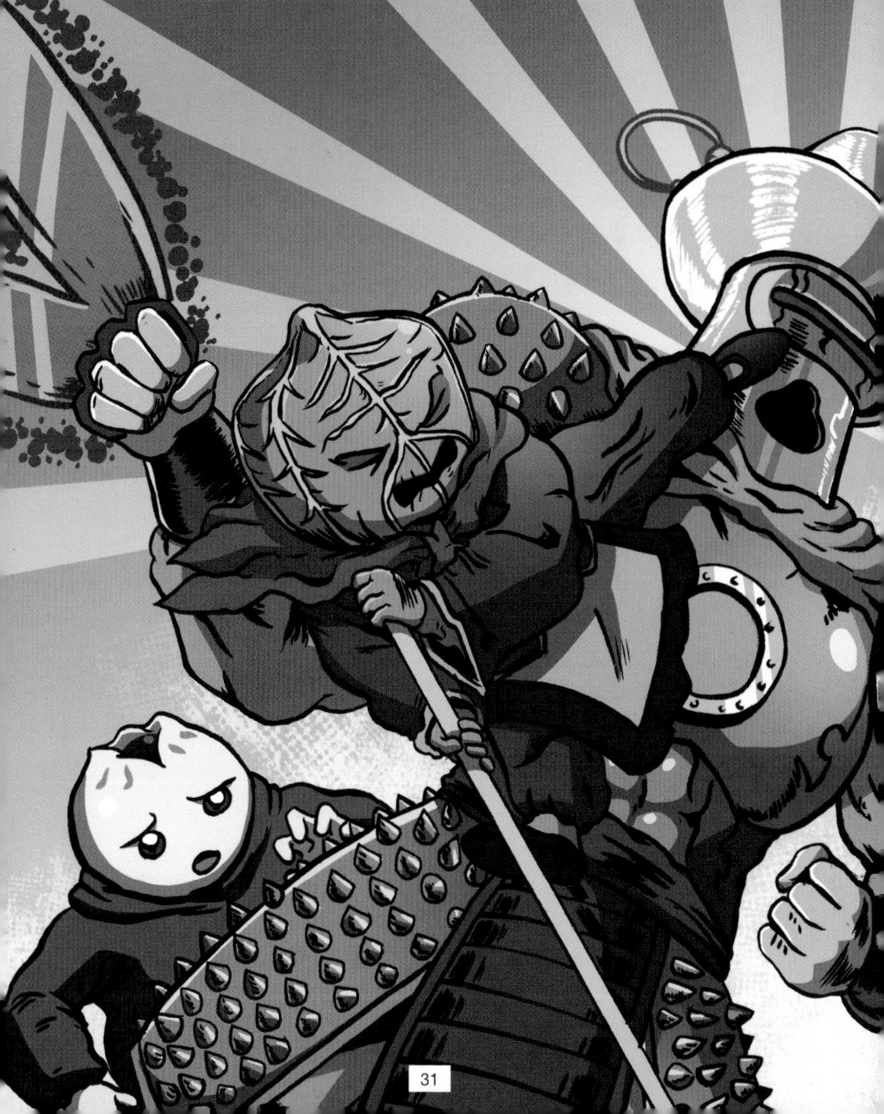

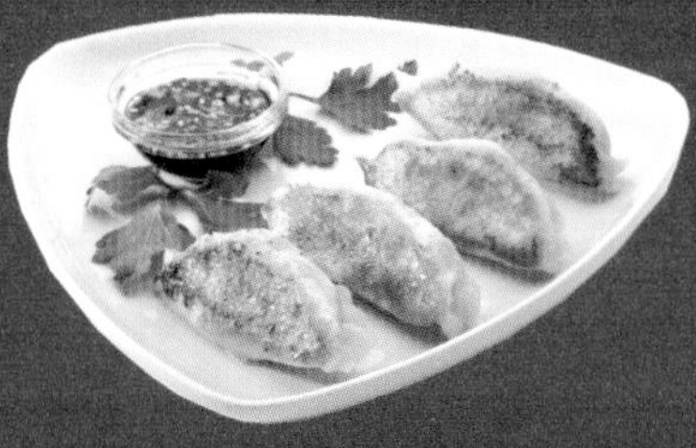

svry/ Shutterstock.com

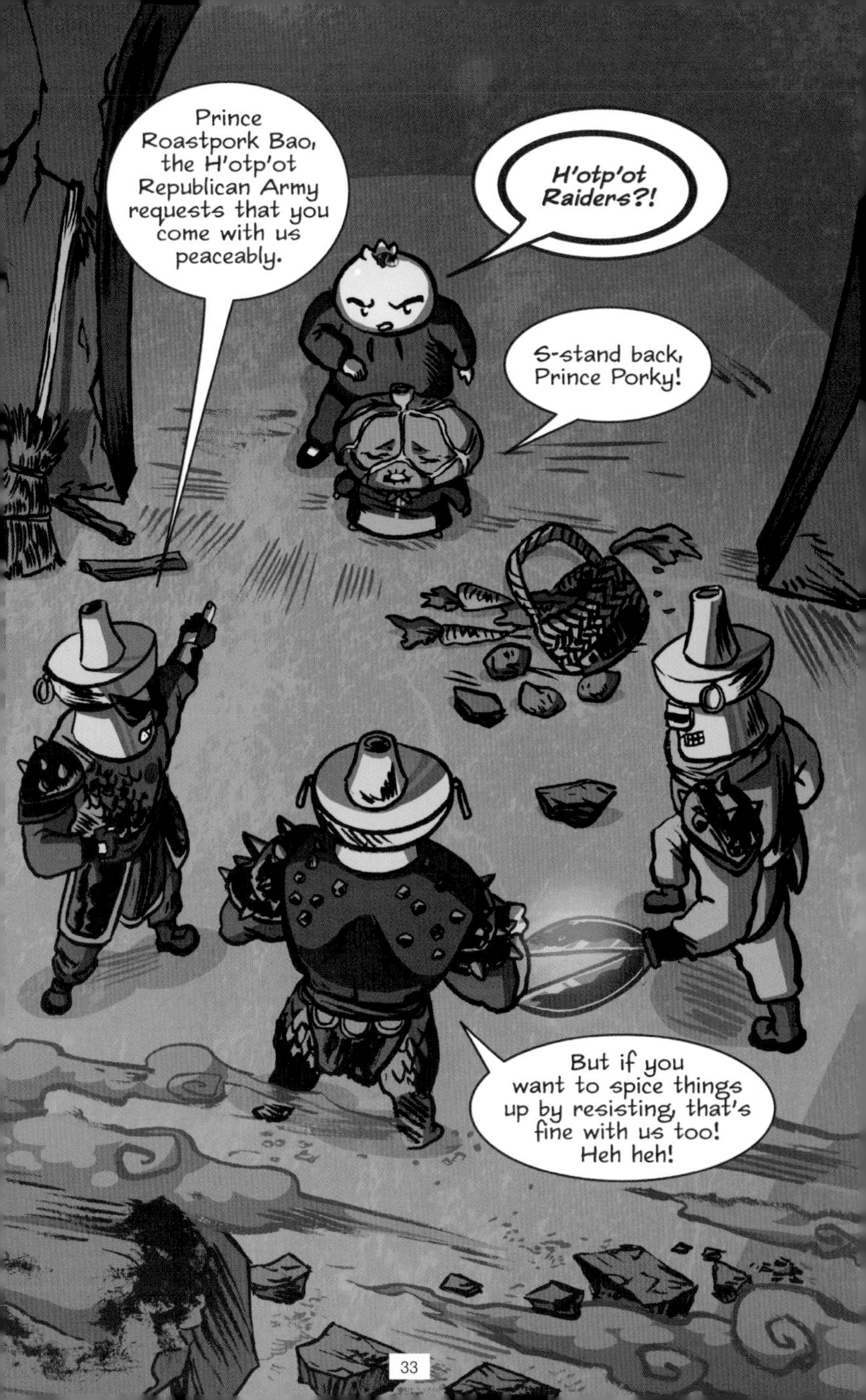
Prince Roastpork Bao, the H'otp'ot Republican Army requests that you come with us peaceably.
H'otp'ot Raiders?!
S-stand back, Prince Porky!
But if you want to spice things up by resisting, that's fine with us too! Heh heh!

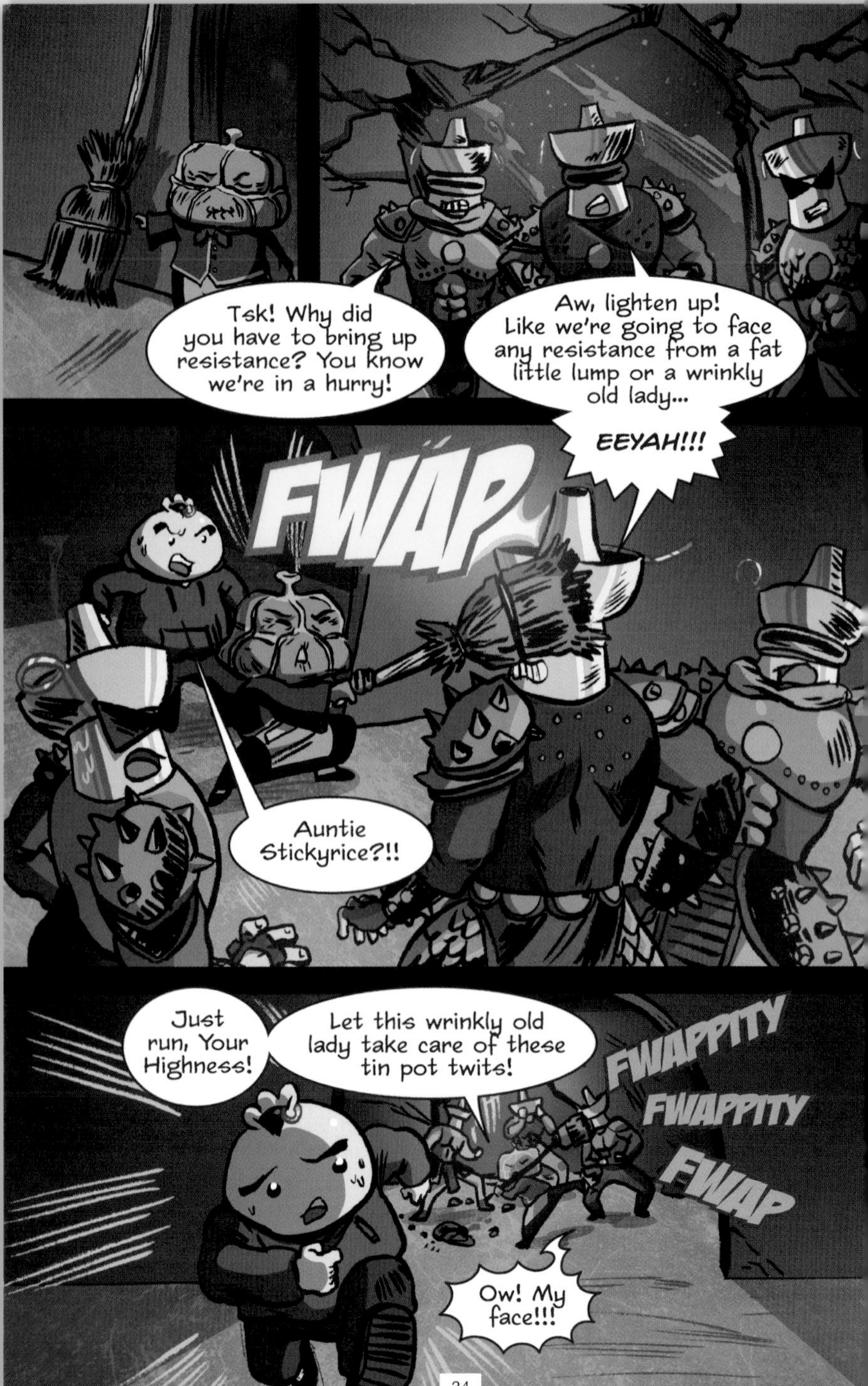

Tsk! Why did you have to bring up resistance? You know we're in a hurry!
Aw, lighten up! Like we're going to face any resistance from a fat little lump or a wrinkly old lady...
EEYAH!!!
FWAP
Auntie Stickyrice?!!
Just run, Your Highness!
Let this wrinkly old lady take care of these tin pot twits!
FWAPPITY
FWAPPITY
FWAP
Ow! My face!!!

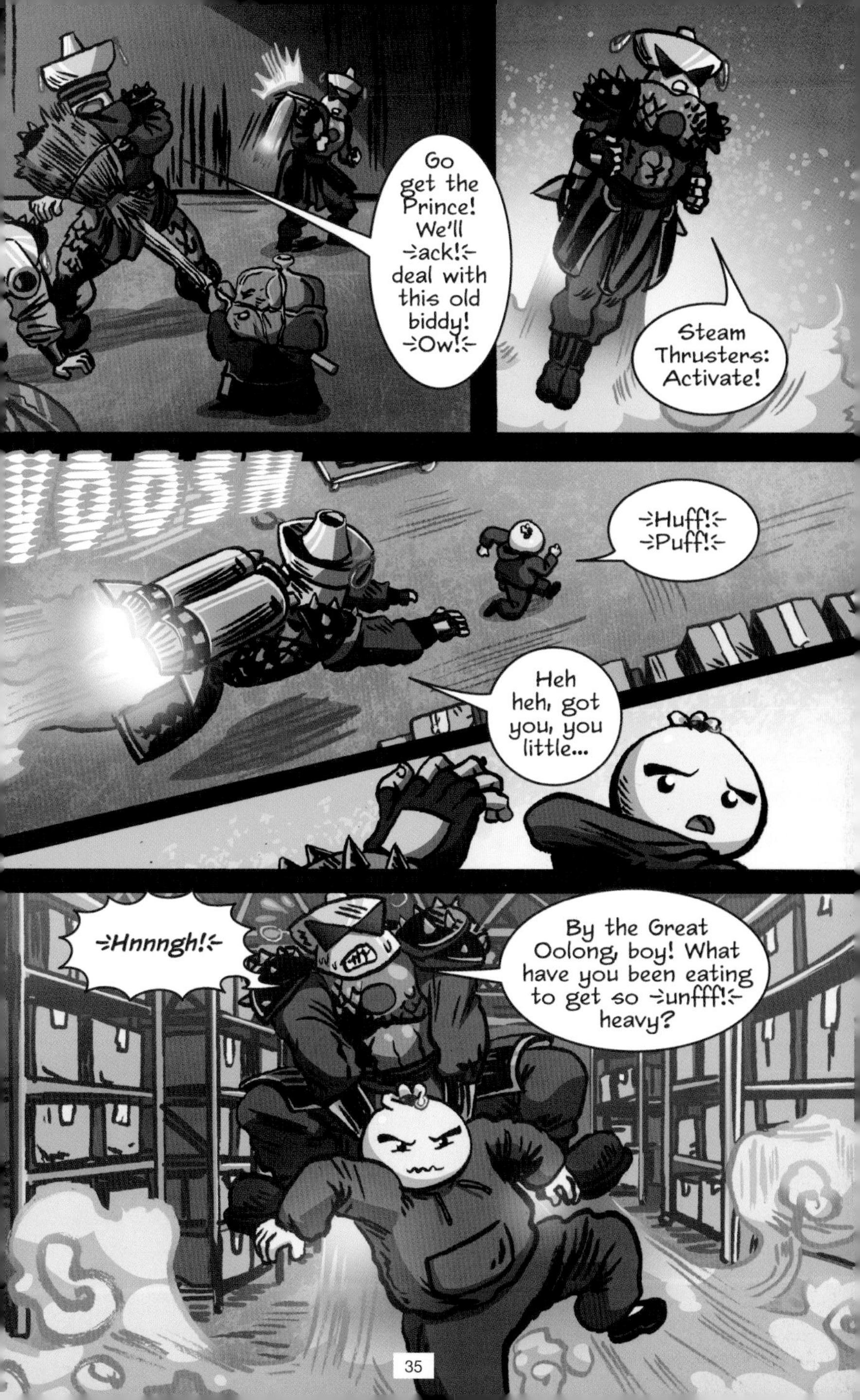
Go get the Prince! We'll =ack!= deal with this old biddy! =Ow!=
Steam Thrusters: Activate!
=Huff!= =Puff!=
Heh heh, got you, you little...
=Hnnngh!=
By the Great Oolong, boy! What have you been eating to get so =unfff!= heavy?

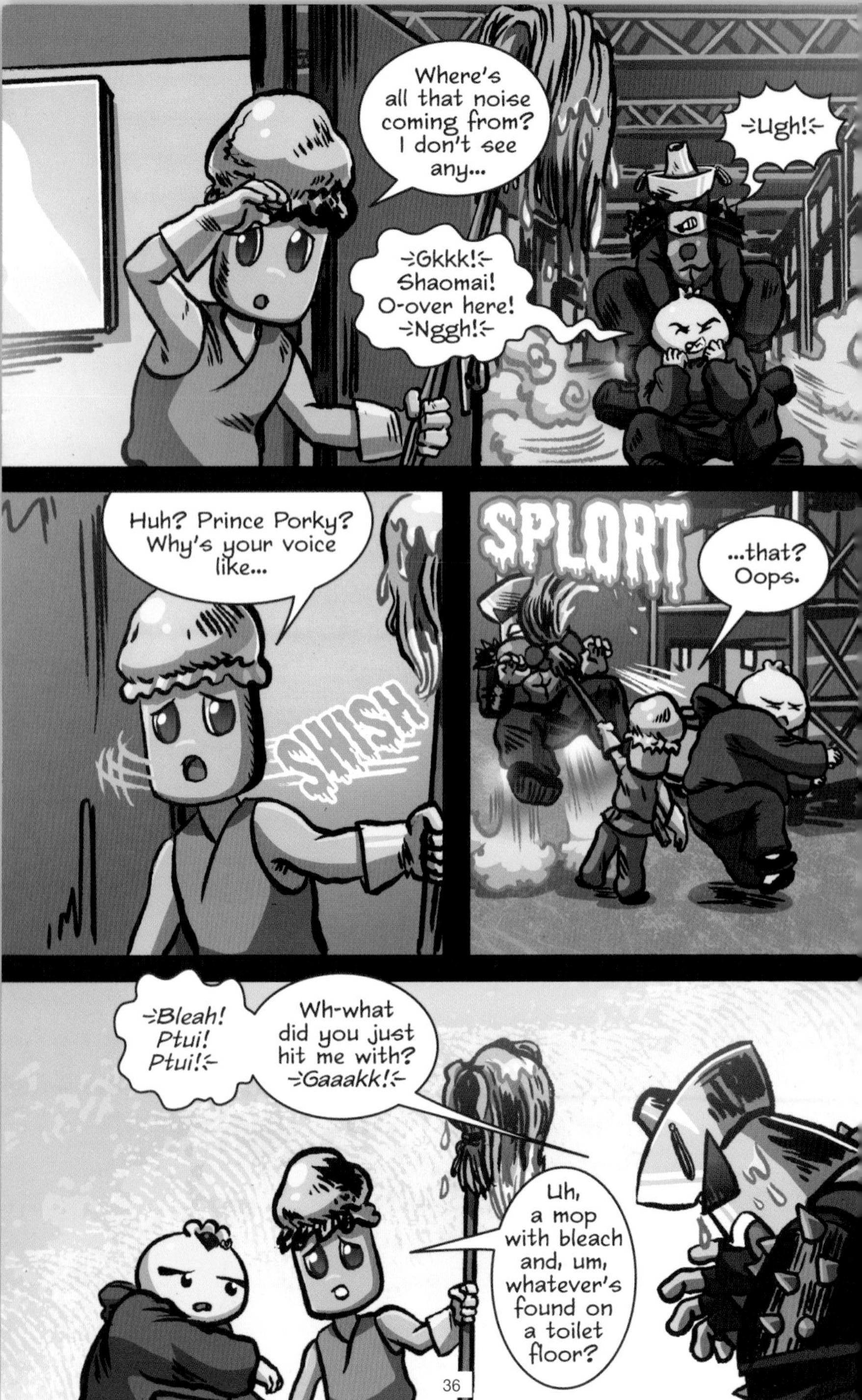
Where's all that noise coming from? I don't see any...
=Ugh!=
=Gkkk!= Shaomai! O-over here! =Nggh!=
Huh? Prince Porky? Why's your voice like...
SHISH
SPLORT
...that? Oops.
=Bleah! Ptui! Ptui!=
Wh-what did you just hit me with? =Gaaakk!=
Uh, a mop with bleach and, um, whatever's found on a toilet floor?

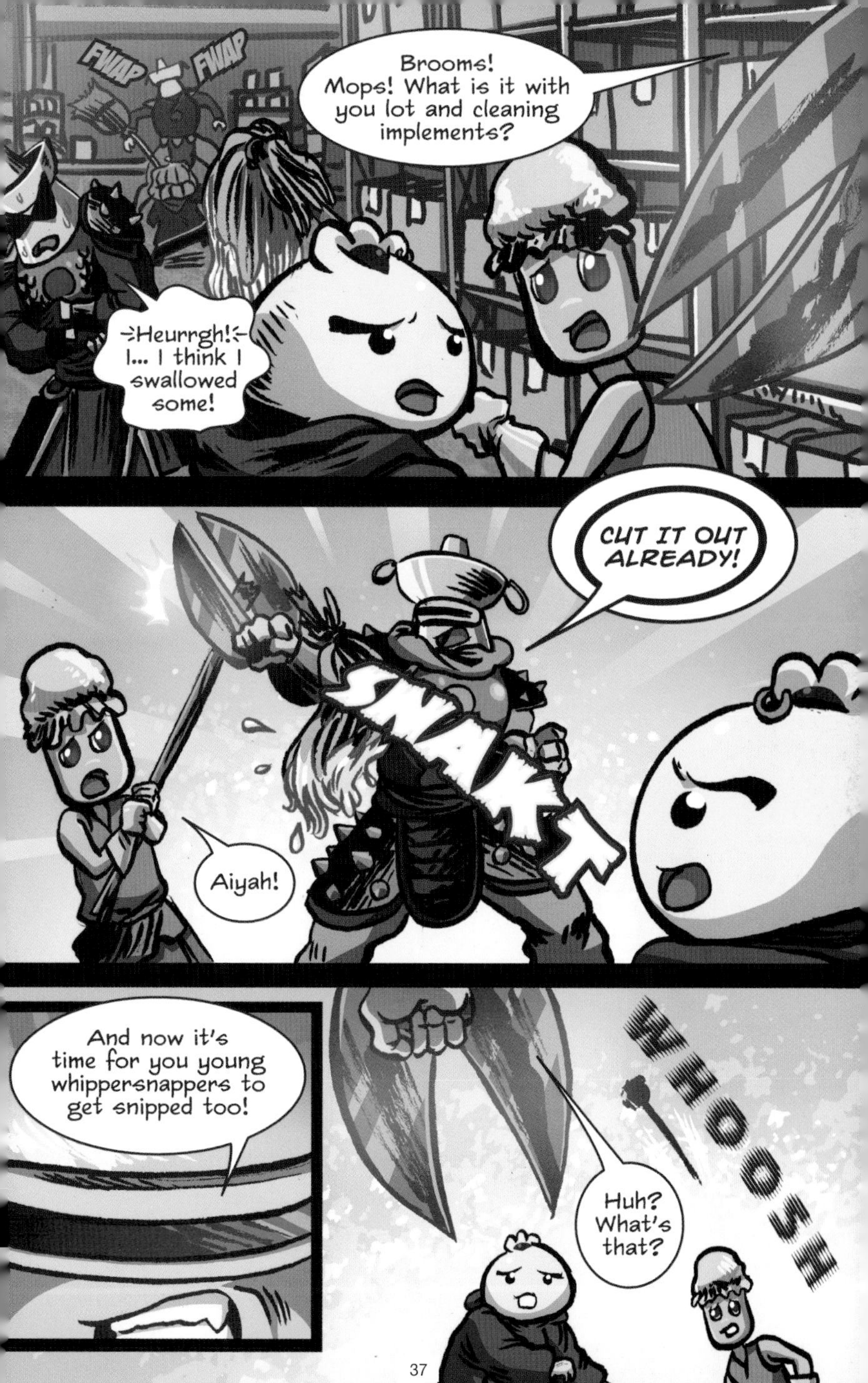
FWAP FWAP
Brooms! Mops! What is it with you lot and cleaning implements?
Heurrgh! I... I think I swallowed some!
CUT IT OUT ALREADY!
SNAKT
Aiyah!
And now it's time for you young whippersnappers to get snipped too!
WHOOSH
Huh? What's that?

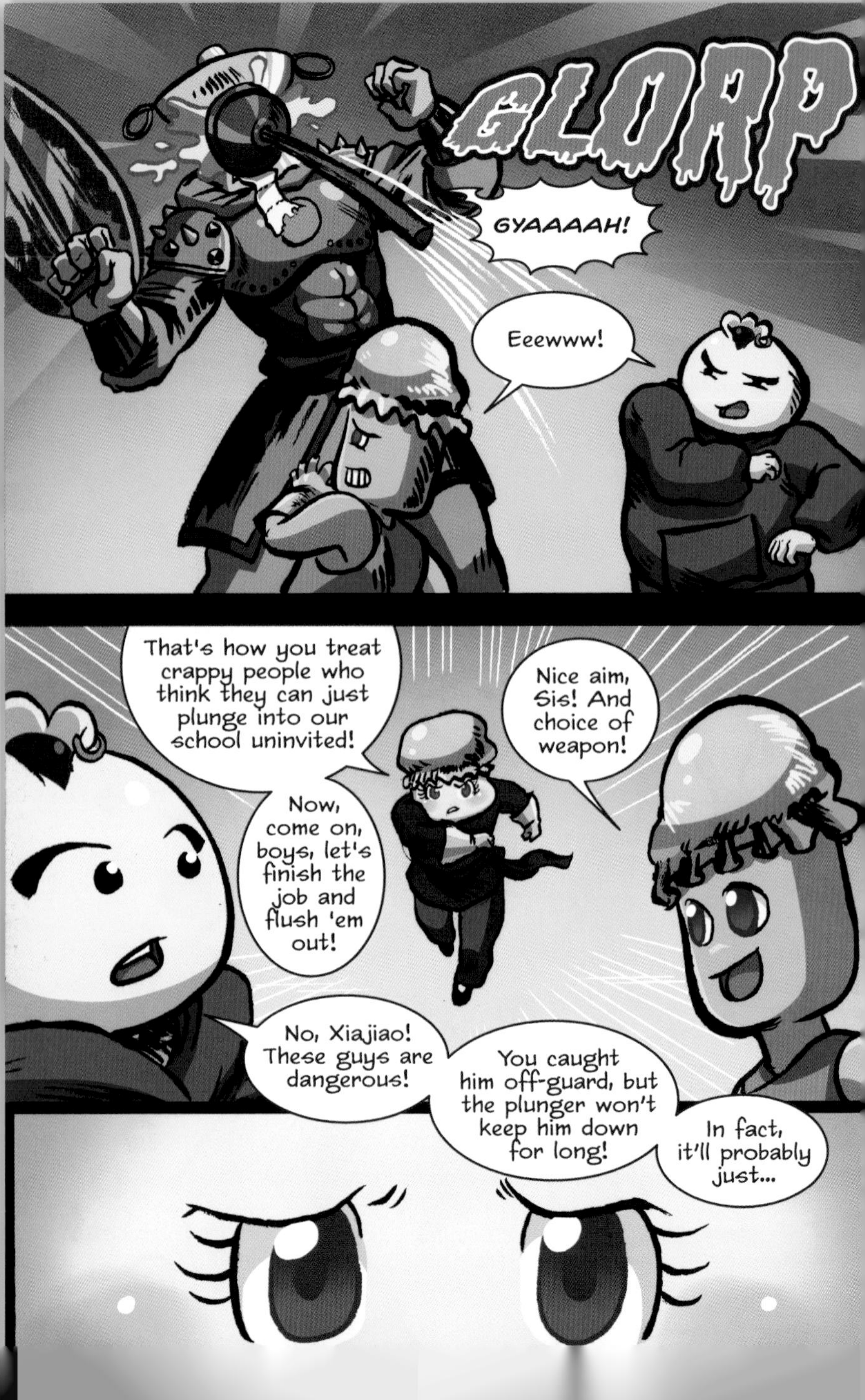
GLORP
GYAAAAH!
Eeewww!
That's how you treat crappy people who think they can just plunge into our school uninvited!
Now, come on, boys, let's finish the job and flush 'em out!
Nice aim, Sis! And choice of weapon!
No, Xiajiao! These guys are dangerous!
You caught him off-guard, but the plunger won't keep him down for long!
In fact, it'll probably just...

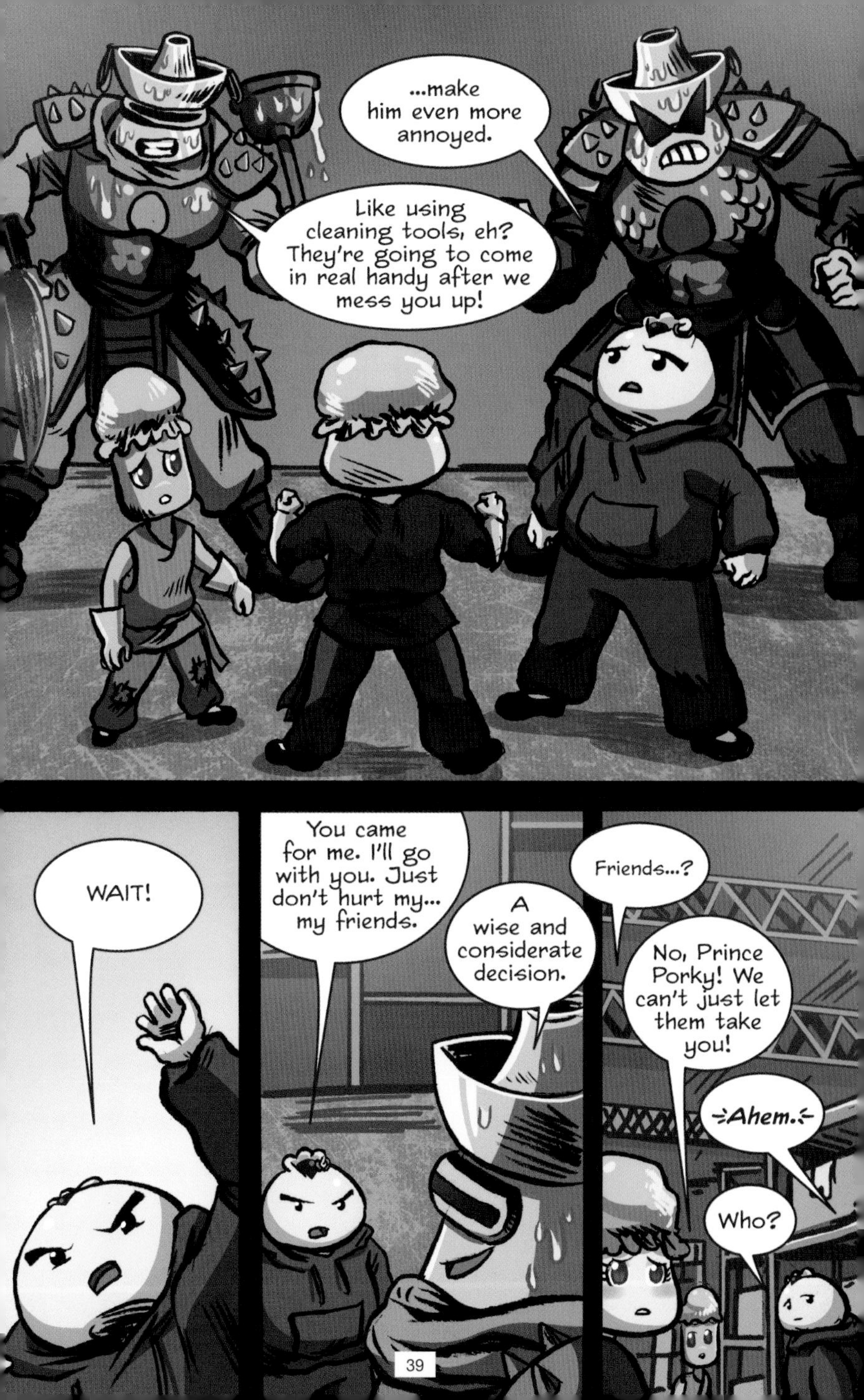
...make him even more annoyed.
Like using cleaning tools, eh? They're going to come in real handy after we mess you up!
WAIT!
You came for me. I'll go with you. Just don't hurt my... my friends.
A wise and considerate decision.
Friends...?
No, Prince Porky! We can't just let them take you!
Ahem.
Who?

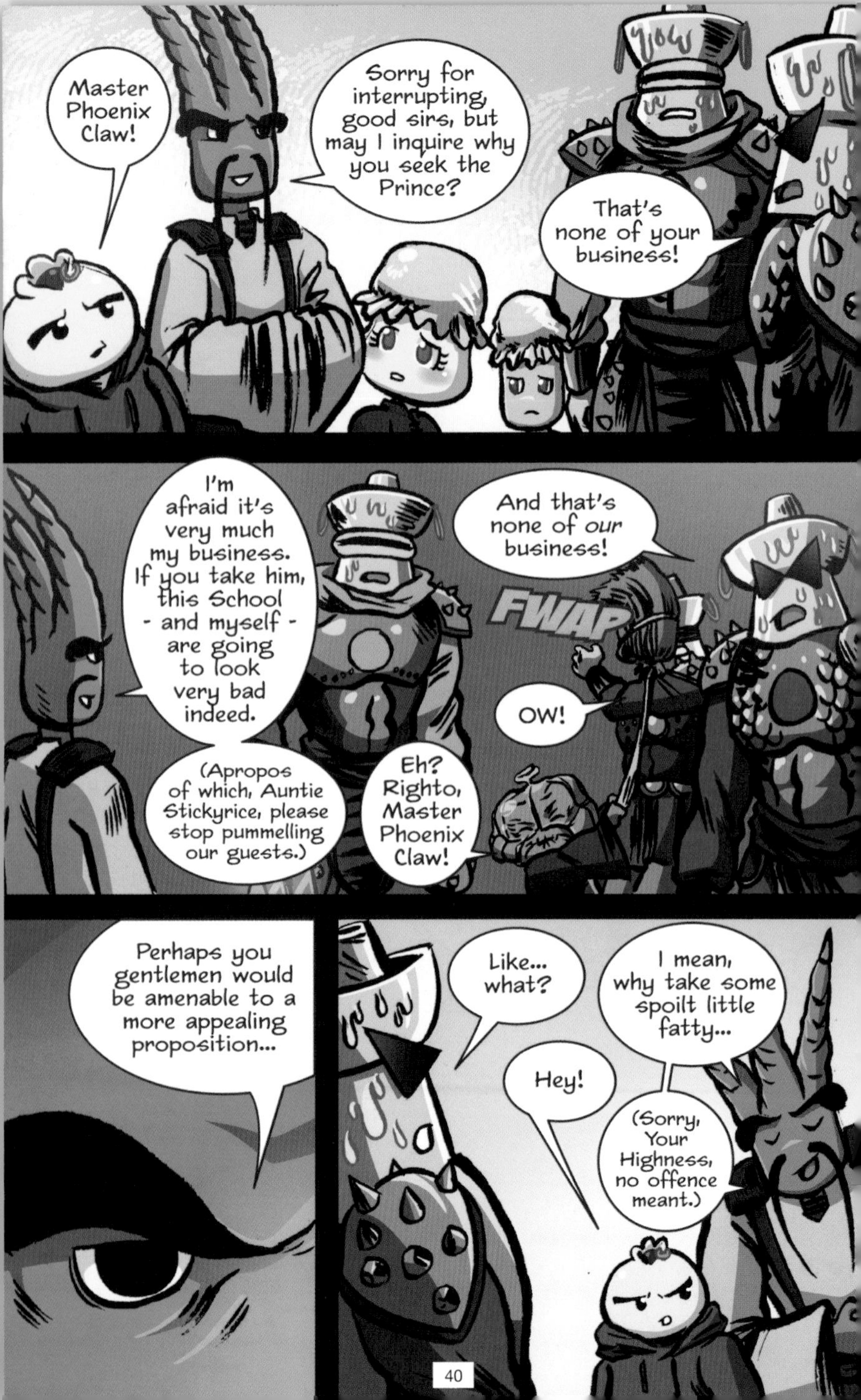
Master Phoenix Claw!
Sorry for interrupting, good sirs, but may I inquire why you seek the Prince?
That's none of your business!
I'm afraid it's very much my business. If you take him, this School - and myself - are going to look very bad indeed.
(Apropos of which, Auntie Stickyrice, please stop pummelling our guests.)
Eh? Righto, Master Phoenix Claw!
And that's none of our business!
FWAP
OW!
Perhaps you gentlemen would be amenable to a more appealing proposition...
Like... what?
I mean, why take some spoilt little fatty...
Hey!
(Sorry, Your Highness, no offence meant.)

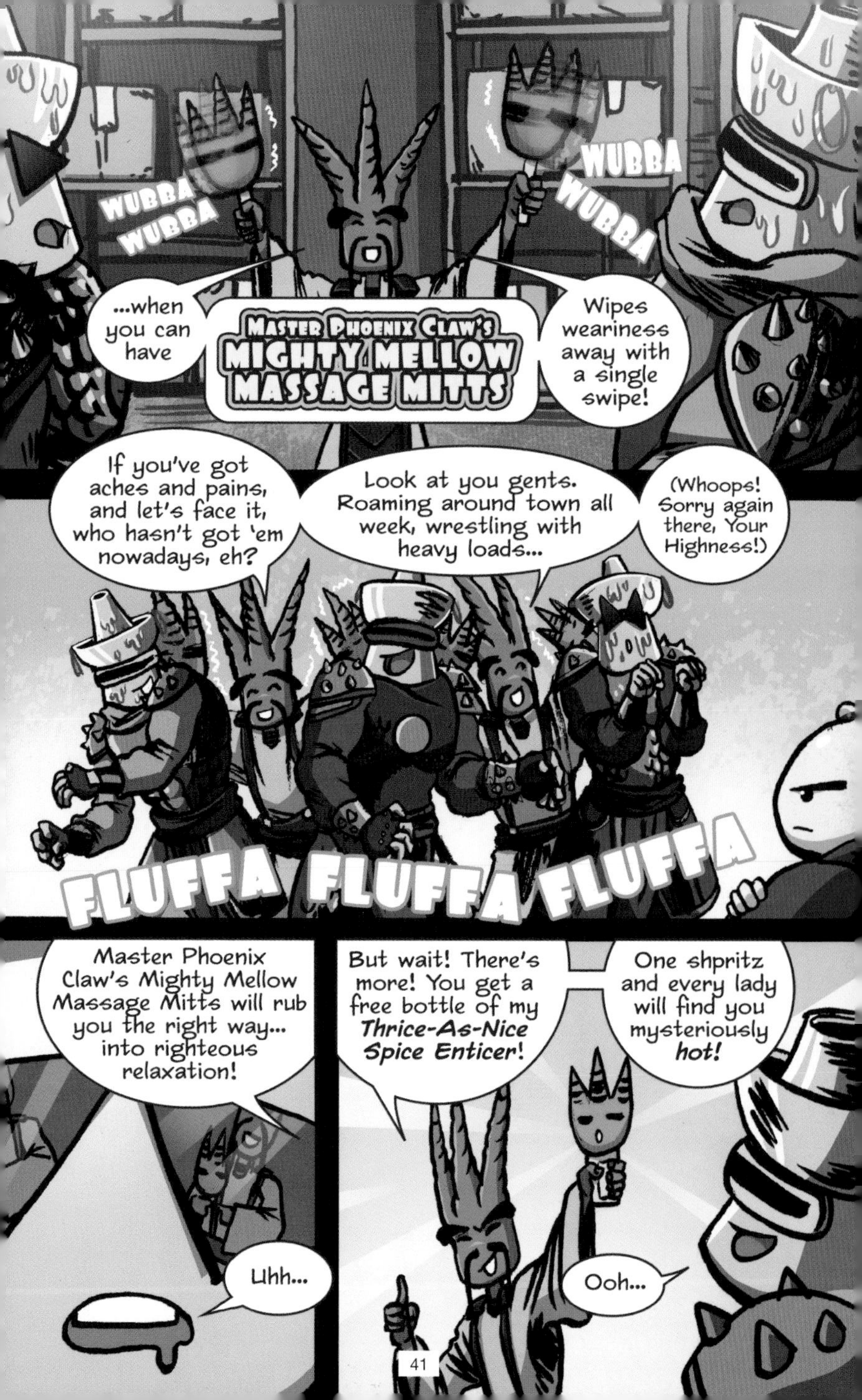
WUBBA WUBBA
WUBBA WUBBA
...when you can have
MASTER PHOENIX CLAW'S MIGHTY MELLOW MASSAGE MITTS
Wipes weariness away with a single swipe!
If you've got aches and pains, and let's face it, who hasn't got 'em nowadays, eh?
Look at you gents. Roaming around town all week, wrestling with heavy loads...
(Whoops! Sorry again there, Your Highness!)
FLUFFA FLUFFA FLUFFA
Master Phoenix Claw's Mighty Mellow Massage Mitts will rub you the right way... into righteous relaxation!
Uhh...
But wait! There's more! You get a free bottle of my *Thrice-As-Nice Spice Enticer*!
One shpritz and every lady will find you mysteriously *hot!*
Ooh...

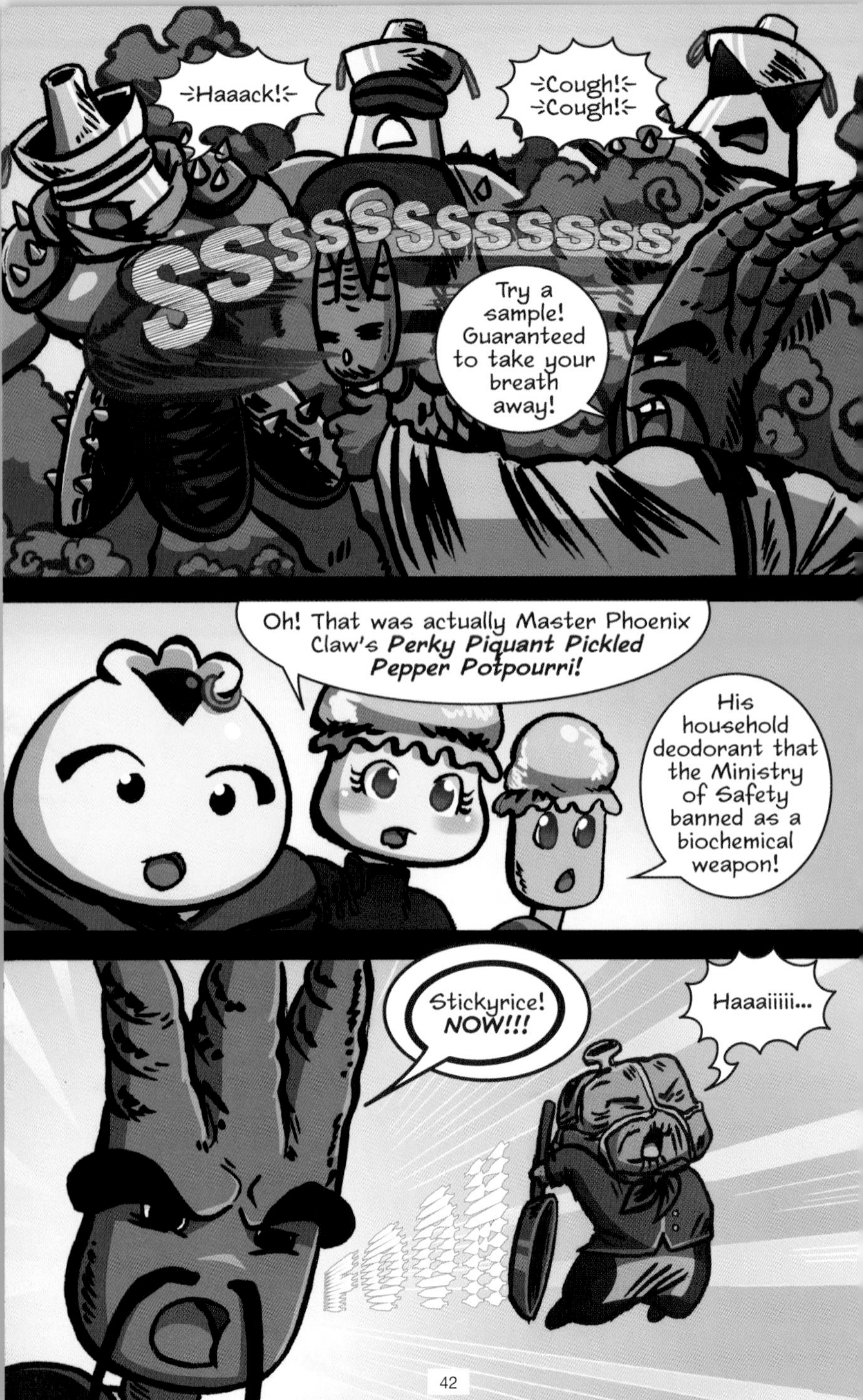

Haaack!
Cough! Cough!
SSSSSSSSSSSSS
Try a sample! Guaranteed to take your breath away!
Oh! That was actually Master Phoenix Claw's ***Perky Piquant Pickled Pepper Potpourri!***
His household deodorant that the Ministry of Safety banned as a biochemical weapon!
Stickyrice! ***NOW!!!***
Haaaiiiii...

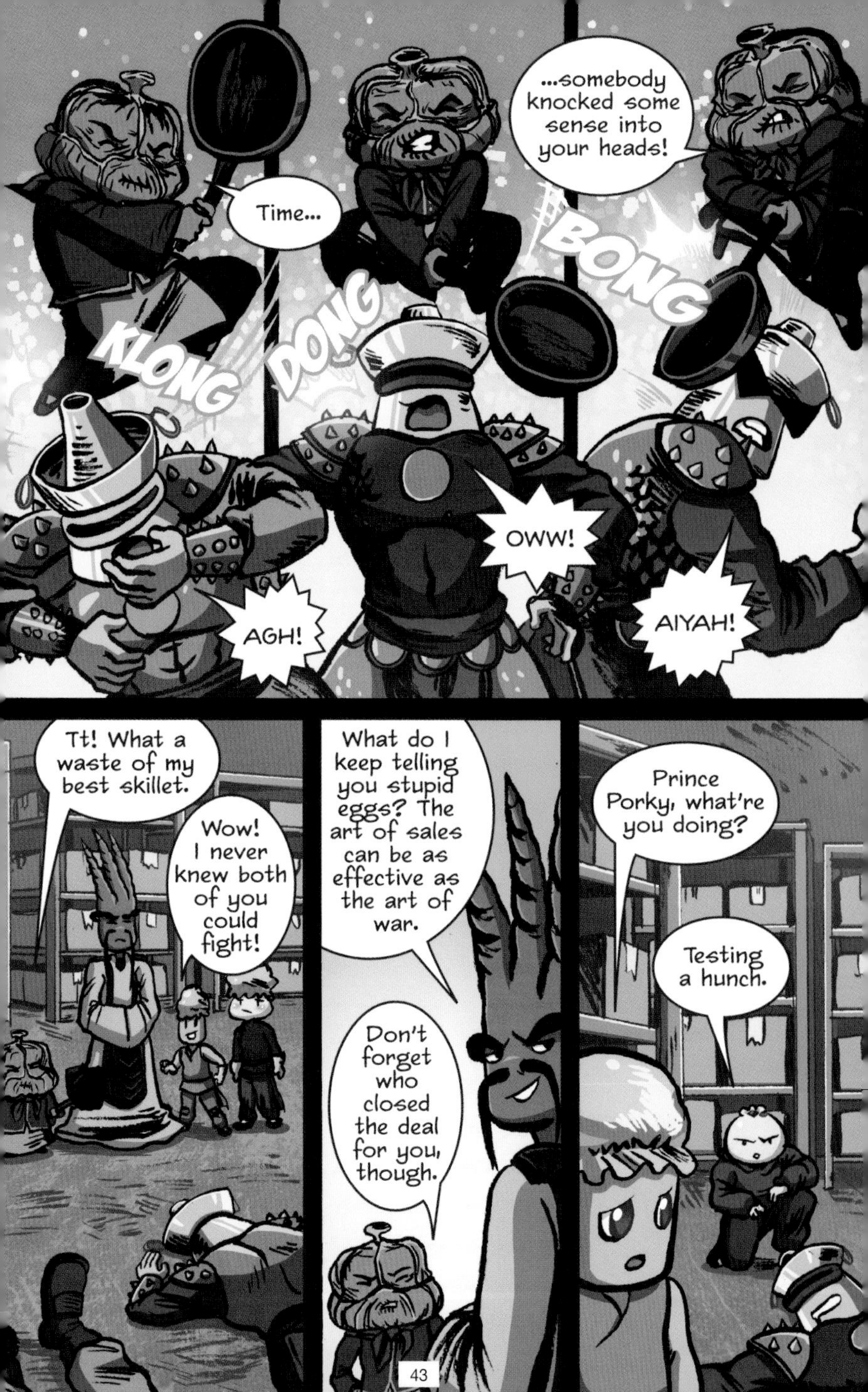
Time...
...somebody knocked some sense into your heads!
KLONG
DONG
BONG
OWW!
AGH!
AIYAH!
Tt! What a waste of my best skillet.
Wow! I never knew both of you could fight!
What do I keep telling you stupid eggs? The art of sales can be as effective as the art of war.
Don't forget who closed the deal for you, though.
Prince Porky, what're you doing?
Testing a hunch.

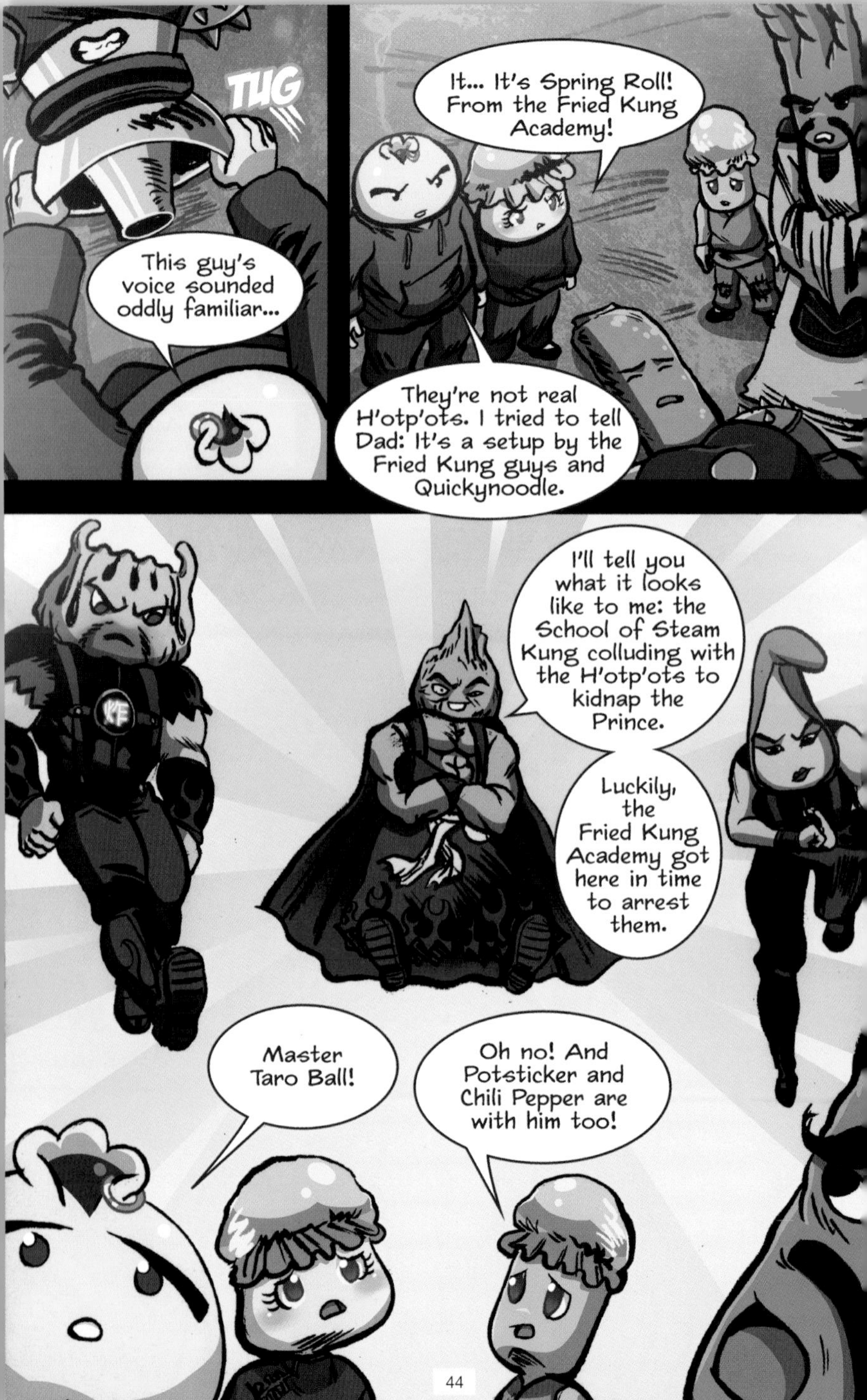
TUG
This guy's voice sounded oddly familiar...
It... It's Spring Roll! From the Fried Kung Academy!
They're not real H'otp'ots. I tried to tell Dad: It's a setup by the Fried Kung guys and Quickynoodle.
I'll tell you what it looks like to me: the School of Steam Kung colluding with the H'otp'ots to kidnap the Prince.
Luckily, the Fried Kung Academy got here in time to arrest them.
Master Taro Ball!
Oh no! And Potsticker and Chili Pepper are with him too!

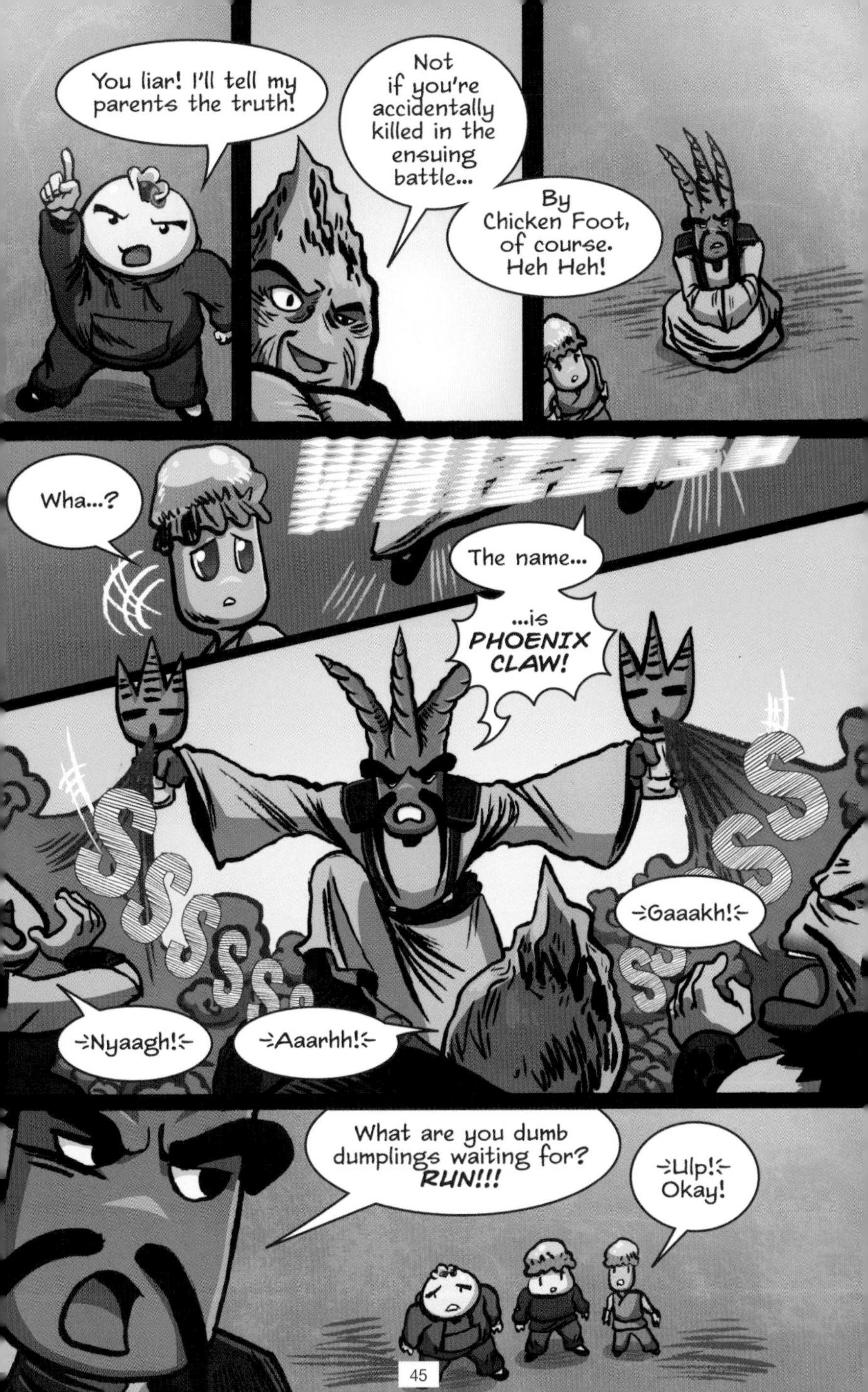

You liar! I'll tell my parents the truth!
Not if you're accidentally killed in the ensuing battle...
By Chicken Foot, of course. Heh Heh!
Wha...?
The name...
...is PHOENIX CLAW!
Gaaakh!
Nyaagh!
Aaarhh!
What are you dumb dumplings waiting for? RUN!!!
Ulp! Okay!

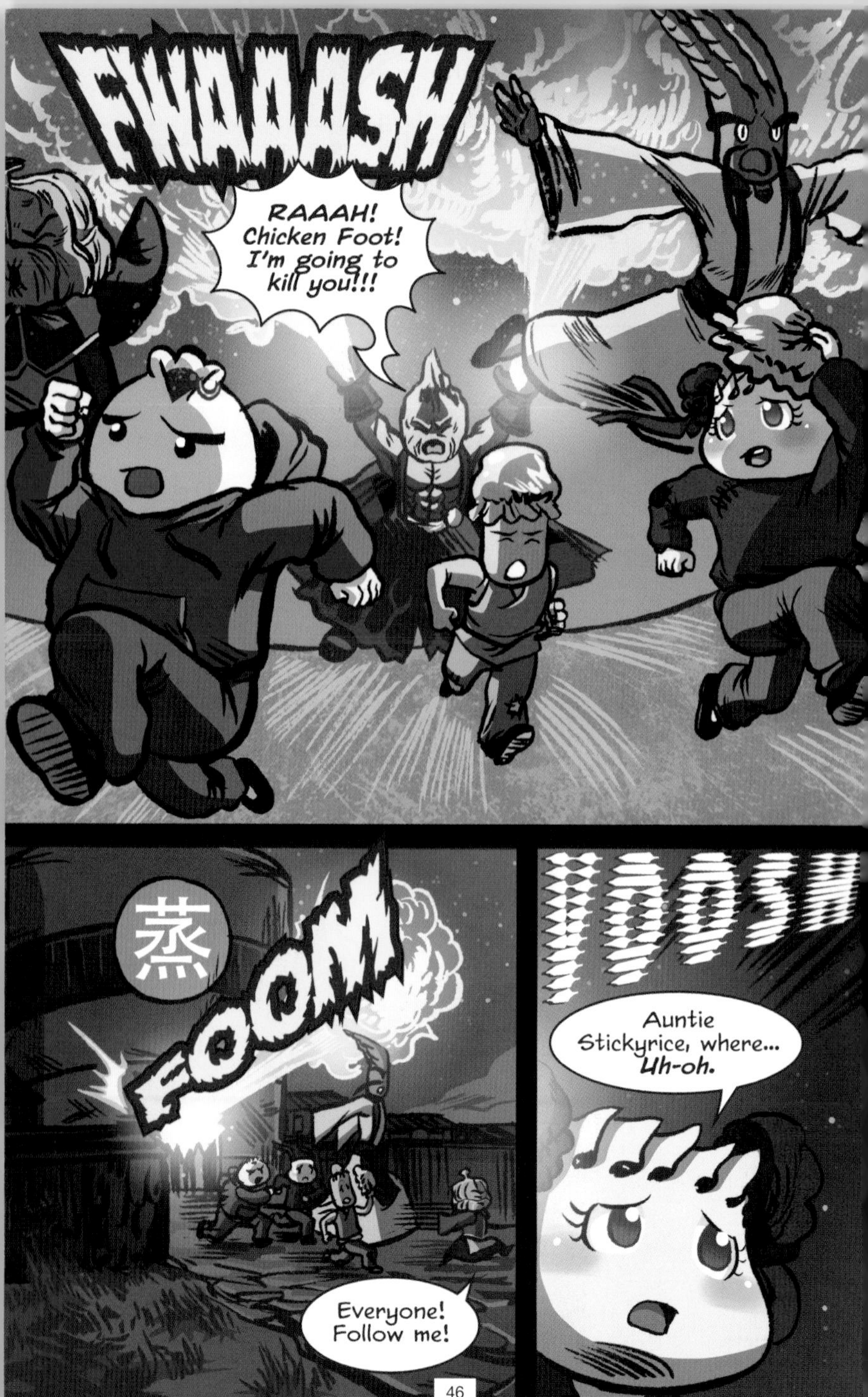
FWAAASH
RAAAH! Chicken Foot! I'm going to kill you!!!
蒸
FOOOM
Everyone! Follow me!
Auntie Stickyrice, where... Uh-oh.

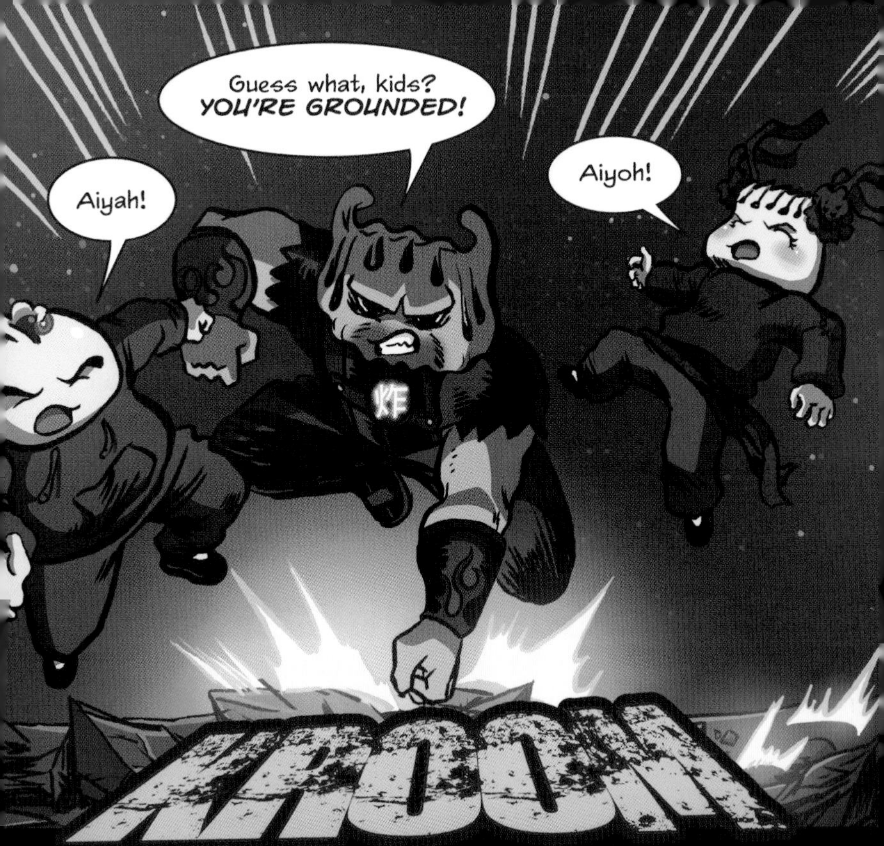
Guess what, kids? ***YOU'RE GROUNDED!***
Aiyah!
Aiyoh!

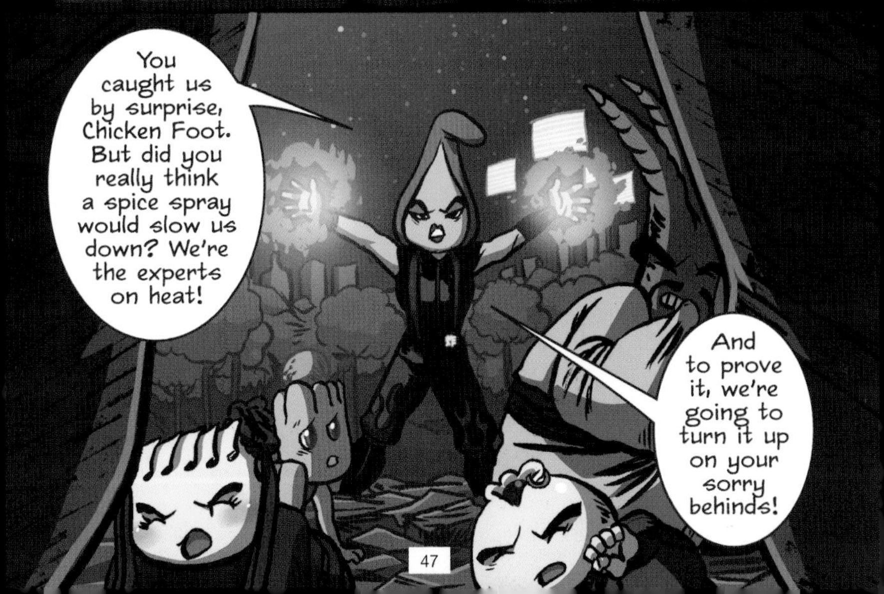
You caught us by surprise, Chicken Foot. But did you really think a spice spray would slow us down? We're the experts on heat!
And to prove it, we're going to turn it up on your sorry behinds!

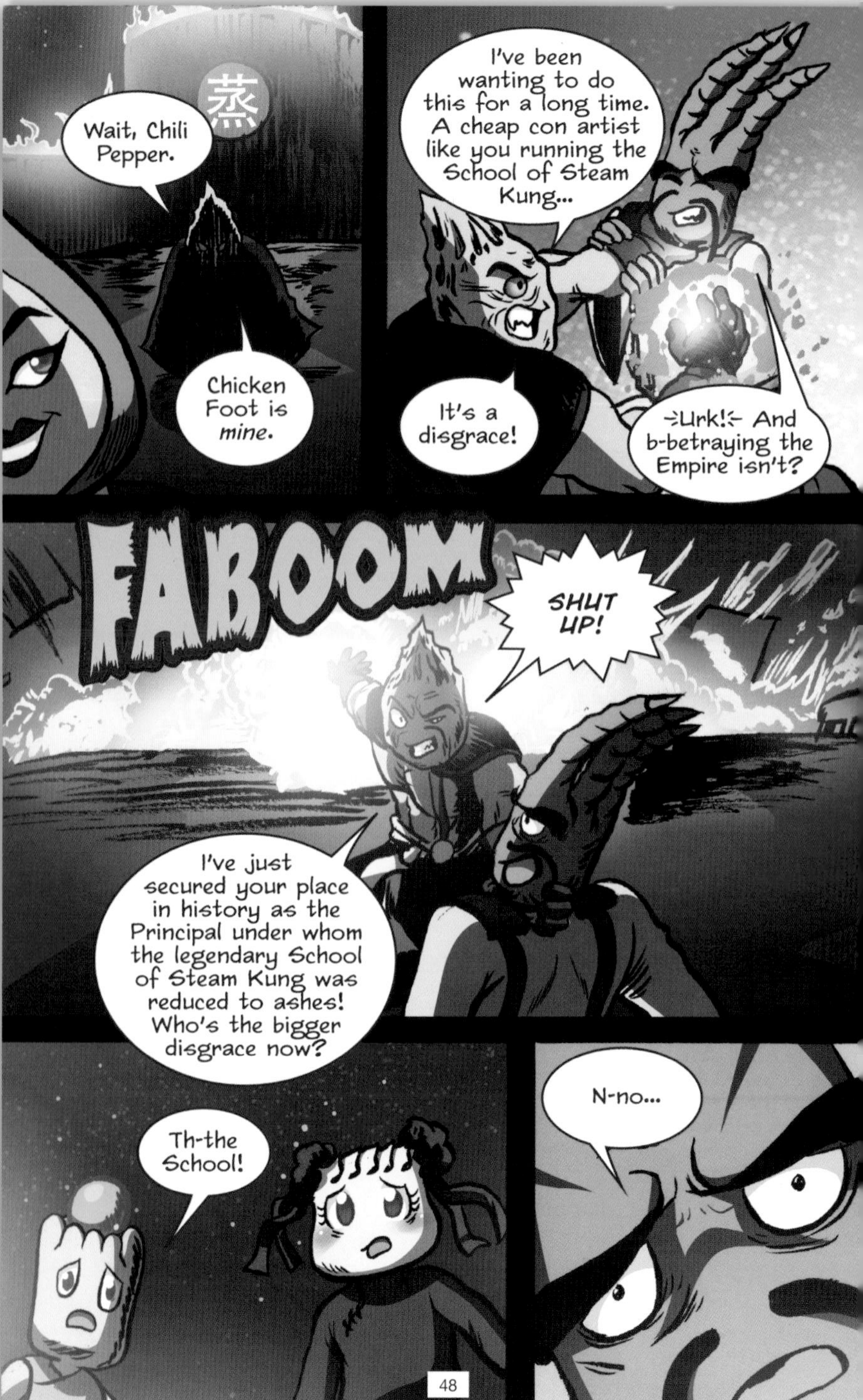
蒸
Wait, Chili Pepper.
Chicken Foot is *mine.*
I've been wanting to do this for a long time. A cheap con artist like you running the School of Steam Kung...
It's a disgrace!
⁼Urk!⁼ And b-betraying the Empire isn't?
FABOOM
SHUT UP!
I've just secured your place in history as the Principal under whom the legendary School of Steam Kung was reduced to ashes! Who's the bigger disgrace now?
Th-the School!
N-no...

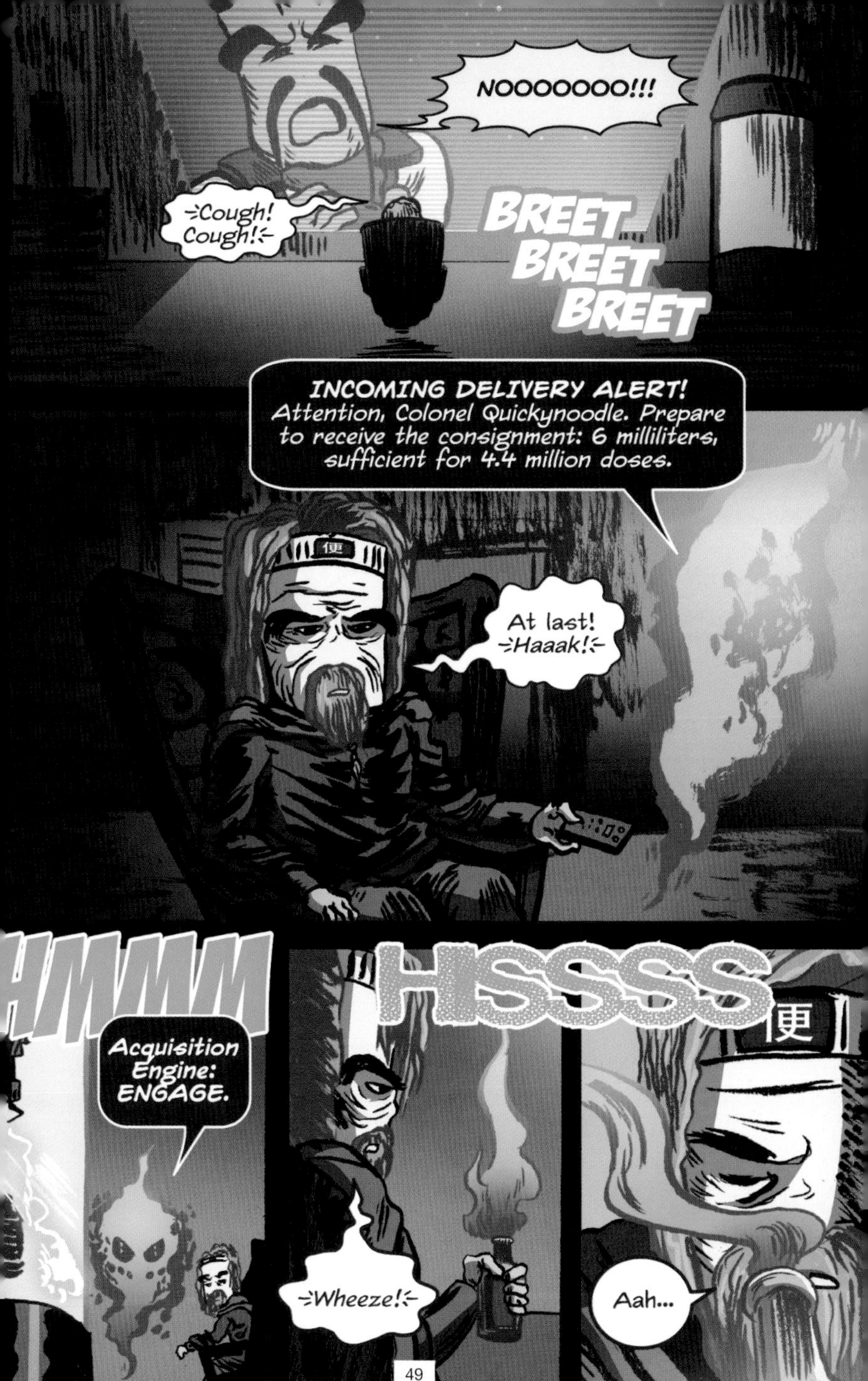

NOOOOOOO!!!
Cough! Cough!
BREET BREET BREET
INCOMING DELIVERY ALERT! Attention, Colonel Quickynoodle. Prepare to receive the consignment: 6 milliliters, sufficient for 4.4 million doses.
At last! Haaak!
HMMM
Acquisition Engine: ENGAGE.
HISSSS
Wheeze!
Aah...

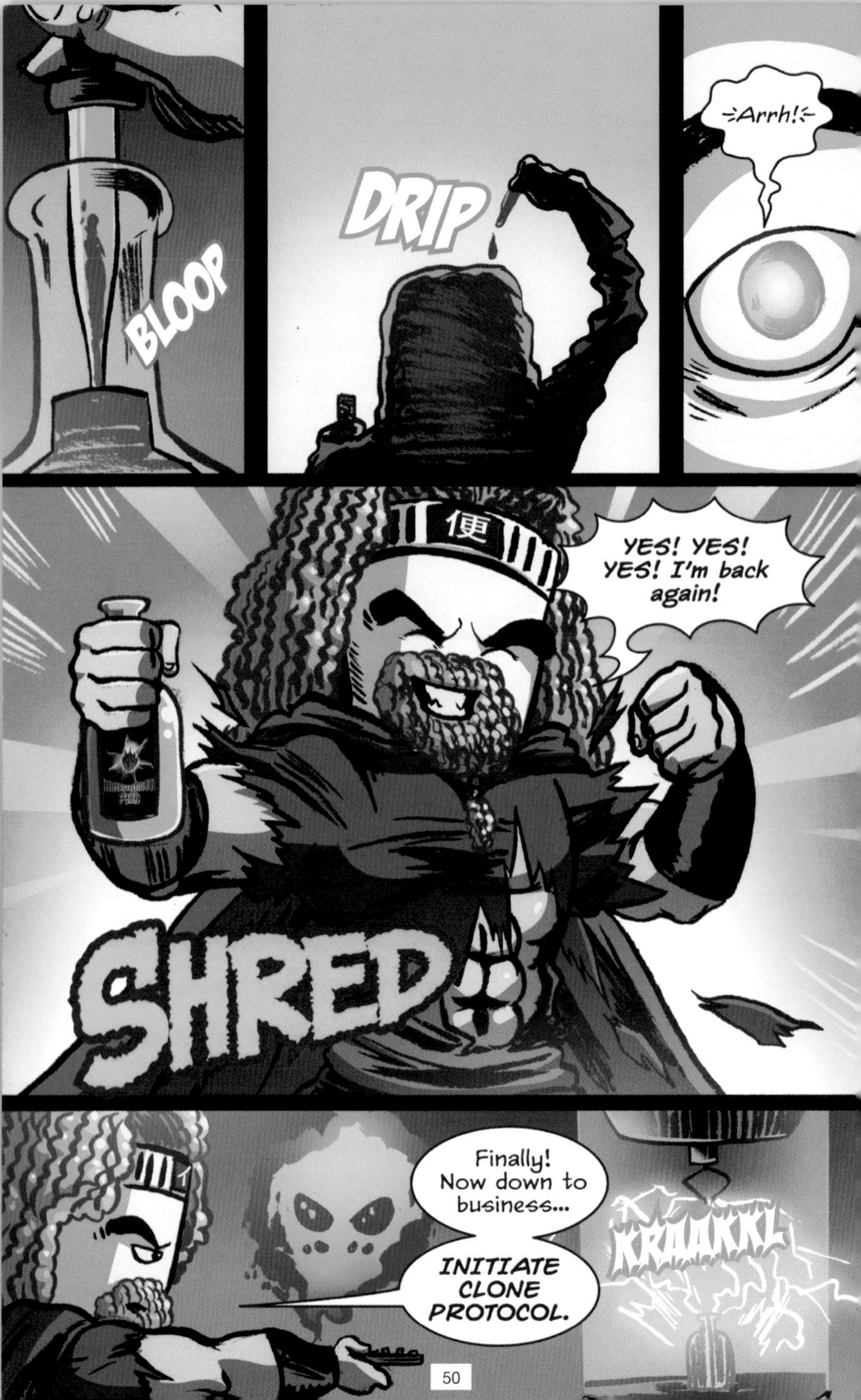
BLOOP
DRIP
Arrh!
YES! YES! YES! I'm back again!
SHRED
Finally! Now down to business...
INITIATE CLONE PROTOCOL.
KRAAKKL

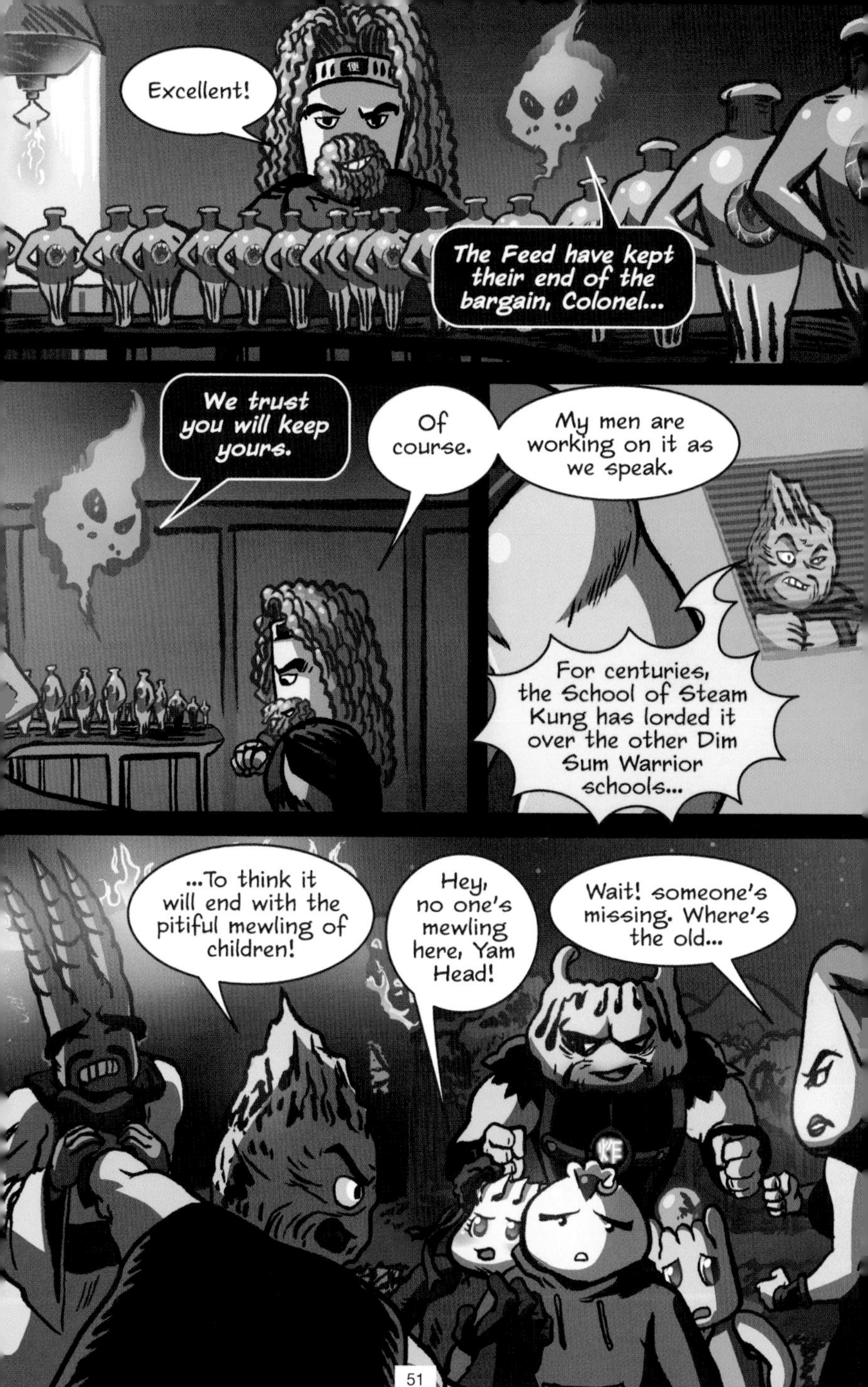
Excellent!
The Feed have kept their end of the bargain, Colonel...
We trust you will keep yours.
Of course.
My men are working on it as we speak.
For centuries, the School of Steam Kung has lorded it over the other Dim Sum Warrior schools...
...To think it will end with the pitiful mewling of children!
Hey, no one's mewling here, Yam Head!
Wait! someone's missing. Where's the old...

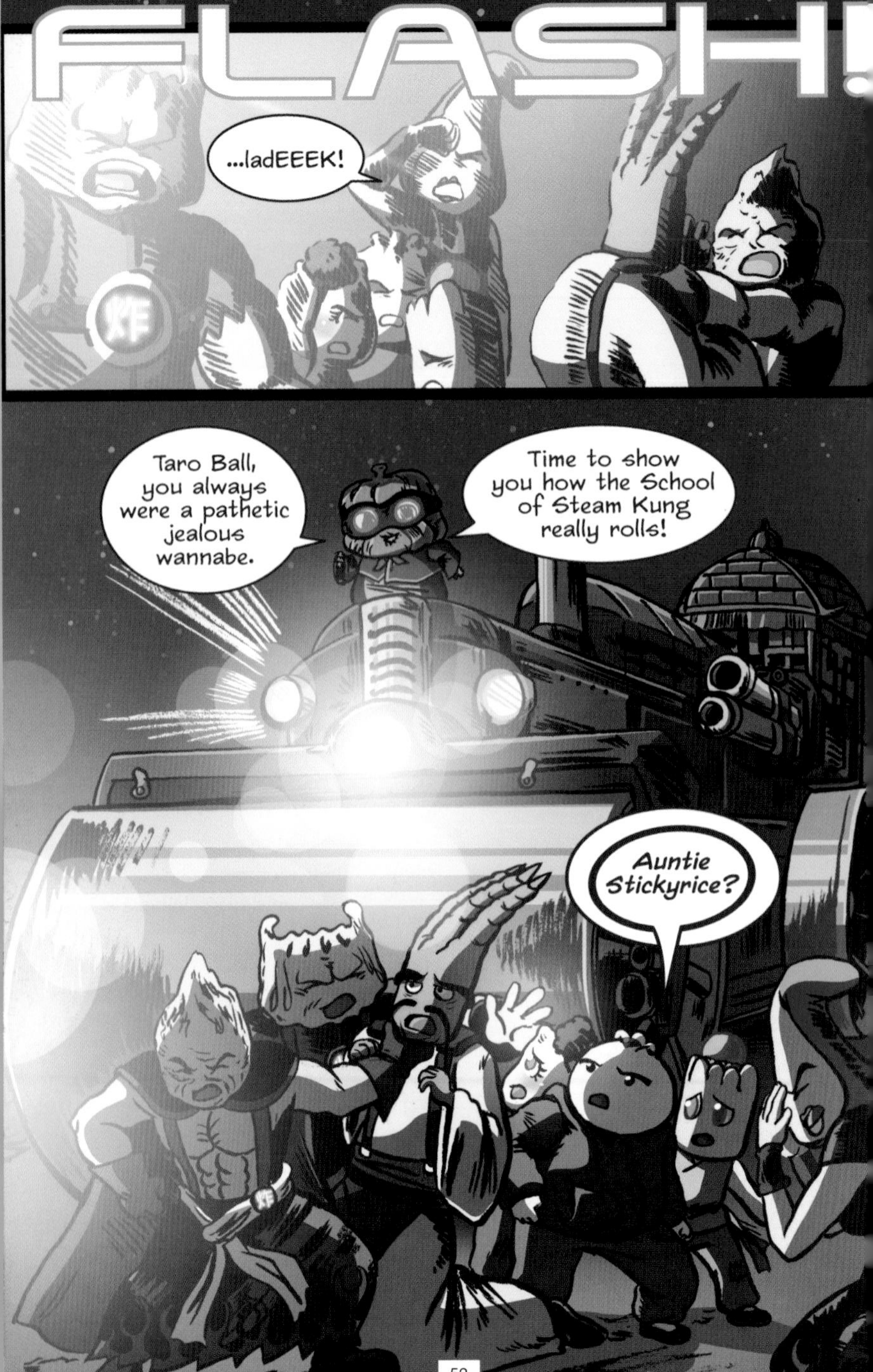
FLASH!
...ladEEEK!
Taro Ball, you always were a pathetic jealous wannabe.
Time to show you how the School of Steam Kung really rolls!
Auntie Stickyrice?

# Chapter 9

# All That We See or Seem is but Steam Within More Steam

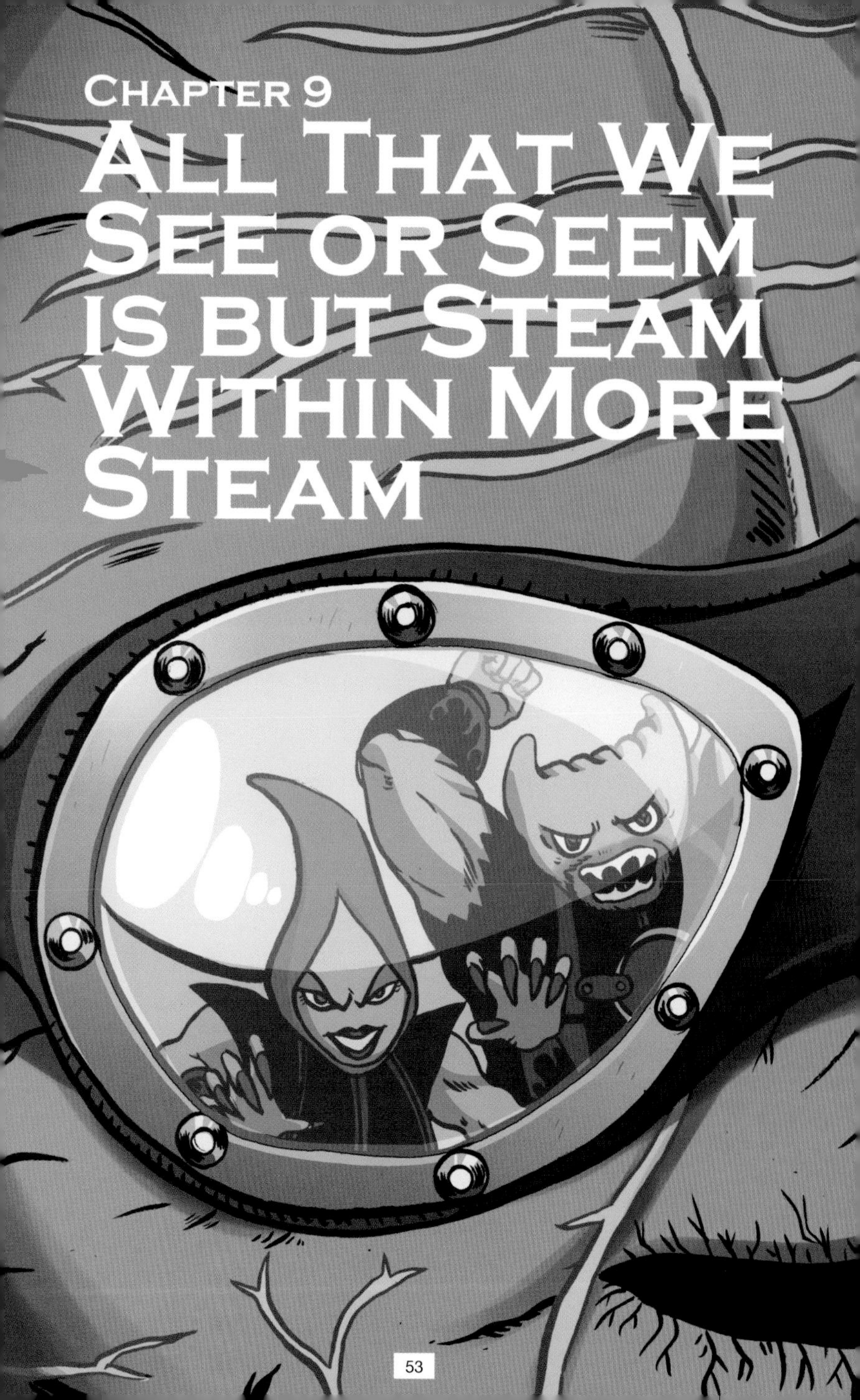

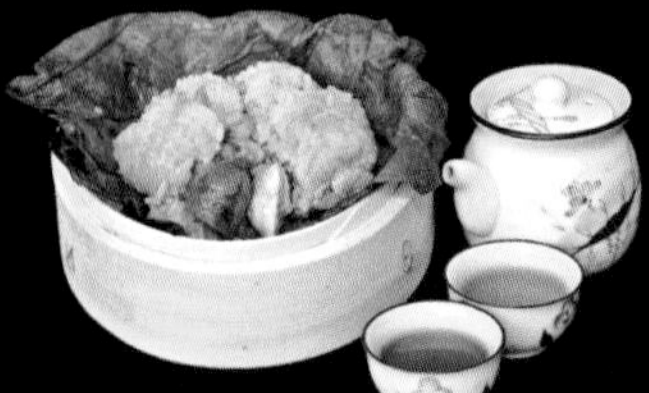

Soon Chung Lim

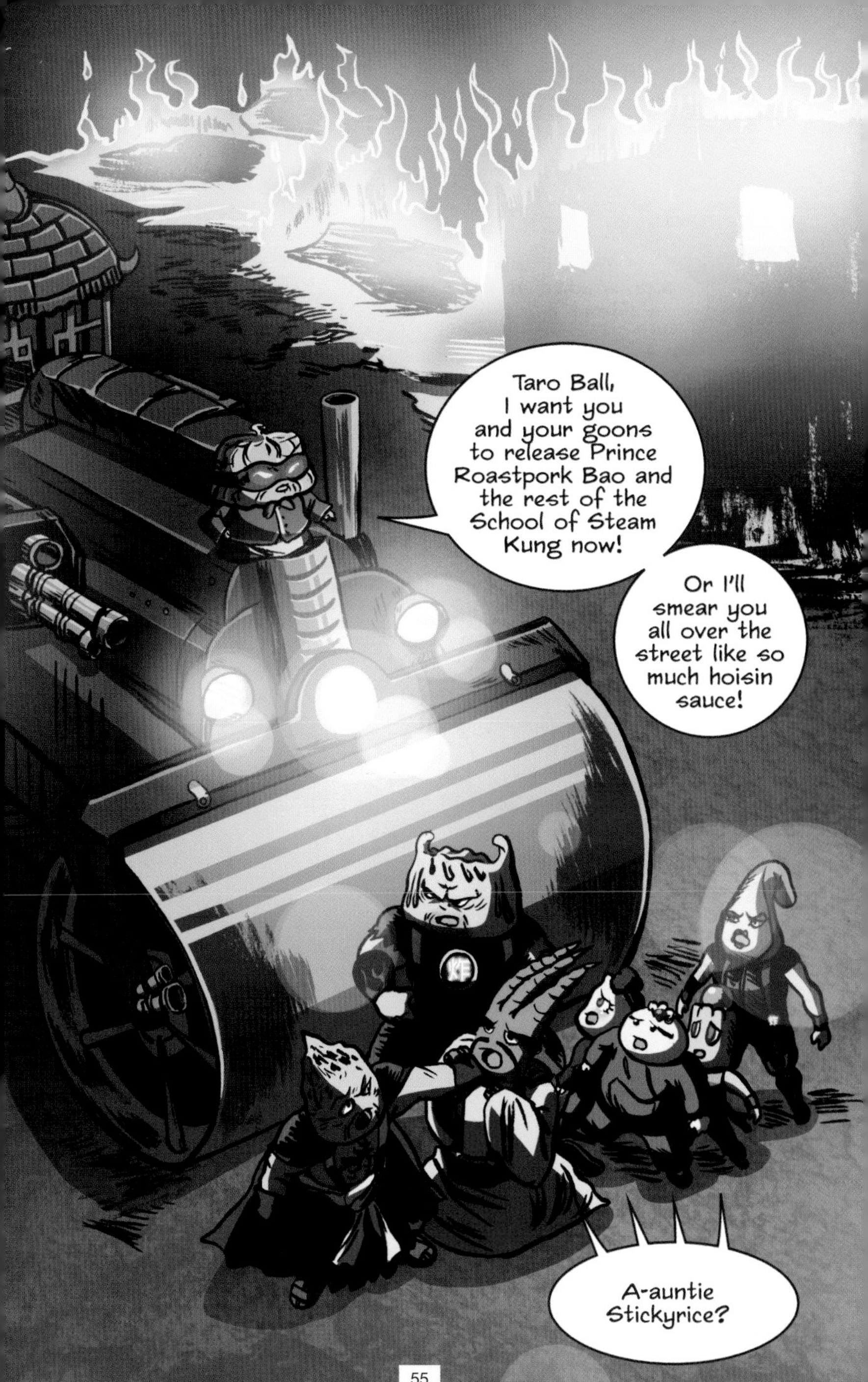
Taro Ball, I want you and your goons to release Prince Roastpork Bao and the rest of the School of Steam Kung now!
Or I'll smear you all over the street like so much hoisin sauce!
A-auntie Stickyrice?

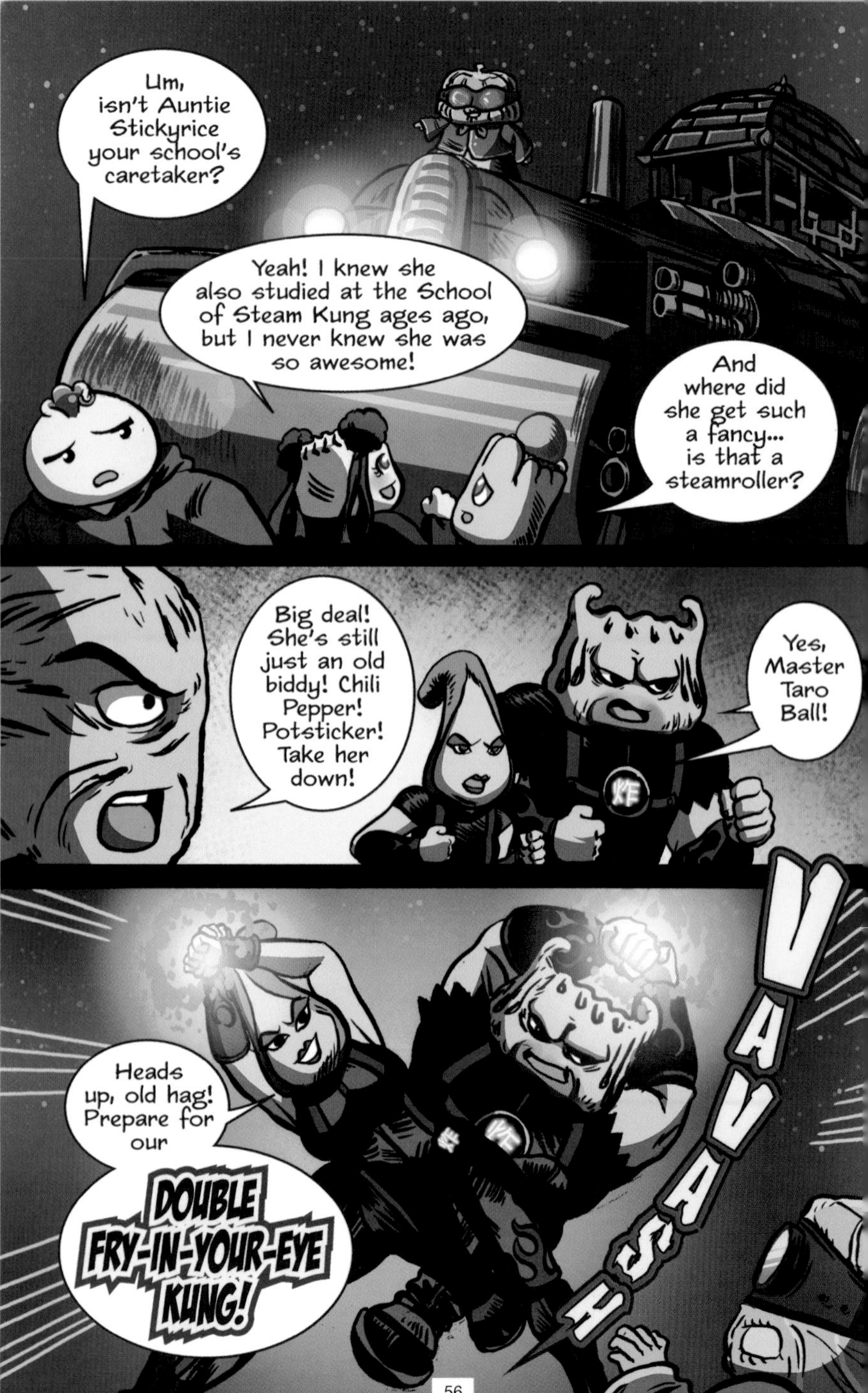
Um, isn't Auntie Stickyrice your school's caretaker?
Yeah! I knew she also studied at the School of Steam Kung ages ago, but I never knew she was so awesome!
And where did she get such a fancy... is that a steamroller?
Big deal! She's still just an old biddy! Chili Pepper! Potsticker! Take her down!
Yes, Master Taro Ball!
Heads up, old hag! Prepare for our
DOUBLE FRY-IN-YOUR-EYE KUNG!
VAVASH

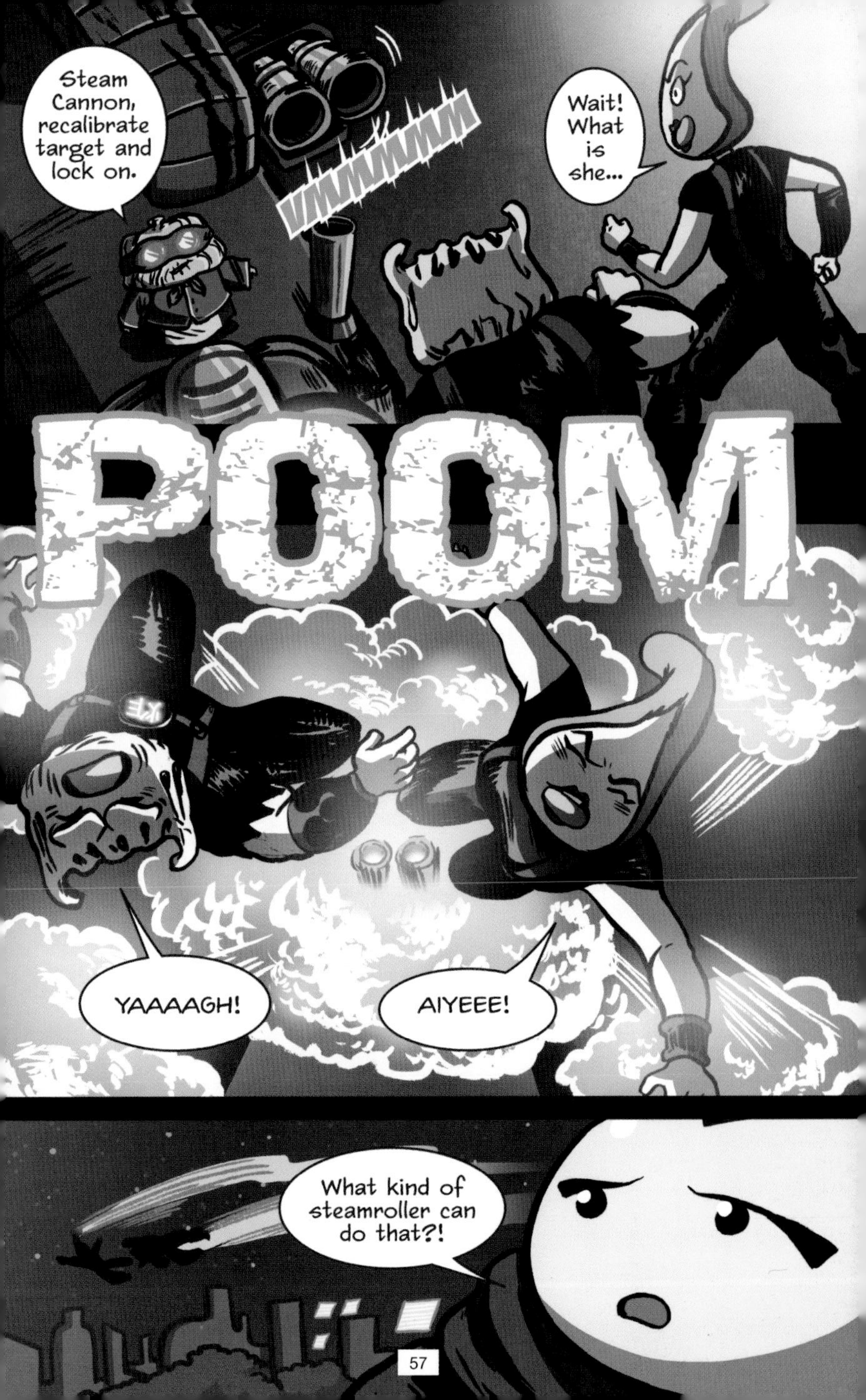
Steam Cannon, recalibrate target and lock on.
VMMMMMM
Wait! What is she...
POOM
YAAAAGH!
AIYEEE!
What kind of steamroller can do that?!

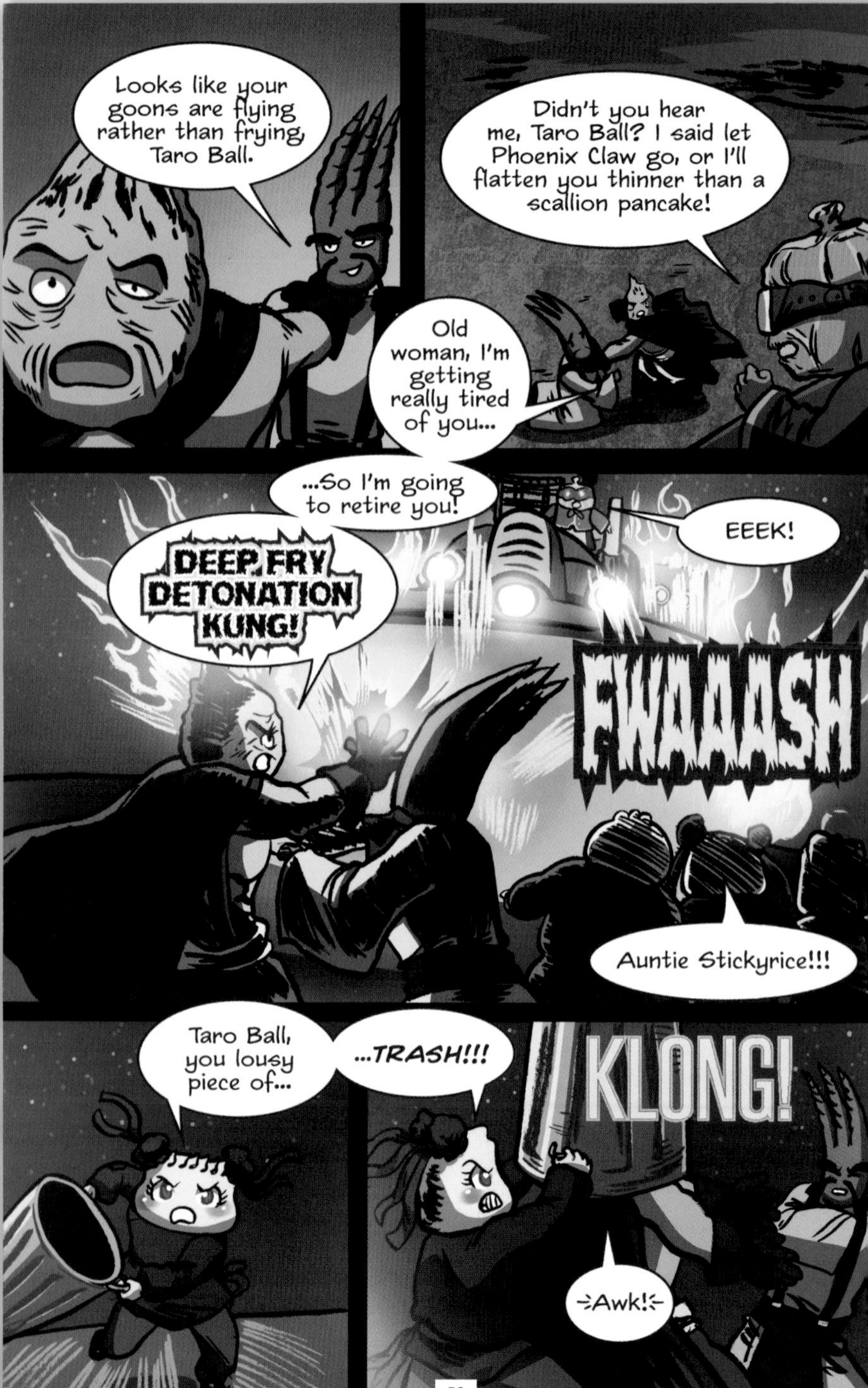
Looks like your goons are flying rather than frying, Taro Ball.
Didn't you hear me, Taro Ball? I said let Phoenix Claw go, or I'll flatten you thinner than a scallion pancake!
Old woman, I'm getting really tired of you...
...So I'm going to retire you!
EEEK!
DEEP FRY DETONATION KUNG!
FWAAASH
Auntie Stickyrice!!!
Taro Ball, you lousy piece of...
...TRASH!!!
KLONG!
Awk!

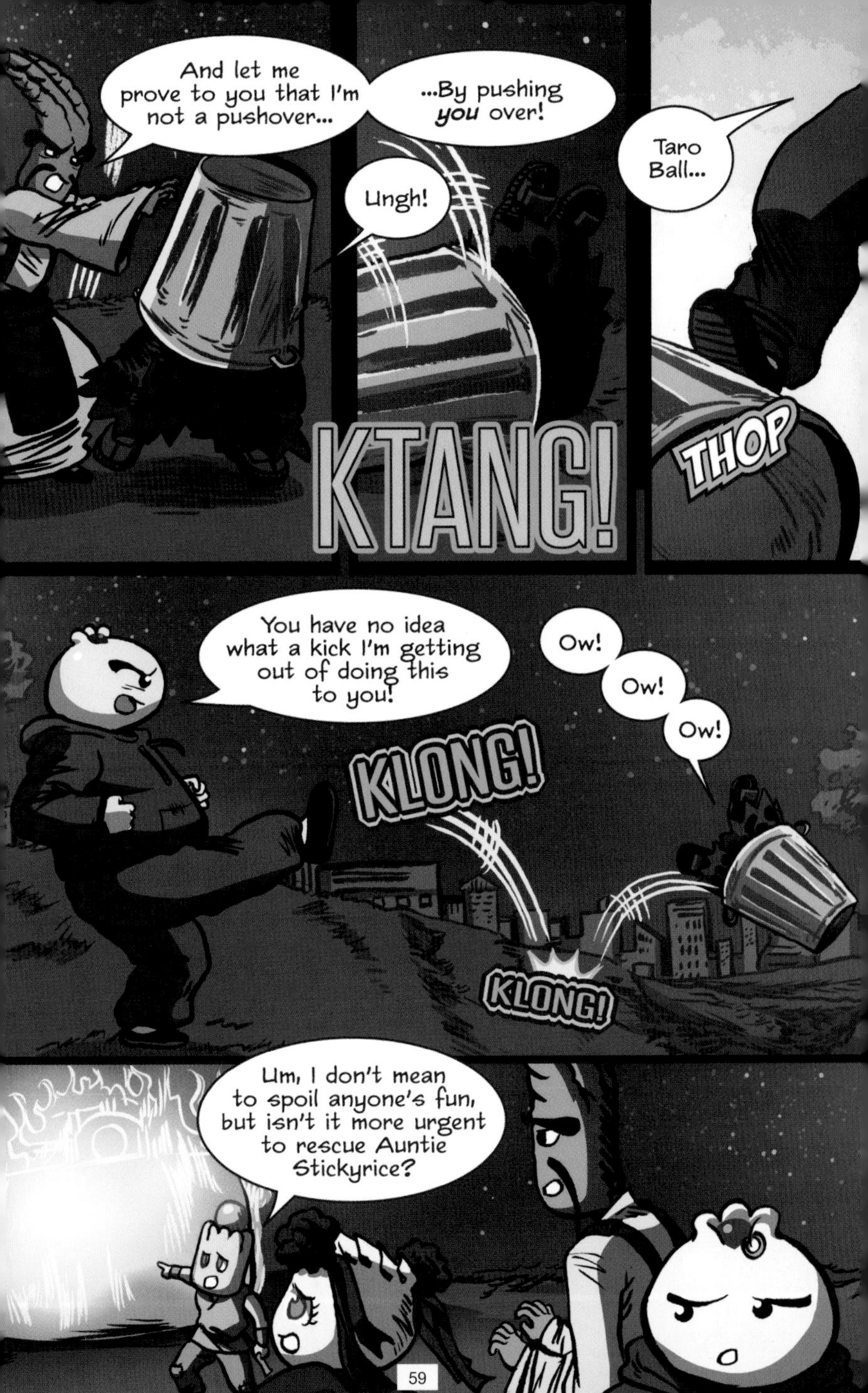
And let me prove to you that I'm not a pushover...
...By pushing *you* over!
Ungh!
KTANG!
Taro Ball...
THOP
You have no idea what a kick I'm getting out of doing this to you!
KLONG!
Ow!
Ow!
Ow!
KLONG!
Um, I don't mean to spoil anyone's fun, but isn't it more urgent to rescue Auntie Stickyrice?

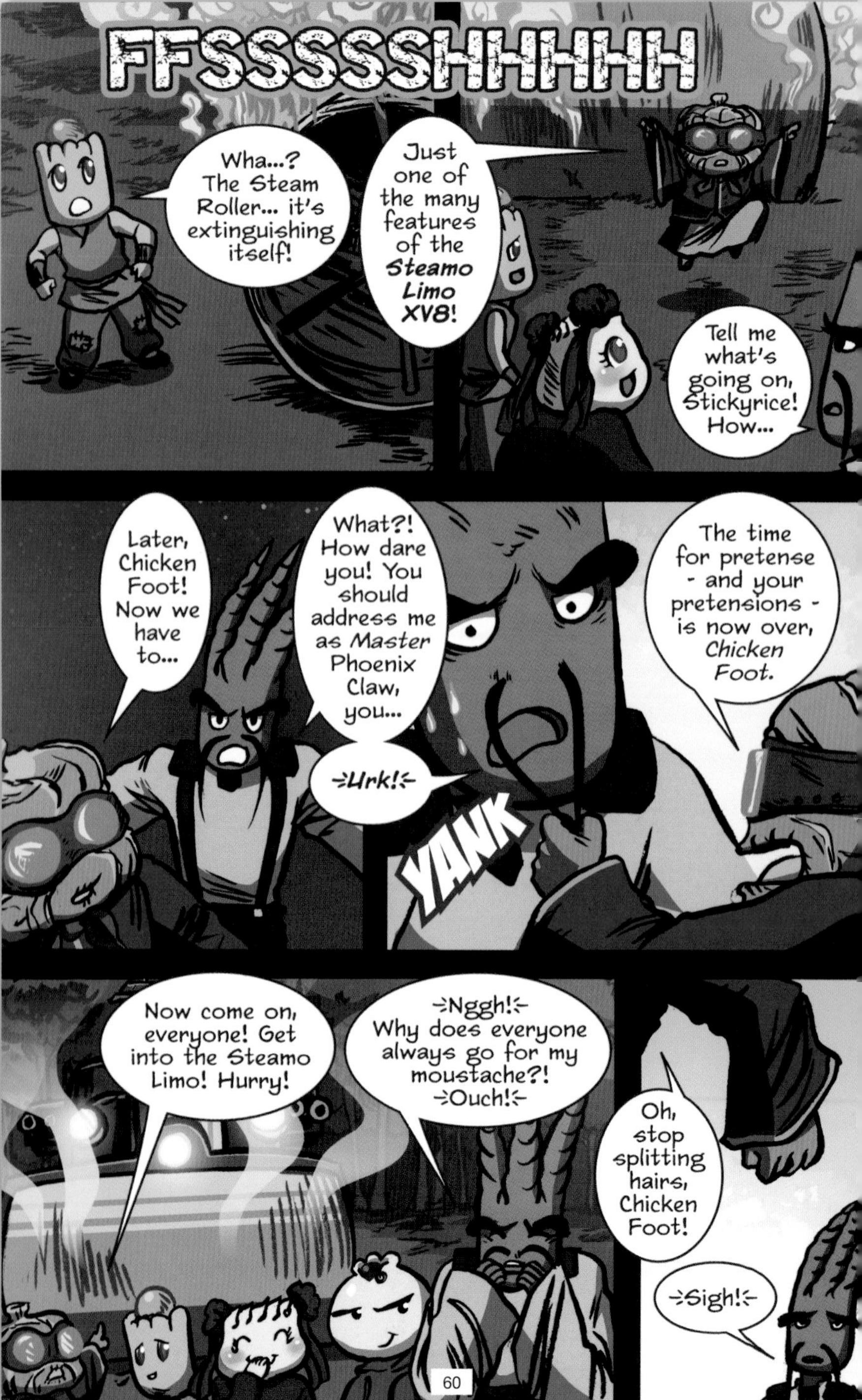
FFSSSSSSHHHHHH
Wha...? The Steam Roller... it's extinguishing itself!
Just one of the many features of the *Steamo Limo XV8*!
Tell me what's going on, Stickyrice! How...
Later, Chicken Foot! Now we have to...
What?! How dare you! You should address me as *Master* Phoenix Claw, you...
⇉Urk!⇇
YANK
The time for pretense - and your pretensions - is now over, *Chicken Foot*.
Now come on, everyone! Get into the Steamo Limo! Hurry!
⇉Nggh!⇇ Why does everyone always go for my moustache?! ⇉Ouch!⇇
Oh, stop splitting hairs, Chicken Foot!
⇉Sigh!⇇

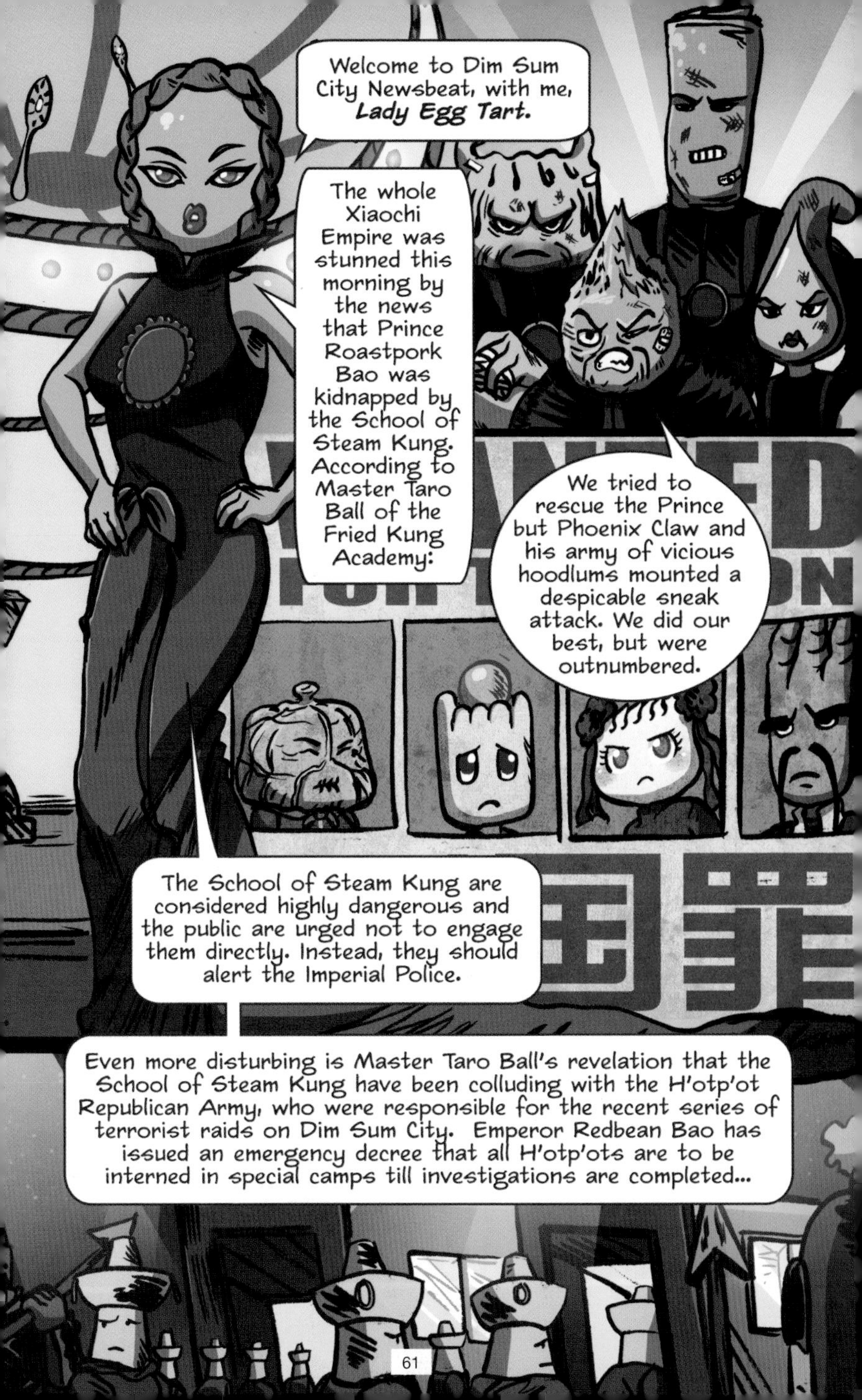

Welcome to Dim Sum City Newsbeat, with me, ***Lady Egg Tart.***
The whole Xiaochi Empire was stunned this morning by the news that Prince Roastpork Bao was kidnapped by the School of Steam Kung. According to Master Taro Ball of the Fried Kung Academy:
We tried to rescue the Prince but Phoenix Claw and his army of vicious hoodlums mounted a despicable sneak attack. We did our best, but were outnumbered.
The School of Steam Kung are considered highly dangerous and the public are urged not to engage them directly. Instead, they should alert the Imperial Police.
Even more disturbing is Master Taro Ball's revelation that the School of Steam Kung have been colluding with the H'otp'ot Republican Army, who were responsible for the recent series of terrorist raids on Dim Sum City. Emperor Redbean Bao has issued an emergency decree that all H'otp'ots are to be interned in special camps till investigations are completed...

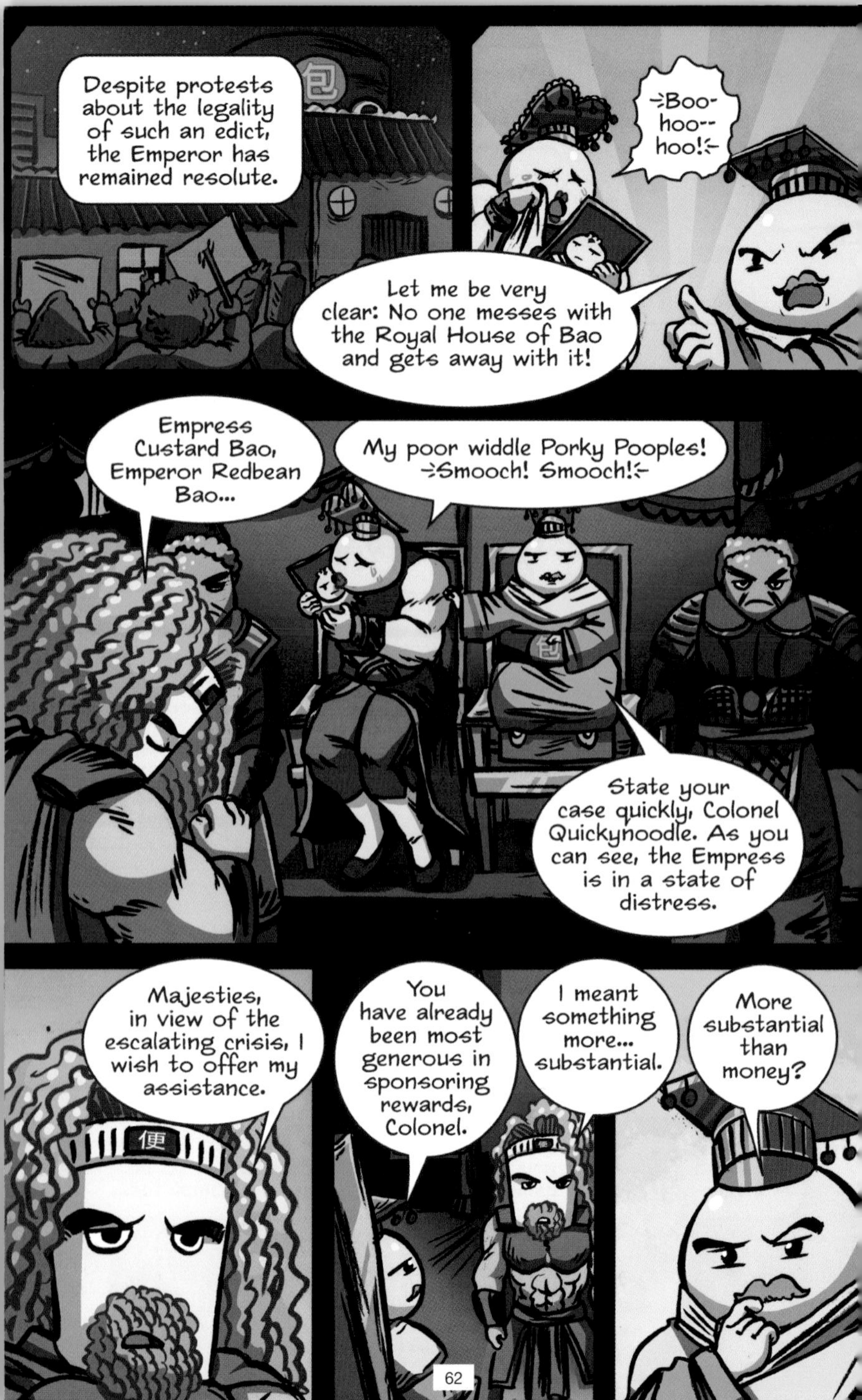
Despite protests about the legality of such an edict, the Emperor has remained resolute.
⇒Boo-hoo--hoo!⇐
Let me be very clear: No one messes with the Royal House of Bao and gets away with it!
Empress Custard Bao, Emperor Redbean Bao...
My poor widdle Porky Pooples! ⇒Smooch! Smooch!⇐
State your case quickly, Colonel Quickynoodle. As you can see, the Empress is in a state of distress.
Majesties, in view of the escalating crisis, I wish to offer my assistance.
You have already been most generous in sponsoring rewards, Colonel.
I meant something more... substantial.
More substantial than money?

Majesties, what you face is not some petty gang of lowlifes.
One of the oldest Dim Sum Warrior schools is conspiring with an entire people. That is a threat of unprecedented scale, which merits an exceptional response.
I am offering to augment the physical abilities of your troops with my InnerStrength elixir. You've seen how it's improved Master Taro Ball and his team. I can do the same for your entire army!
I've already taken the liberty of giving your praetorian guard a dose...
Oh. I thought they'd just been working out more...
And you've definitely seen its benefits on Her Majesty the Empress, even over these few short weeks.
Eh? Me?

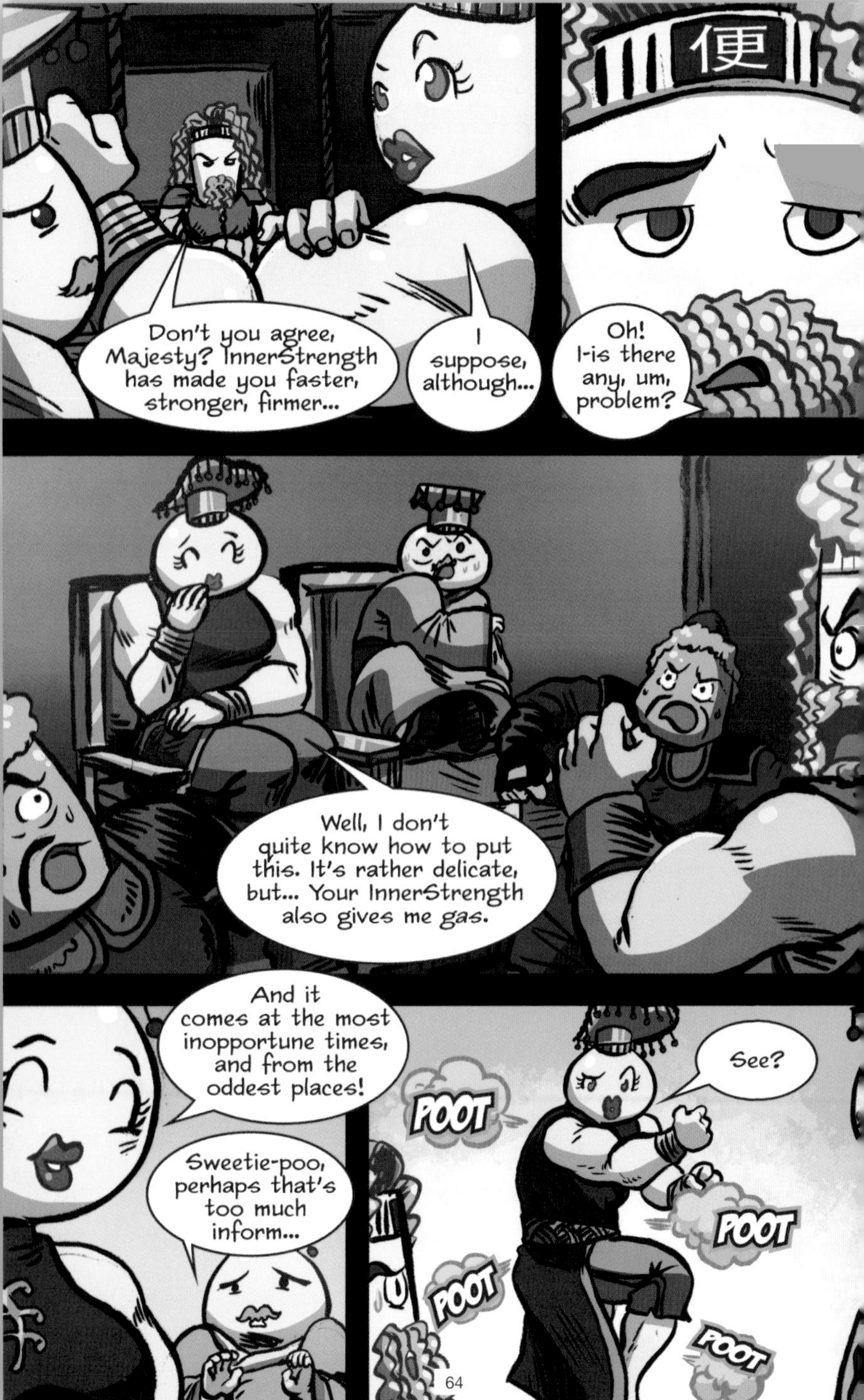

Don't you agree, Majesty? InnerStrength has made you faster, stronger, firmer...
I suppose, although...
便
Oh! I-is there any, um, problem?
Well, I don't quite know how to put this. It's rather delicate, but... Your InnerStrength also gives me gas.
And it comes at the most inopportune times, and from the oddest places!
Sweetie-poo, perhaps that's too much inform...
POOT
See?
POOT
POOT
POOT

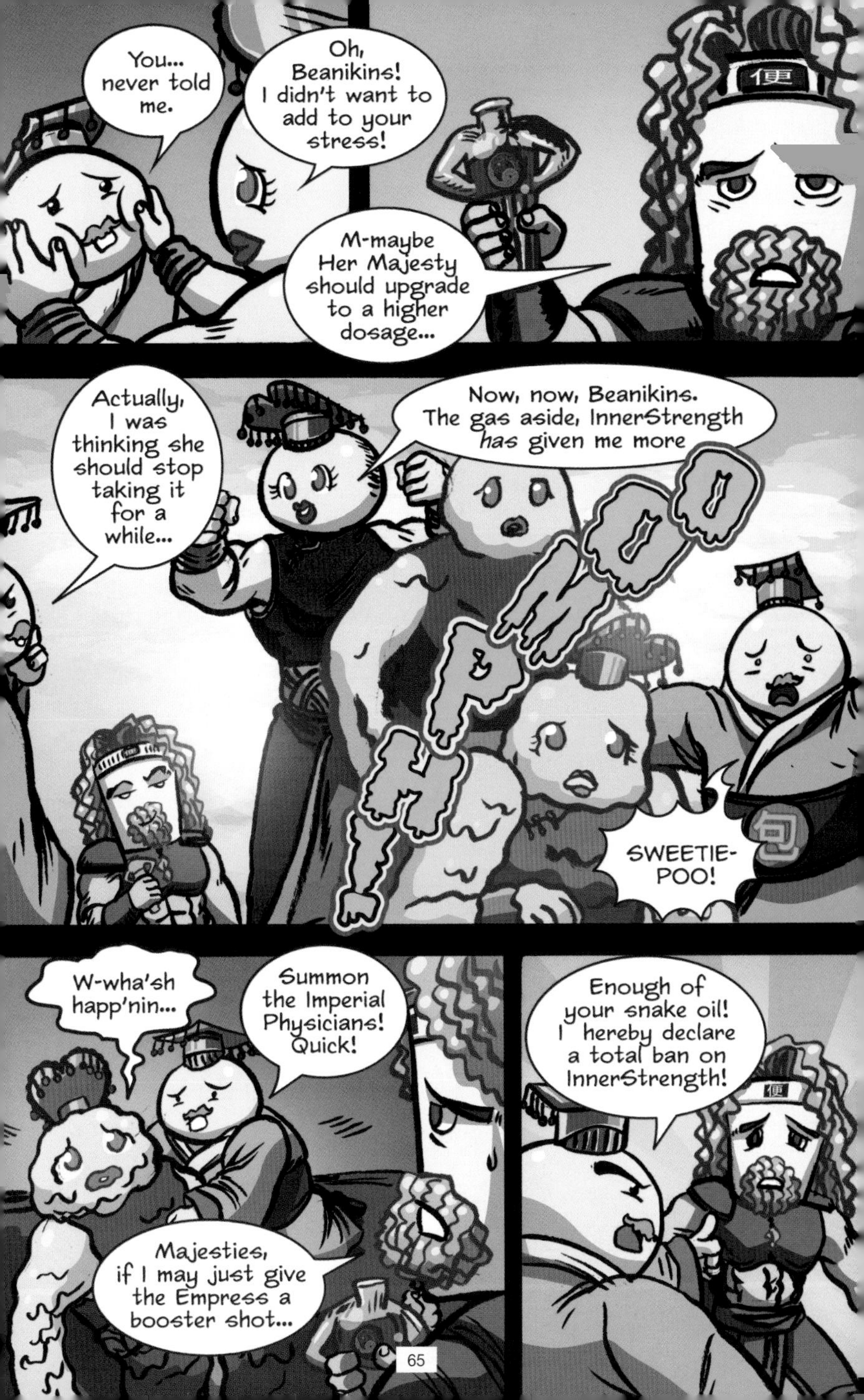

You... never told me.
Oh, Beanikins! I didn't want to add to your stress!
M-maybe Her Majesty should upgrade to a higher dosage...
Actually, I was thinking she should stop taking it for a while...
Now, now, Beanikins. The gas aside, InnerStrength has given me more
PHOO
SWEETIE-POO!
W-wha'sh happ'nin...
Summon the Imperial Physicians! Quick!
Majesties, if I may just give the Empress a booster shot...
Enough of your snake oil! I hereby declare a total ban on InnerStrength!

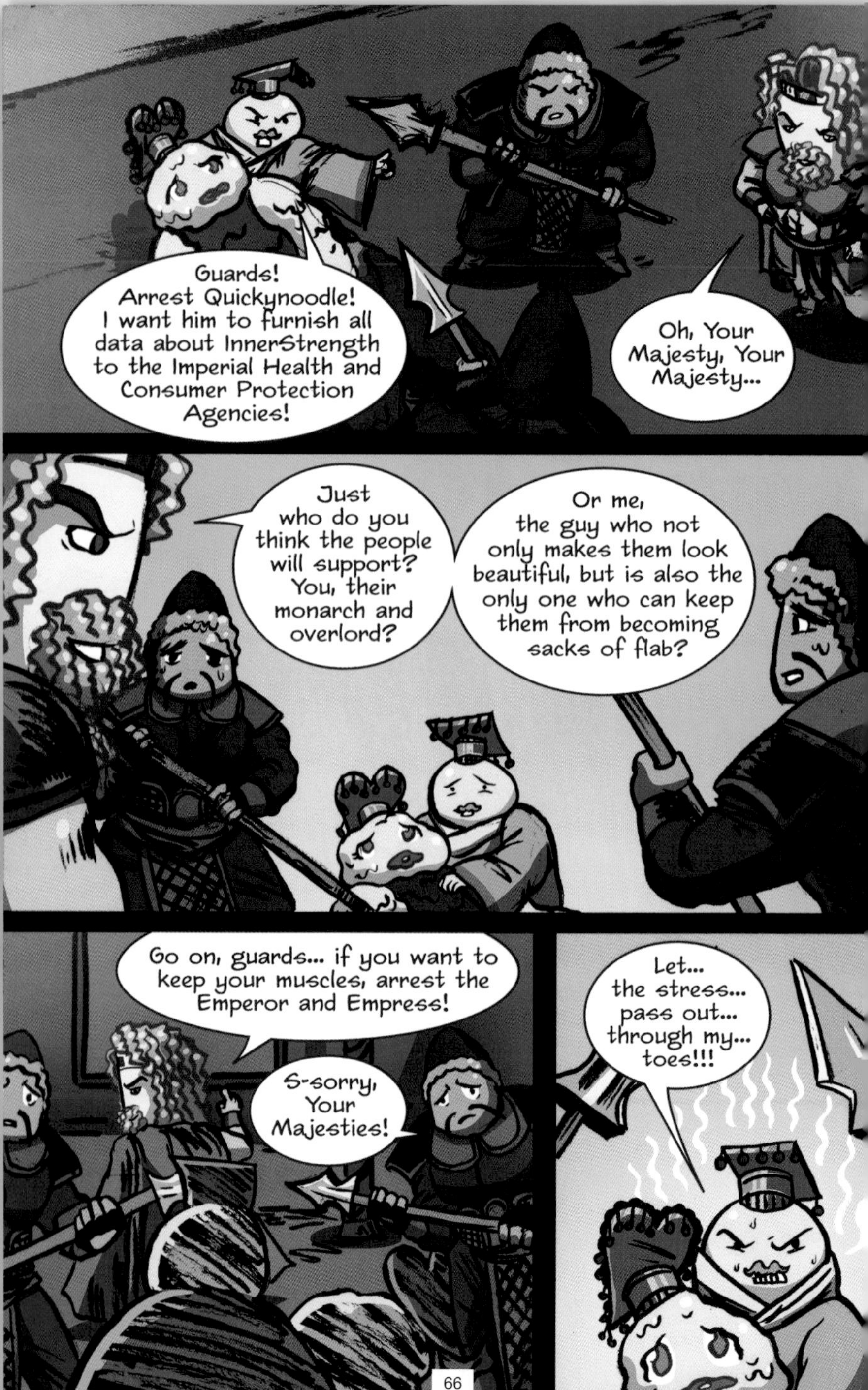
Guards! Arrest Quickynoodle! I want him to furnish all data about InnerStrength to the Imperial Health and Consumer Protection Agencies!
Oh, Your Majesty, Your Majesty...
Just who do you think the people will support? You, their monarch and overlord?
Or me, the guy who not only makes them look beautiful, but is also the only one who can keep them from becoming sacks of flab?
Go on, guards... if you want to keep your muscles, arrest the Emperor and Empress!
S-sorry, Your Majesties!
Let... the stress... pass out... through my... toes!!!

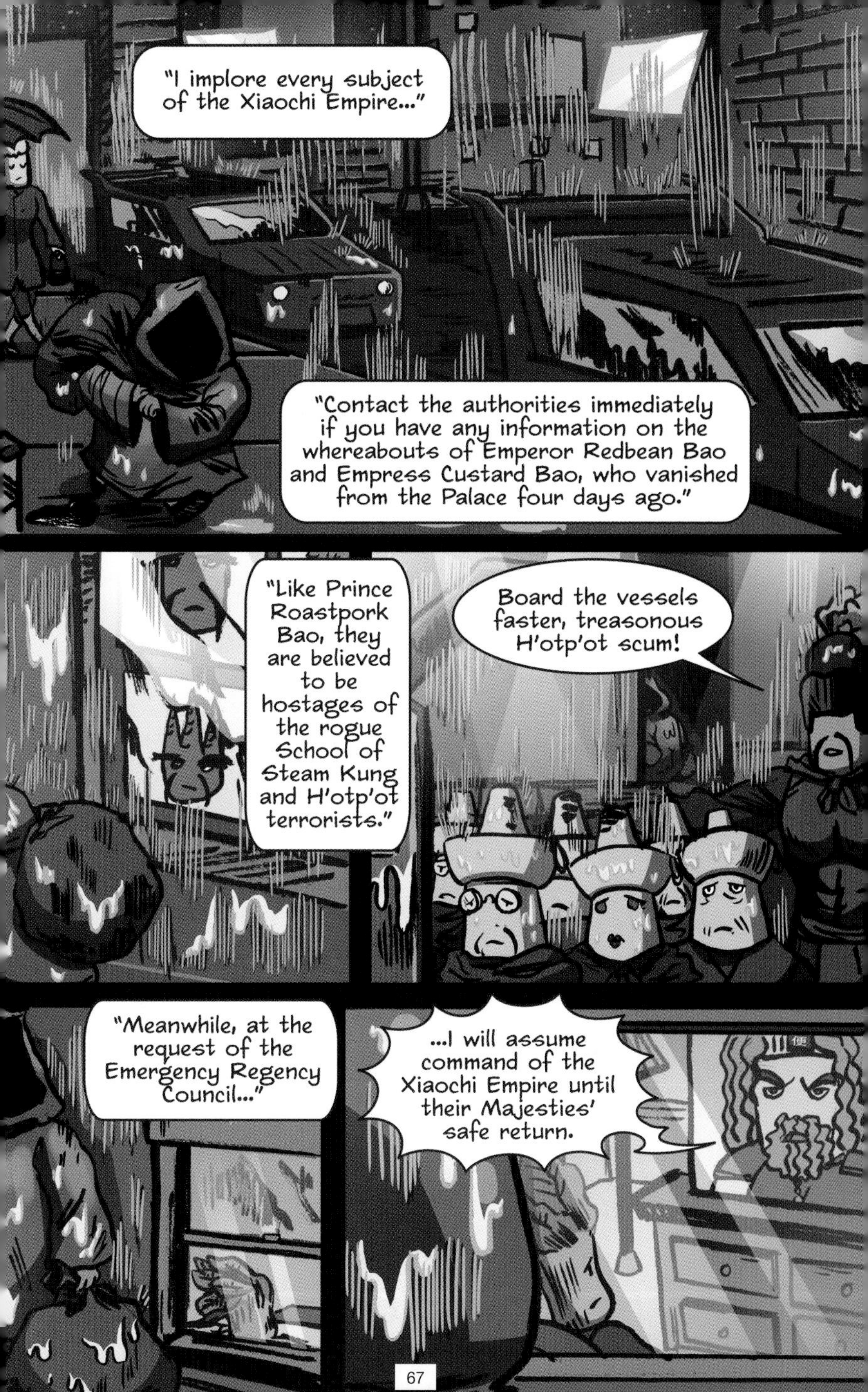
"I implore every subject of the Xiaochi Empire..."
"Contact the authorities immediately if you have any information on the whereabouts of Emperor Redbean Bao and Empress Custard Bao, who vanished from the Palace four days ago."
"Like Prince Roastpork Bao, they are believed to be hostages of the rogue School of Steam Kung and H'otp'ot terrorists."
Board the vessels faster, treasonous H'otp'ot scum!
"Meanwhile, at the request of the Emergency Regency Council..."
...I will assume command of the Xiaochi Empire until their Majesties' safe return.

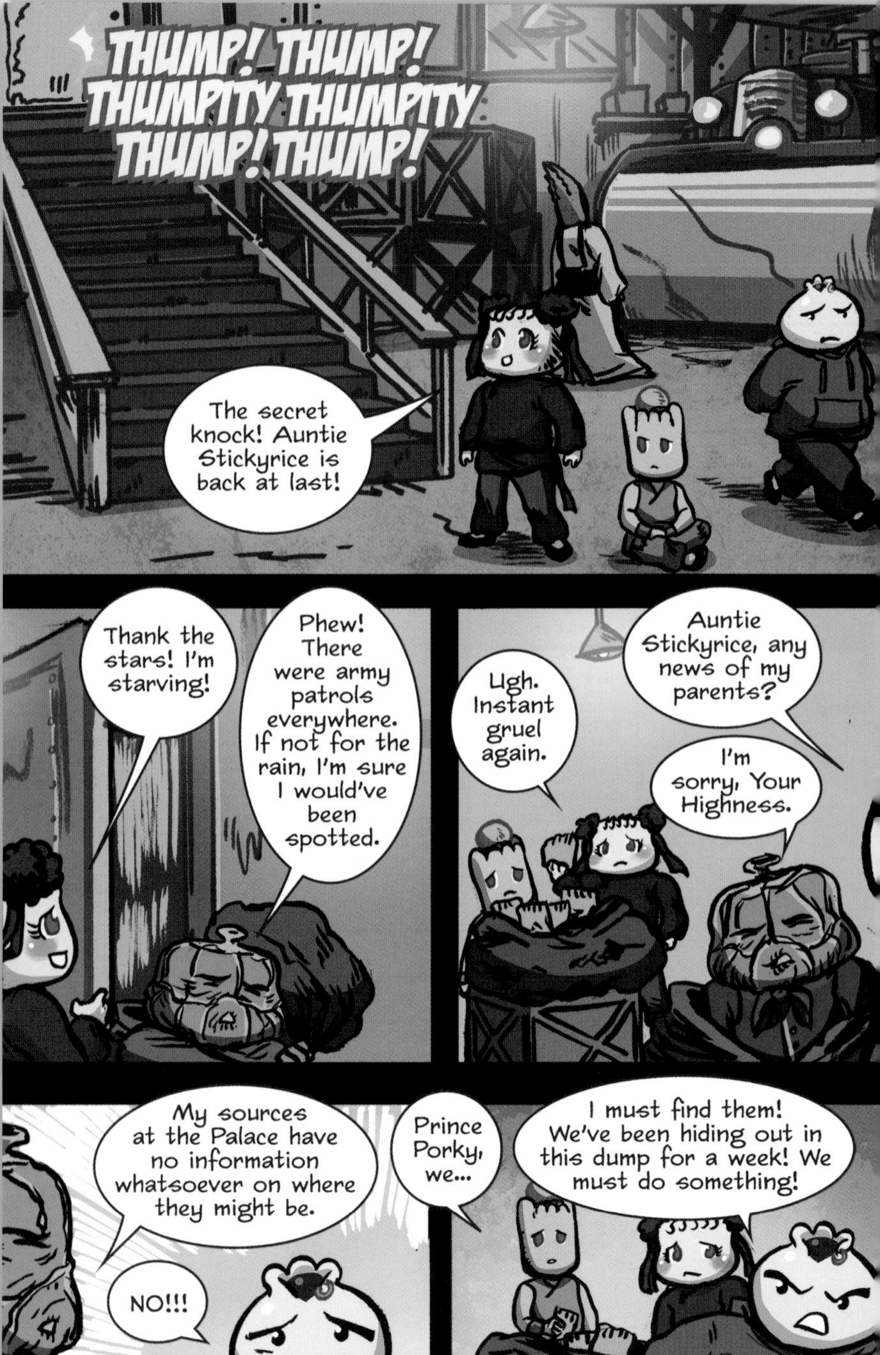
THUMP! THUMP! THUMPITY THUMPITY THUMP! THUMP!
The secret knock! Auntie Stickyrice is back at last!
Thank the stars! I'm starving!
Phew! There were army patrols everywhere. If not for the rain, I'm sure I would've been spotted.
Ugh. Instant gruel again.
Auntie Stickyrice, any news of my parents?
I'm sorry, Your Highness.
My sources at the Palace have no information whatsoever on where they might be.
NO!!!
Prince Porky, we...
I must find them! We've been hiding out in this dump for a week! We must do something!

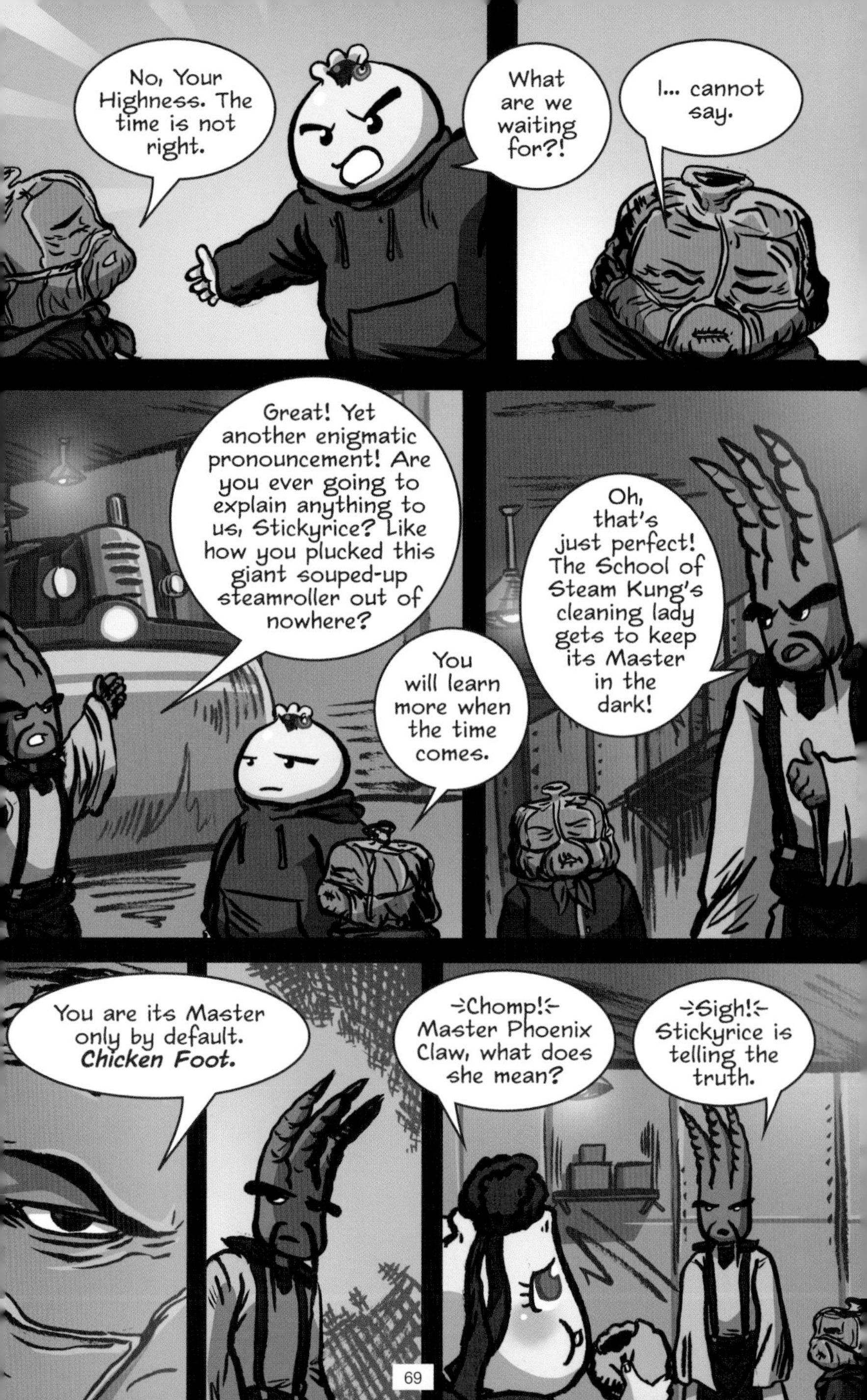
No, Your Highness. The time is not right.
What are we waiting for?!
I... cannot say.
Great! Yet another enigmatic pronouncement! Are you ever going to explain anything to us, Stickyrice? Like how you plucked this giant souped-up steamroller out of nowhere?
You will learn more when the time comes.
Oh, that's just perfect! The School of Steam Kung's cleaning lady gets to keep its Master in the dark!
You are its Master only by default. ***Chicken Foot.***
-Chomp!- Master Phoenix Claw, what does she mean?
-Sigh!- Stickyrice is telling the truth.

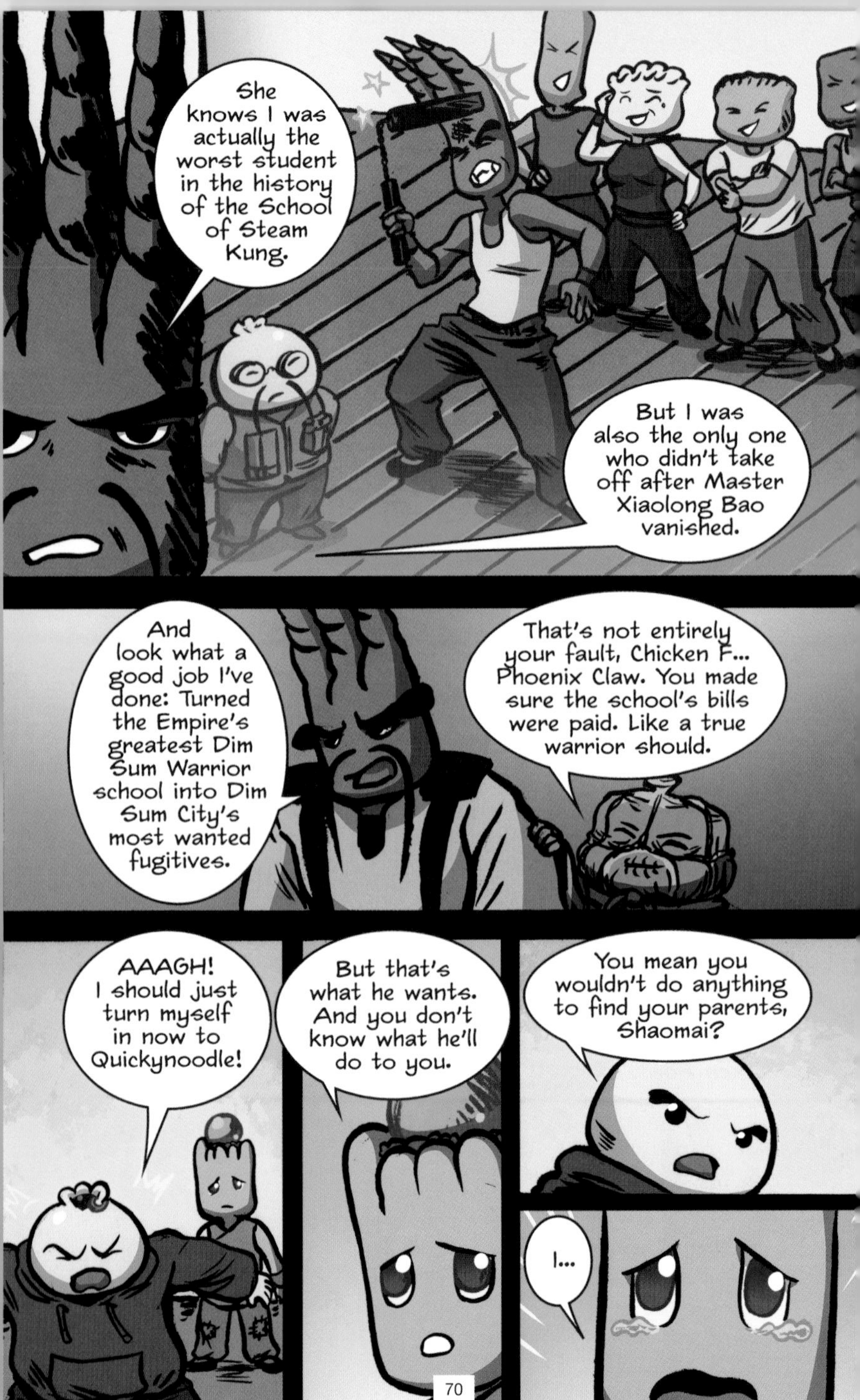
She knows I was actually the worst student in the history of the School of Steam Kung.
But I was also the only one who didn't take off after Master Xiaolong Bao vanished.
And look what a good job I've done: Turned the Empire's greatest Dim Sum Warrior school into Dim Sum City's most wanted fugitives.
That's not entirely your fault, Chicken F... Phoenix Claw. You made sure the school's bills were paid. Like a true warrior should.
AAAGH! I should just turn myself in now to Quickynoodle!
But that's what he wants. And you don't know what he'll do to you.
You mean you wouldn't do anything to find your parents, Shaomai?
I...

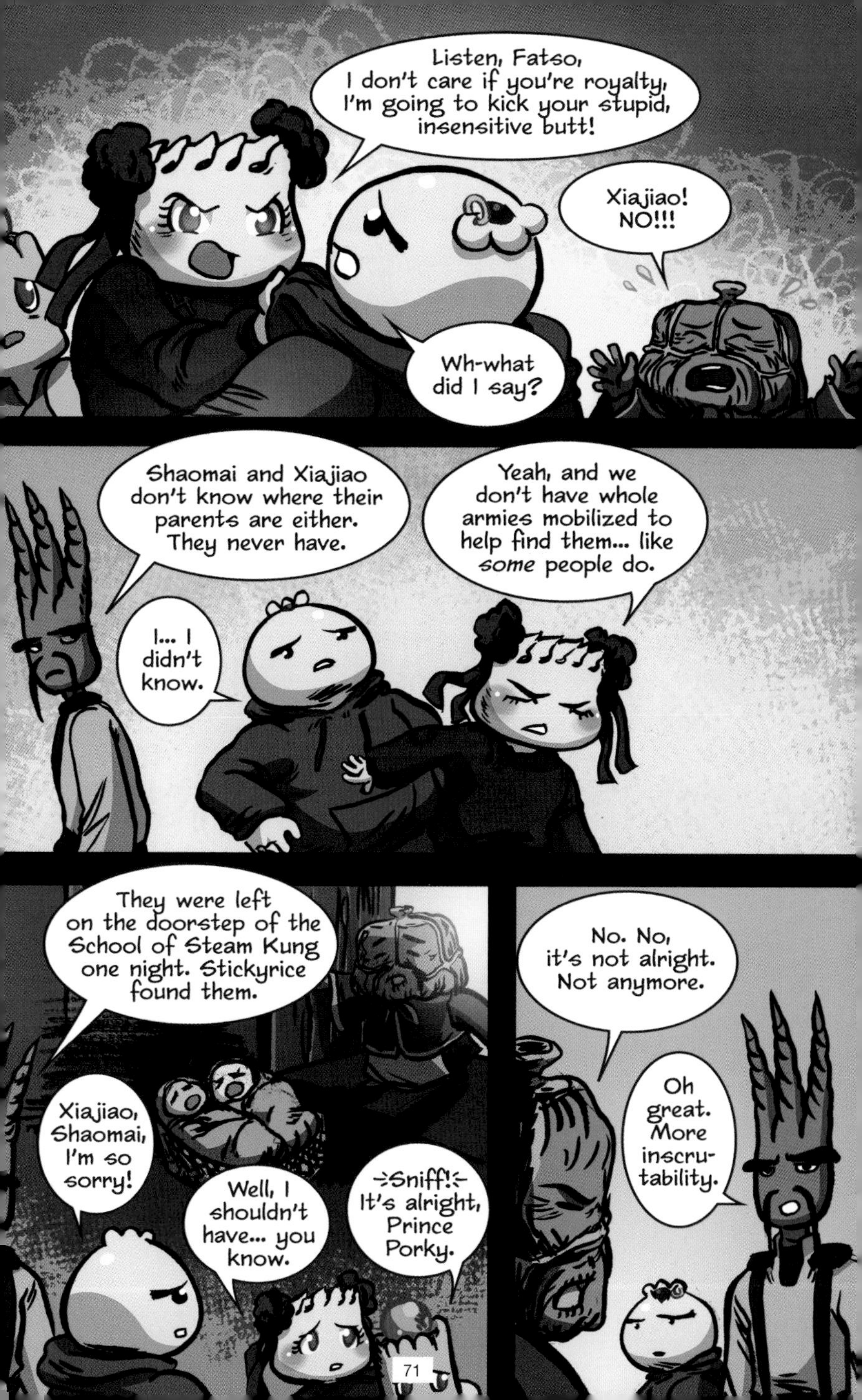
Listen, Fatso, I don't care if you're royalty, I'm going to kick your stupid, insensitive butt!
Xiajiao! NO!!!
Wh-what did I say?
Shaomai and Xiajiao don't know where their parents are either. They never have.
Yeah, and we don't have whole armies mobilized to help find them... like *some* people do.
I... I didn't know.
They were left on the doorstep of the School of Steam Kung one night. Stickyrice found them.
Xiajiao, Shaomai, I'm so sorry!
Well, I shouldn't have... you know.
Sniff! It's alright, Prince Porky.
No. No, it's not alright. Not anymore.
Oh great. More inscru-tability.

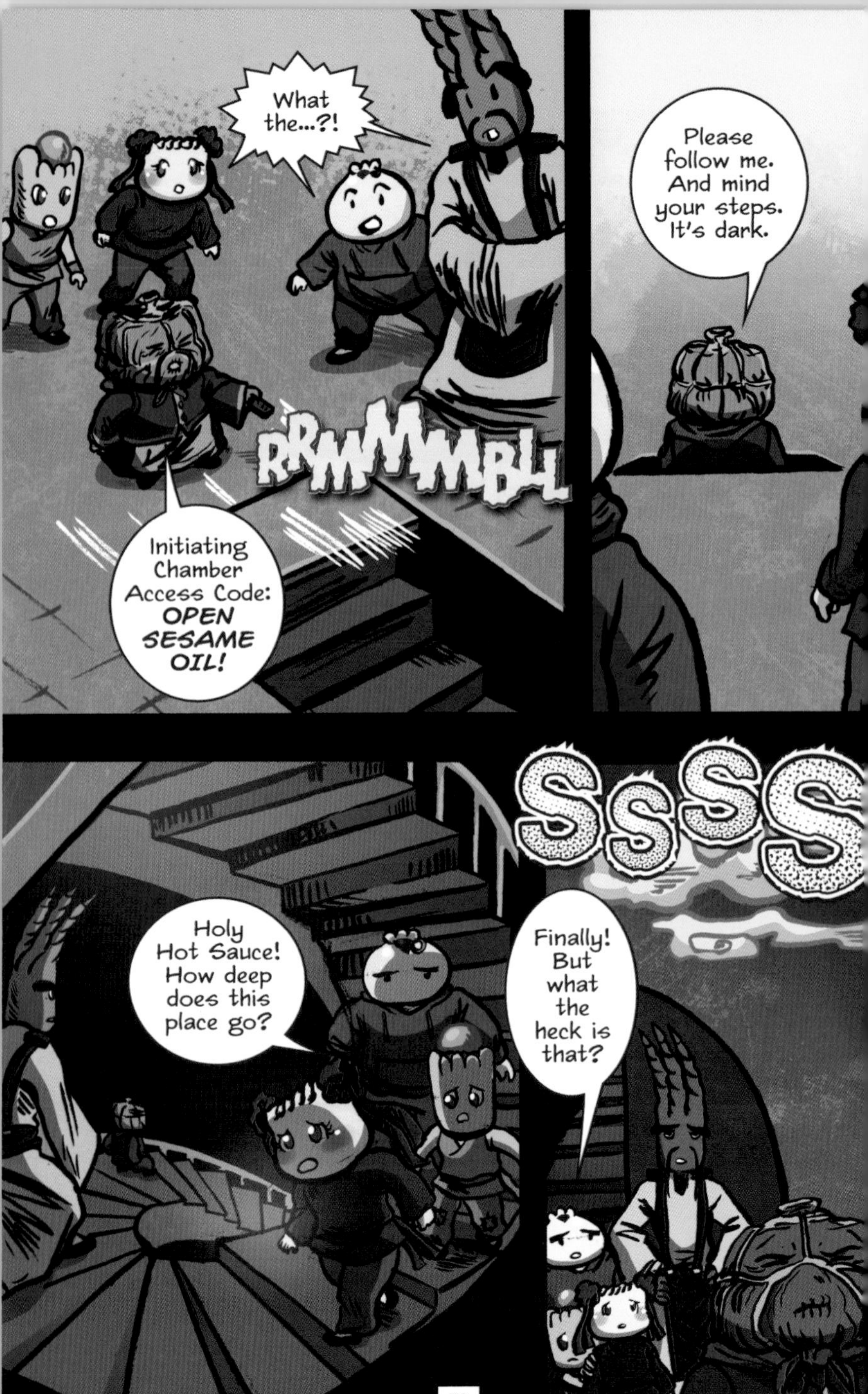
What the...?!
RRMMMMBLL
Initiating Chamber Access Code: OPEN SESAME OIL!
Please follow me. And mind your steps. It's dark.
SSSS
Holy Hot Sauce! How deep does this place go?
Finally! But what the heck is that?

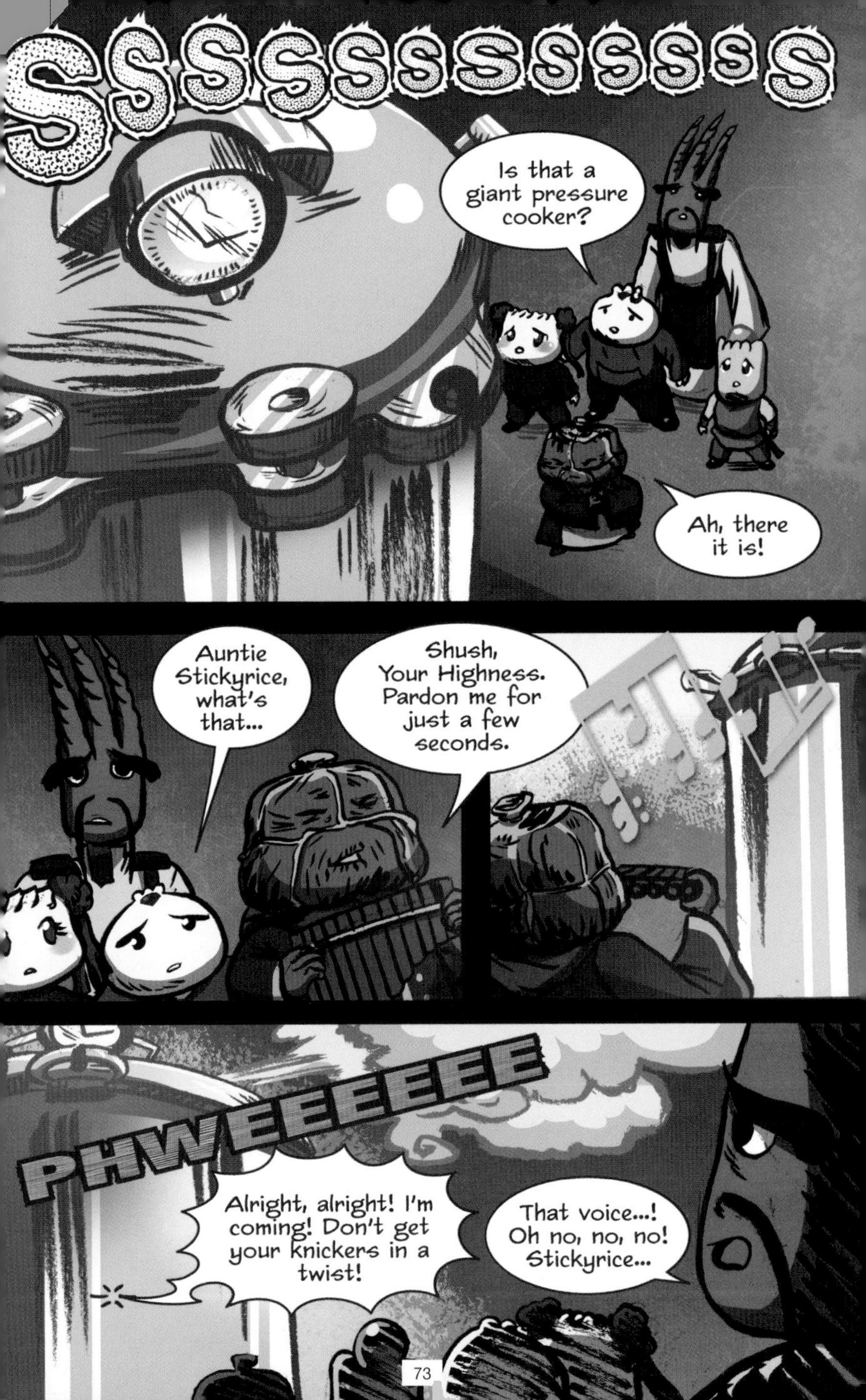
SSSSSSSSSSS
Is that a giant pressure cooker?
Ah, there it is!
Auntie Stickyrice, what's that...
Shush, Your Highness. Pardon me for just a few seconds.
PHWEEEEEEE
Alright, alright! I'm coming! Don't get your knickers in a twist!
That voice...! Oh no, no, no! Stickyrice...

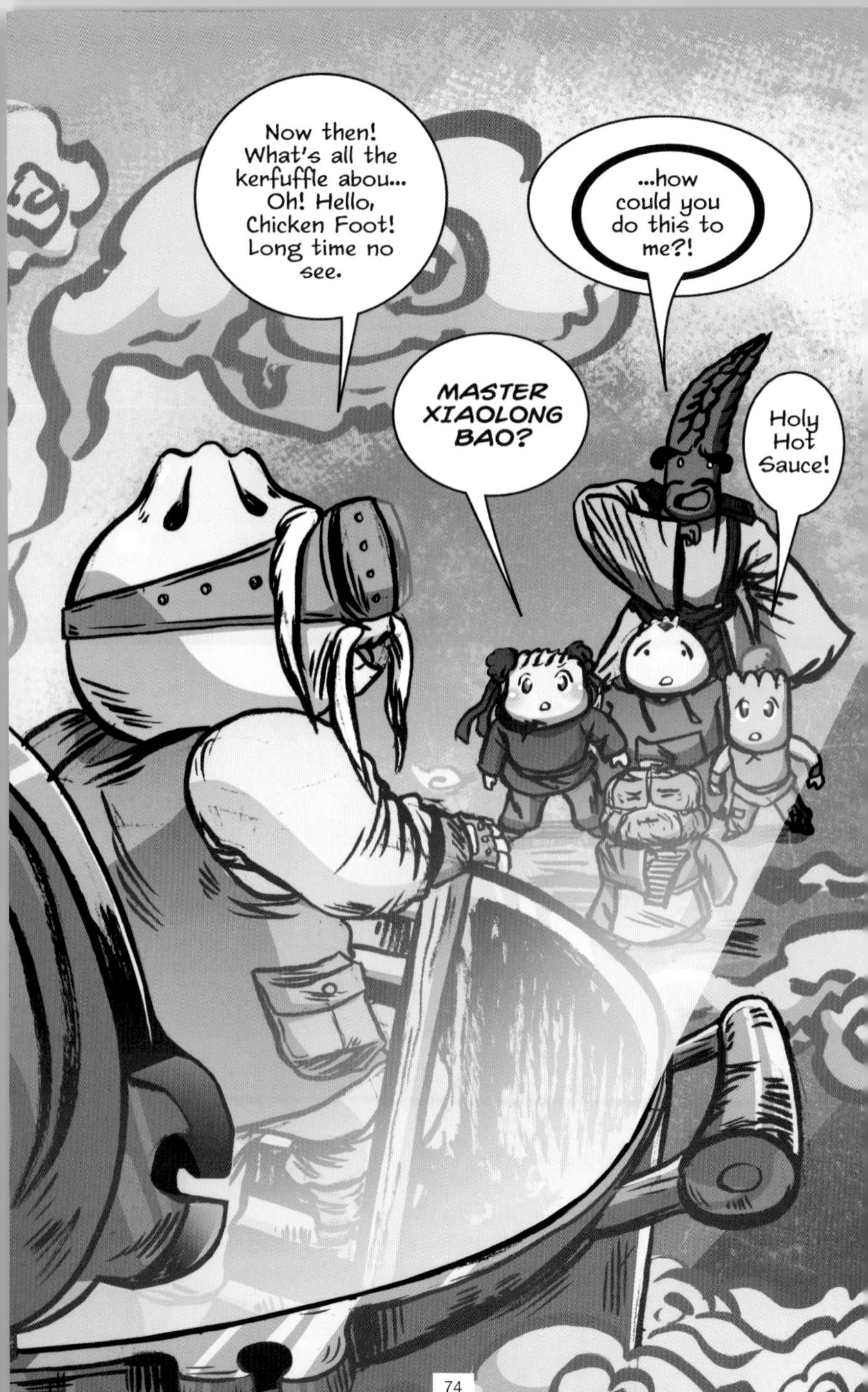

Now then! What's all the kerfuffle abou... Oh! Hello, Chicken Foot! Long time no see.
...how could you do this to me?!
MASTER XIAOLONG BAO?
Holy Hot Sauce!

# Chapter 10
# Unraveling the Noodle

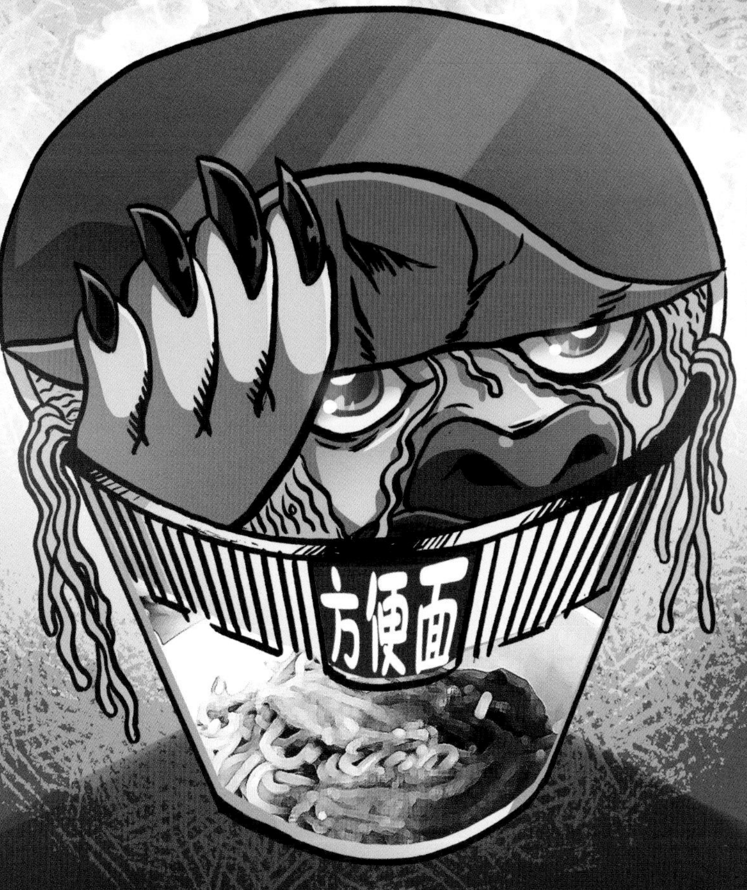
方便面

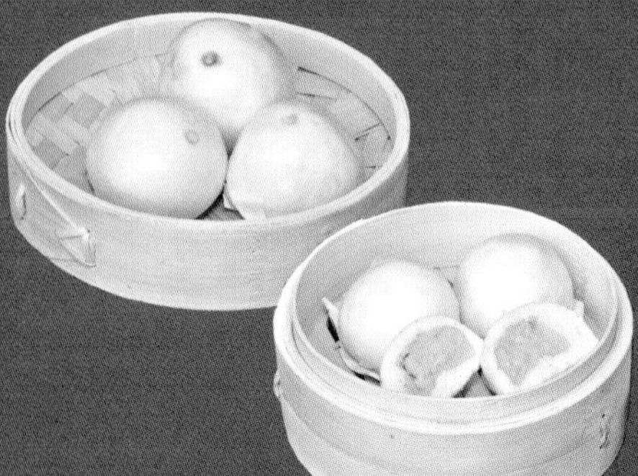

Soon Chung Lim

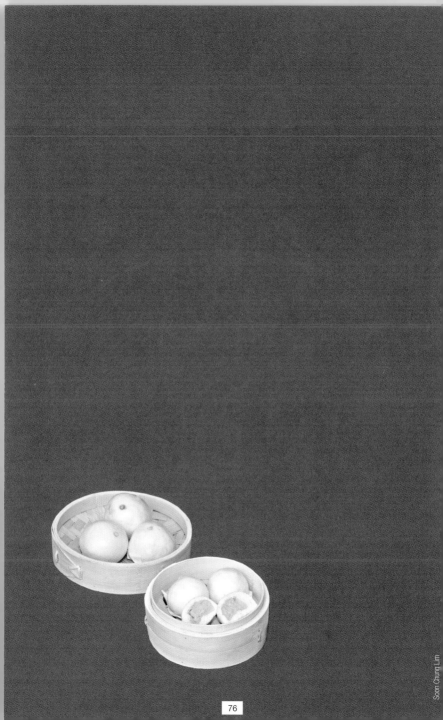

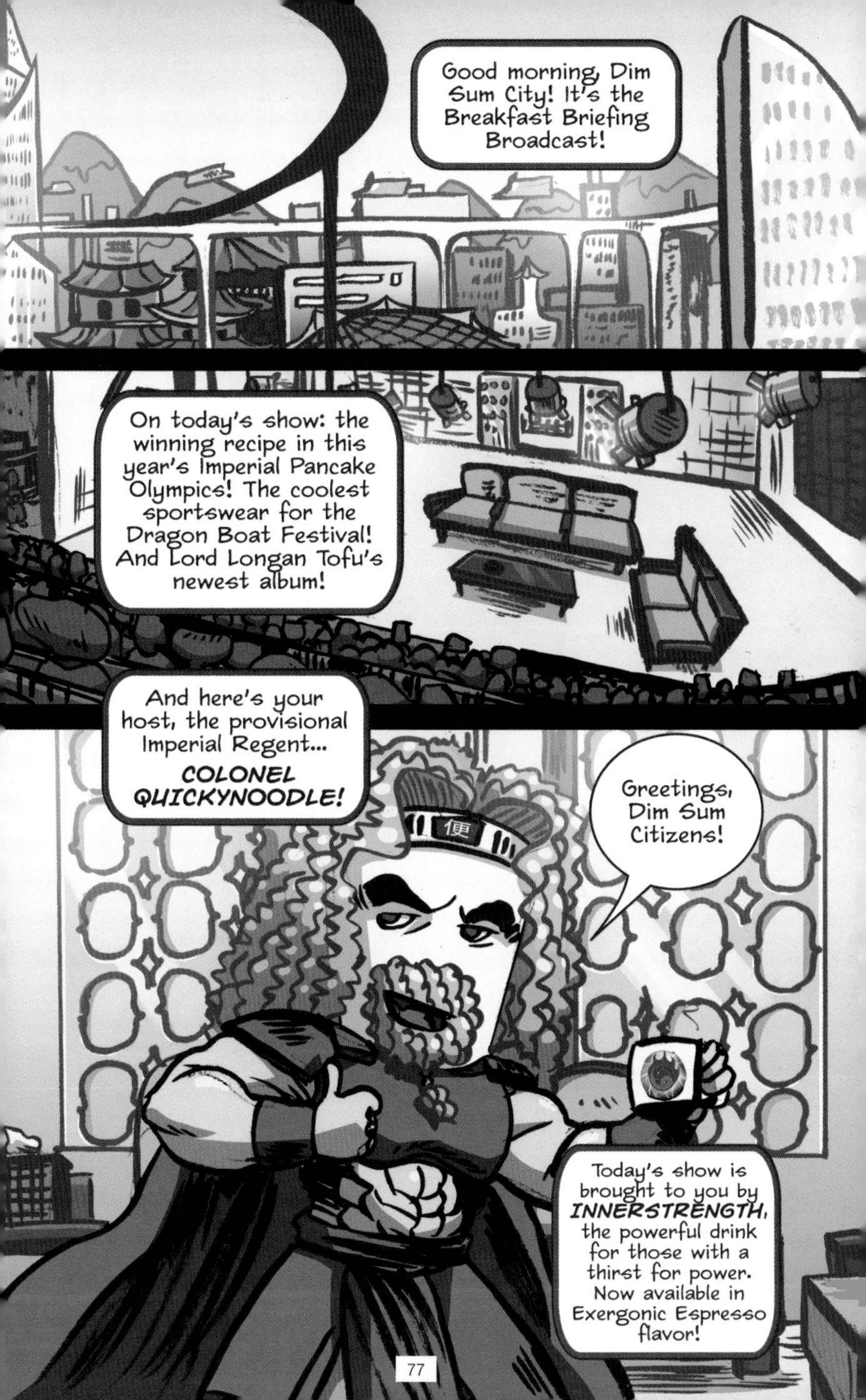
Good morning, Dim Sum City! It's the Breakfast Briefing Broadcast!
On today's show: the winning recipe in this year's Imperial Pancake Olympics! The coolest sportswear for the Dragon Boat Festival! And Lord Longan Tofu's newest album!
And here's your host, the provisional Imperial Regent... COLONEL QUICKYNOODLE!
便
Greetings, Dim Sum Citizens!
Today's show is brought to you by INNERSTRENGTH, the powerful drink for those with a thirst for power. Now available in Exergonic Espresso flavor!

And now, Excellencies and gathered dignitaries from the United Nourishments: an update about the search for Emperor Redbean Bao, Empress Custard Bao and Prince Roastpork Bao, who are believed to have been kidnapped by the rogue Dim Sum Warrior group, the School of Steam Kung...
Nope. Nothing new to report. Oh well.
Now if there are no ques... Oh! Yes...
Ambassador Baconburger of the United Sandwiches of Ambrosia?
Ahem! Colonel, could you explain to me and my fellow delegates just how you, a private businessman, came to be appointed the provisional ruler?

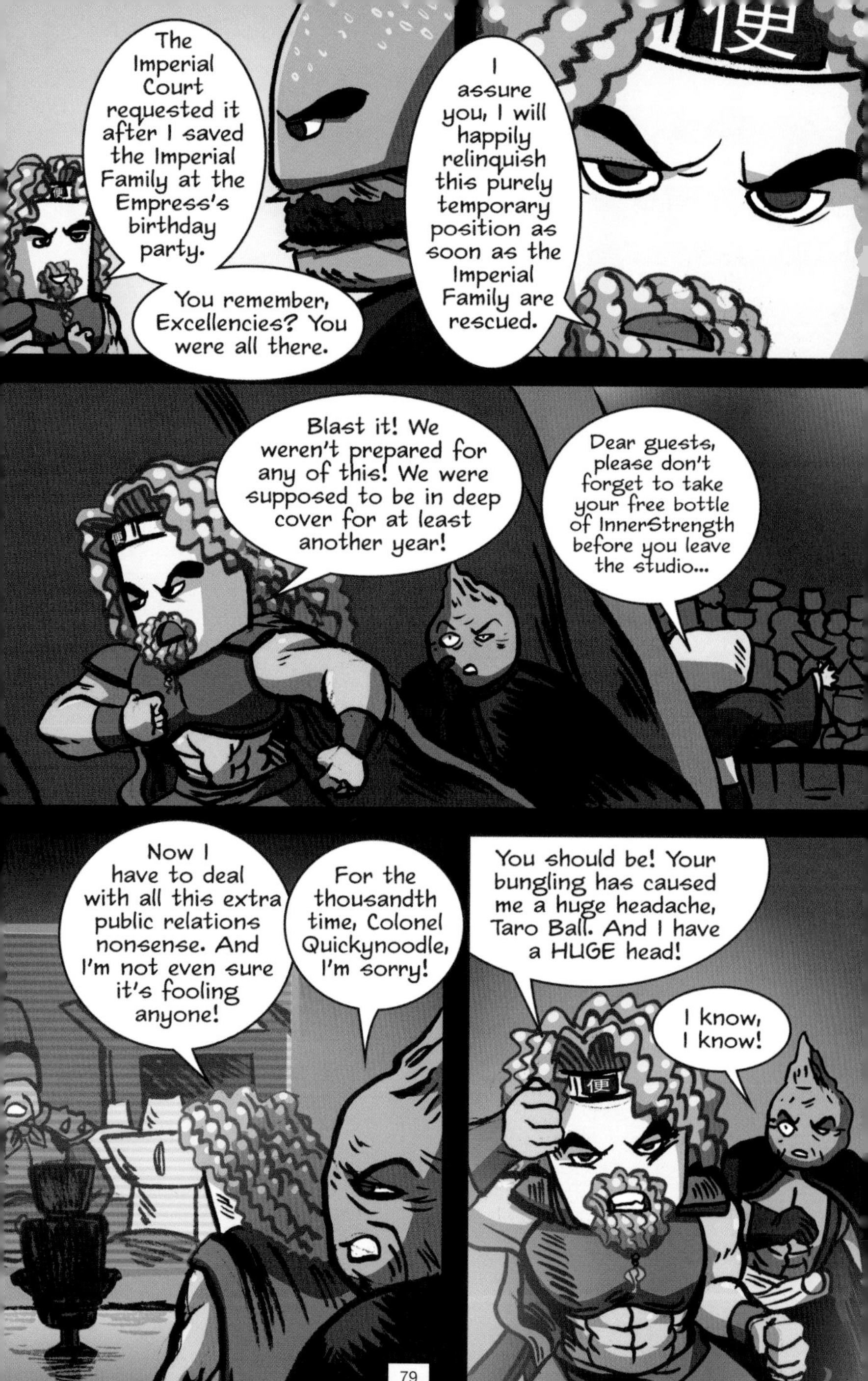
The Imperial Court requested it after I saved the Imperial Family at the Empress's birthday party.
You remember, Excellencies? You were all there.
I assure you, I will happily relinquish this purely temporary position as soon as the Imperial Family are rescued.
Blast it! We weren't prepared for any of this! We were supposed to be in deep cover for at least another year!
Dear guests, please don't forget to take your free bottle of InnerStrength before you leave the studio...
Now I have to deal with all this extra public relations nonsense. And I'm not even sure it's fooling anyone!
For the thousandth time, Colonel Quickynoodle, I'm sorry!
You should be! Your bungling has caused me a huge headache, Taro Ball. And I have a HUGE head!
I know, I know!

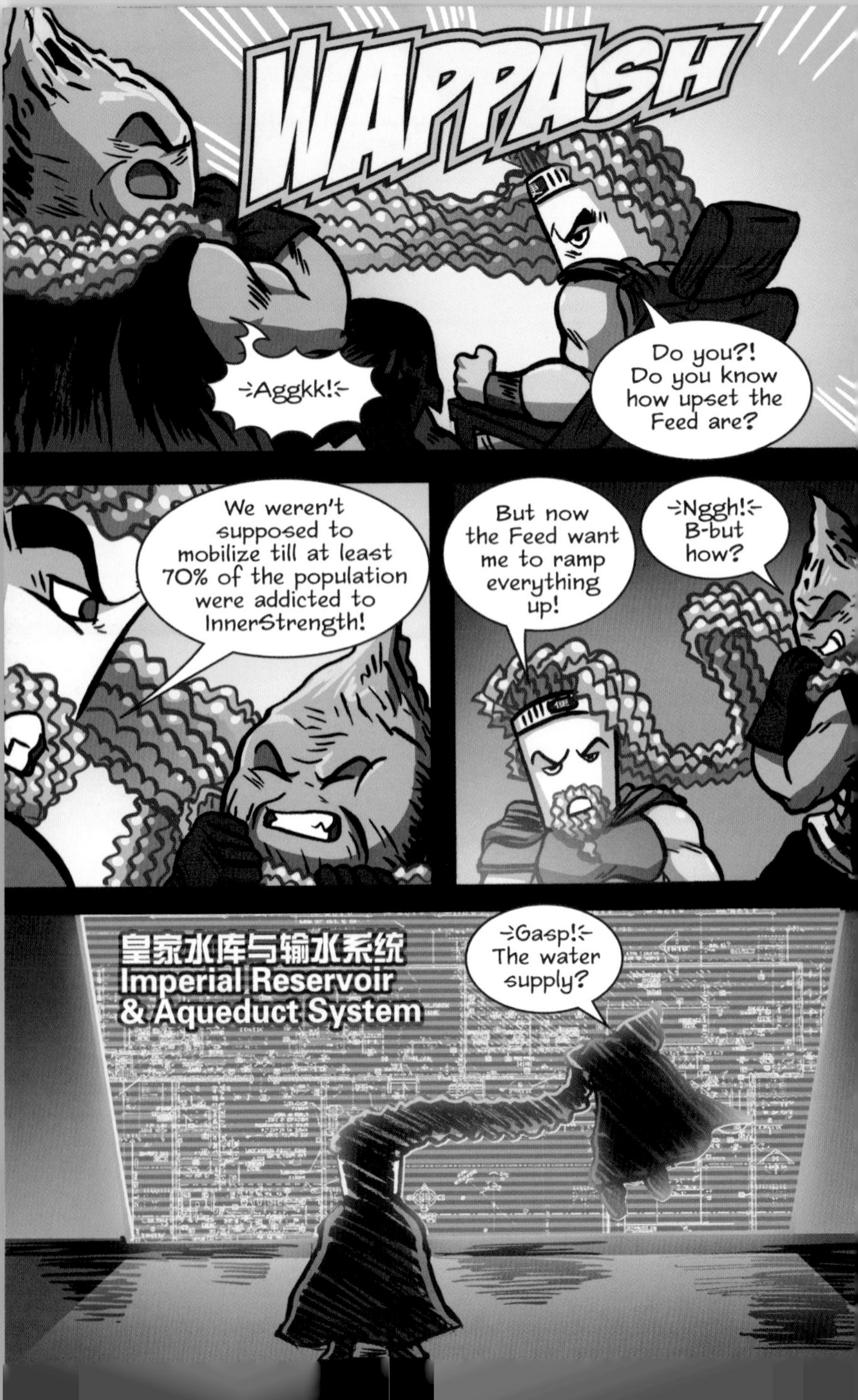
WAPPASH
Aggkk!
Do you?! Do you know how upset the Feed are?
We weren't supposed to mobilize till at least 70% of the population were addicted to InnerStrength!
But now the Feed want me to ramp everything up!
Nggh! B-but how?
皇家水库与输水系统
Imperial Reservoir & Aqueduct System
Gasp! The water supply?

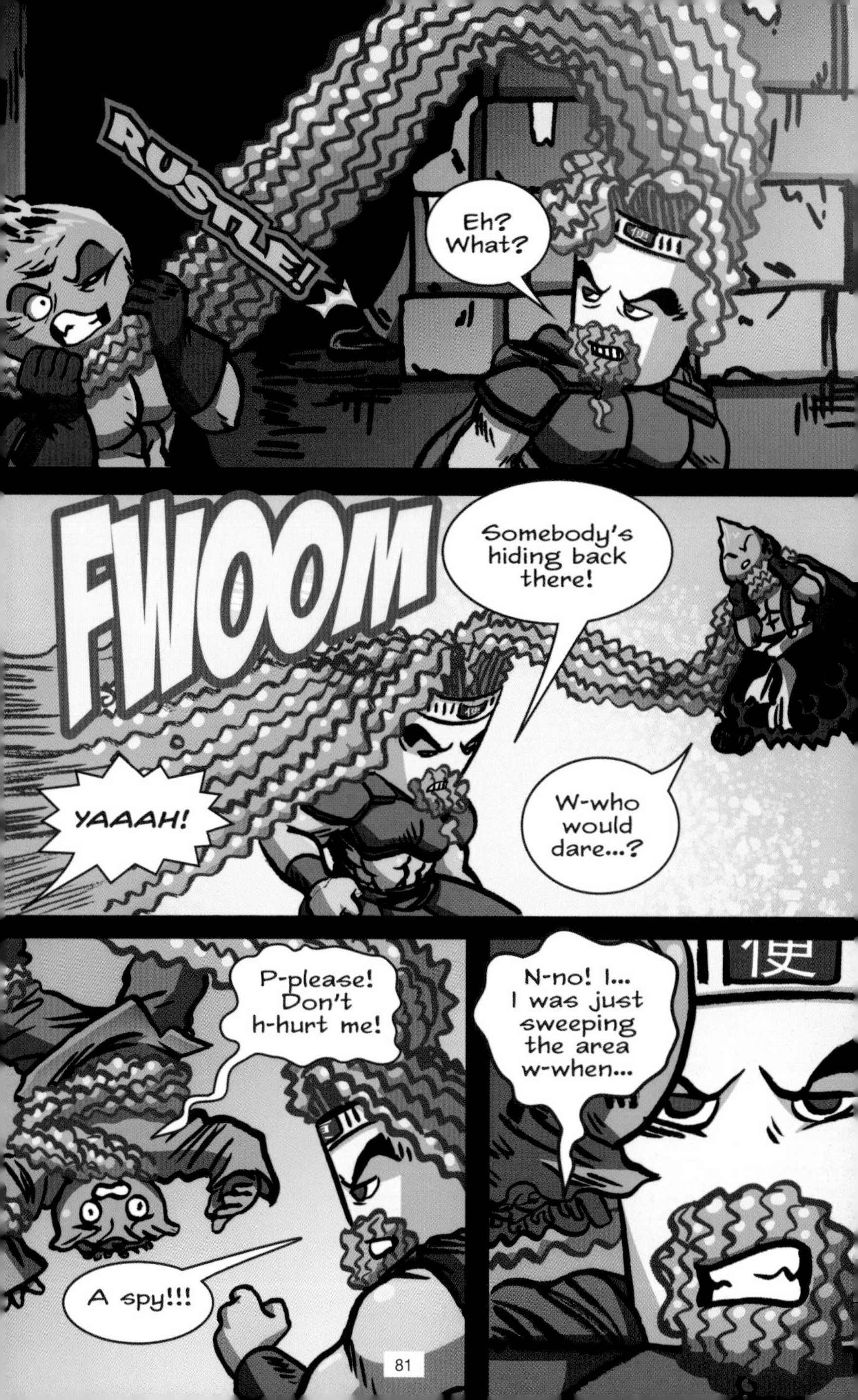
RUSTLE!
Eh? What?
FWOOM
Somebody's hiding back there!
YAAAH!
W-who would dare...?
P-please! Don't h-hurt me!
A spy!!!
N-no! I... I was just sweeping the area w-when...
使

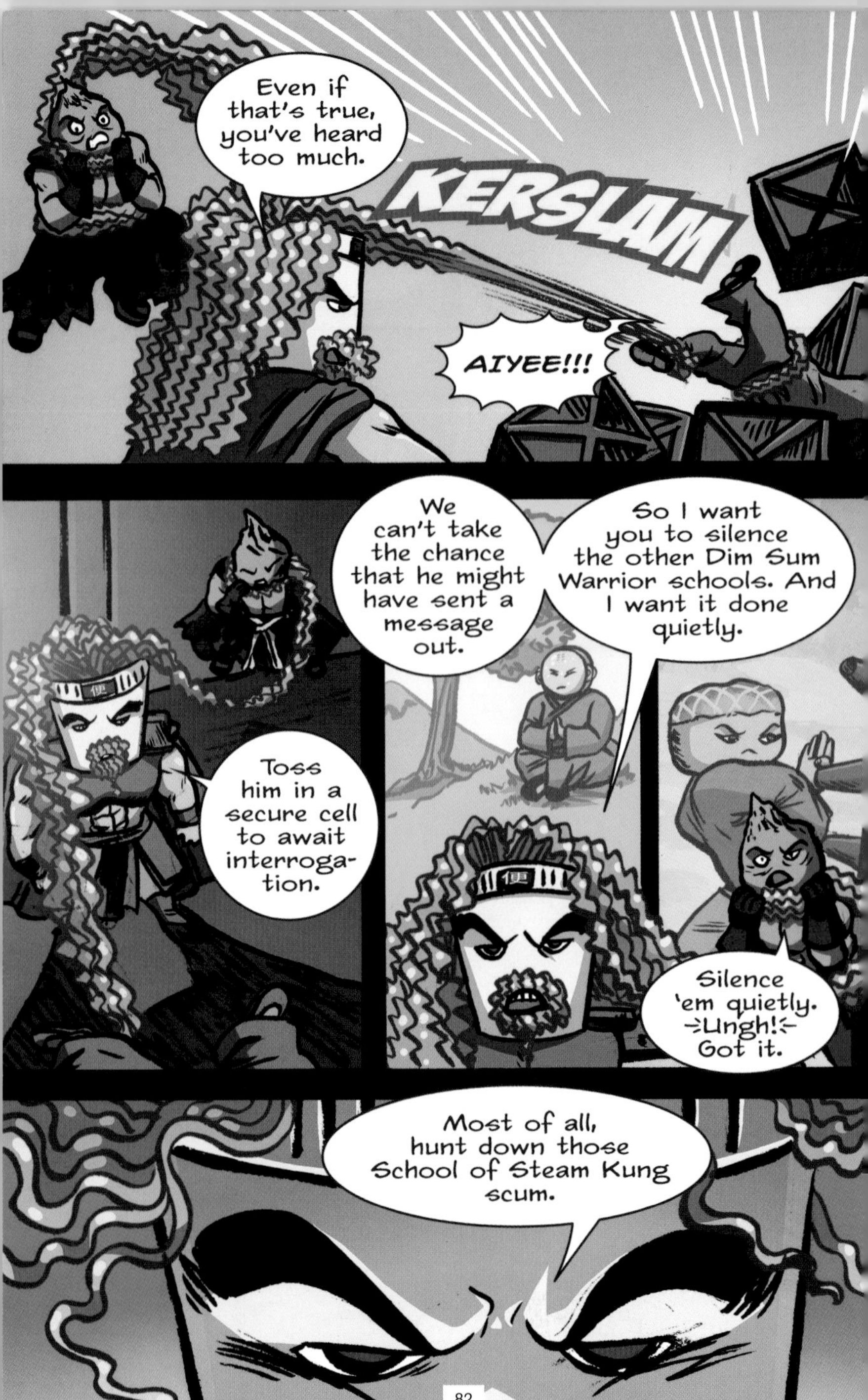
Even if that's true, you've heard too much.
KERSLAM
AIYEE!!!
Toss him in a secure cell to await interrogation.
We can't take the chance that he might have sent a message out.
So I want you to silence the other Dim Sum Warrior schools. And I want it done quietly.
Silence 'em quietly. ≈Ungh!≈ Got it.
Most of all, hunt down those School of Steam Kung scum.

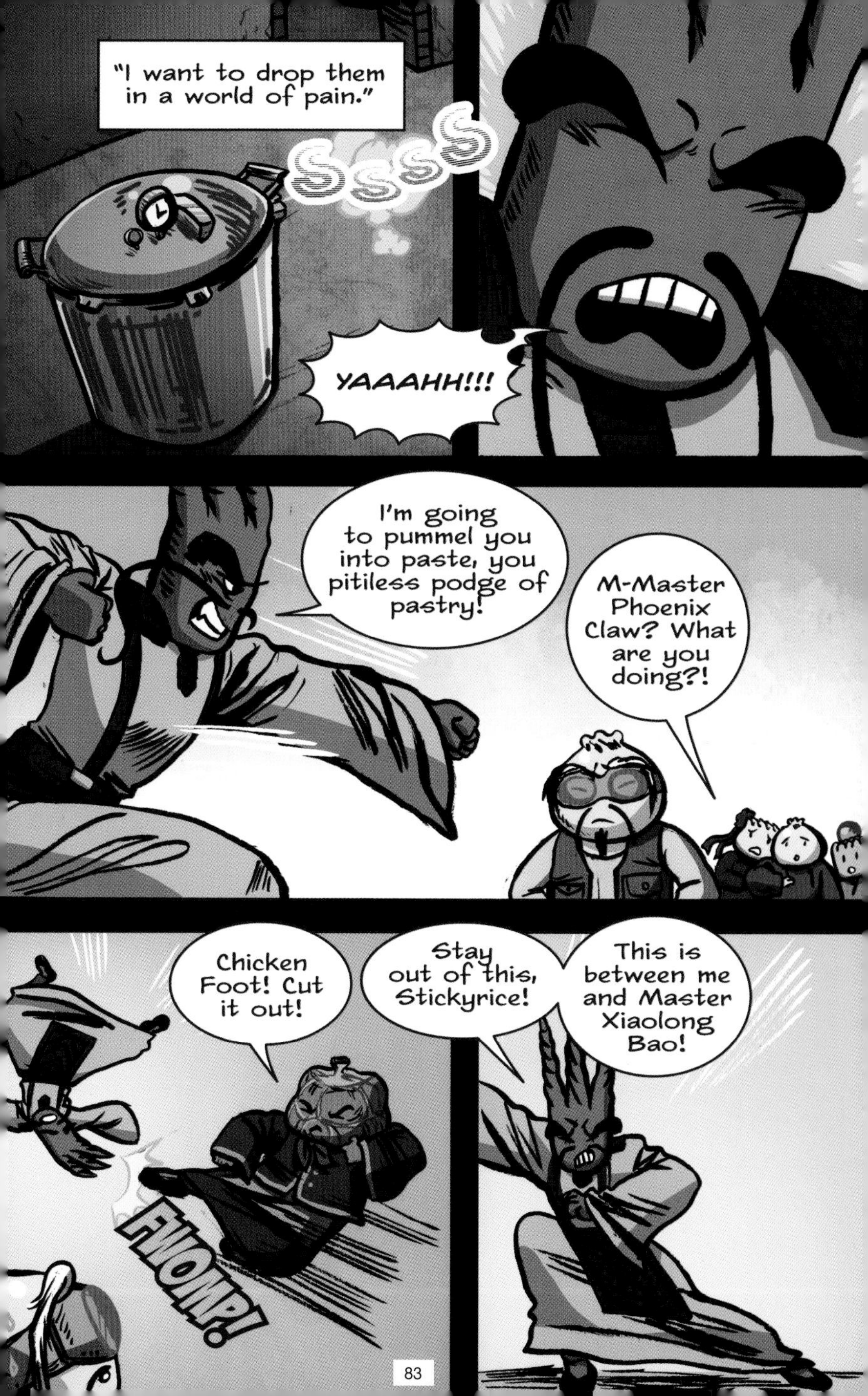
"I want to drop them in a world of pain."
SSSS
YAAAHH!!!
I'm going to pummel you into paste, you pitiless podge of pastry!
M-Master Phoenix Claw? What are you doing?!
Chicken Foot! Cut it out!
FWOMP!
Stay out of this, Stickyrice!
This is between me and Master Xiaolong Bao!

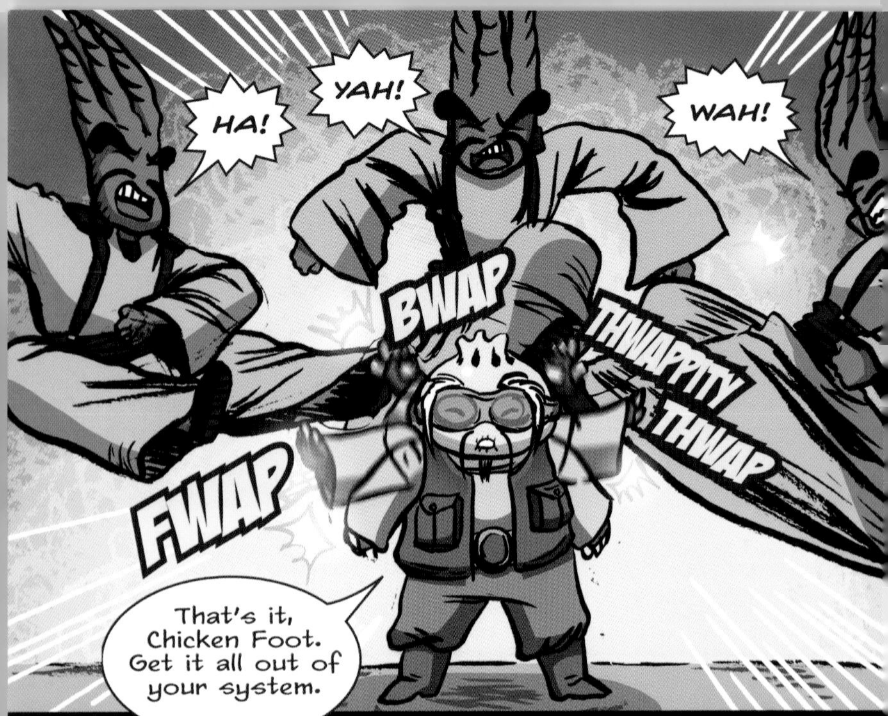
HA!
YAH!
WAH!
BWAP
THWAPPITY
THWAP
FWAP
That's it, Chicken Foot. Get it all out of your system.

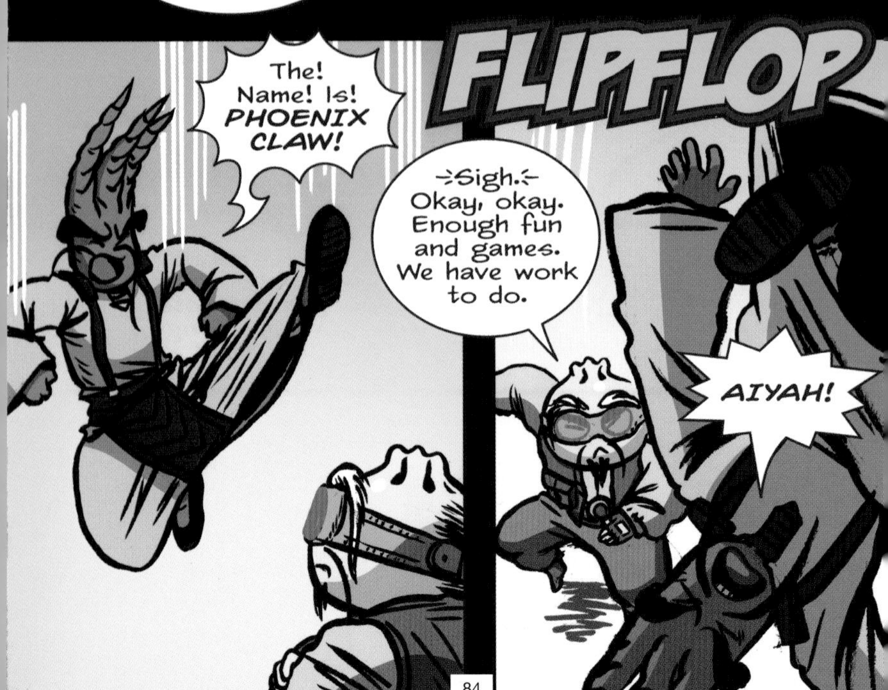
The! Name! Is! PHOENIX CLAW!
FLIPFLOP
-Sigh.- Okay, okay. Enough fun and games. We have work to do.
AIYAH!

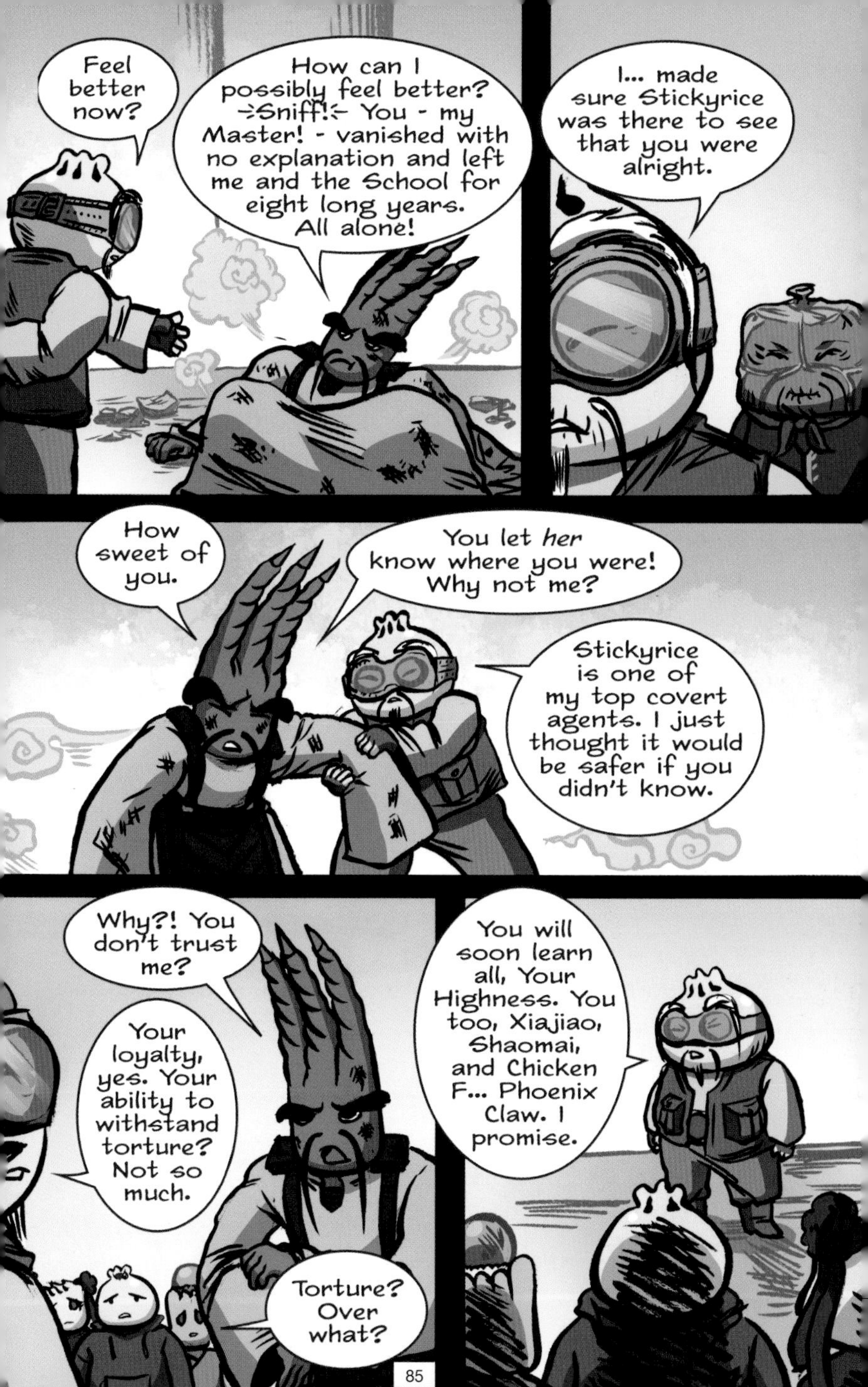
Feel better now?
How can I possibly feel better? ⇒Sniff!⇐ You - my Master! - vanished with no explanation and left me and the School for eight long years. All alone!
I... made sure Stickyrice was there to see that you were alright.
How sweet of you.
You let *her* know where you were! Why not me?
Stickyrice is one of my top covert agents. I just thought it would be safer if you didn't know.
Why?! You don't trust me?
Your loyalty, yes. Your ability to withstand torture? Not so much.
Torture? Over what?
You will soon learn all, Your Highness. You too, Xiajiao, Shaomai, and Chicken F... Phoenix Claw. I promise.

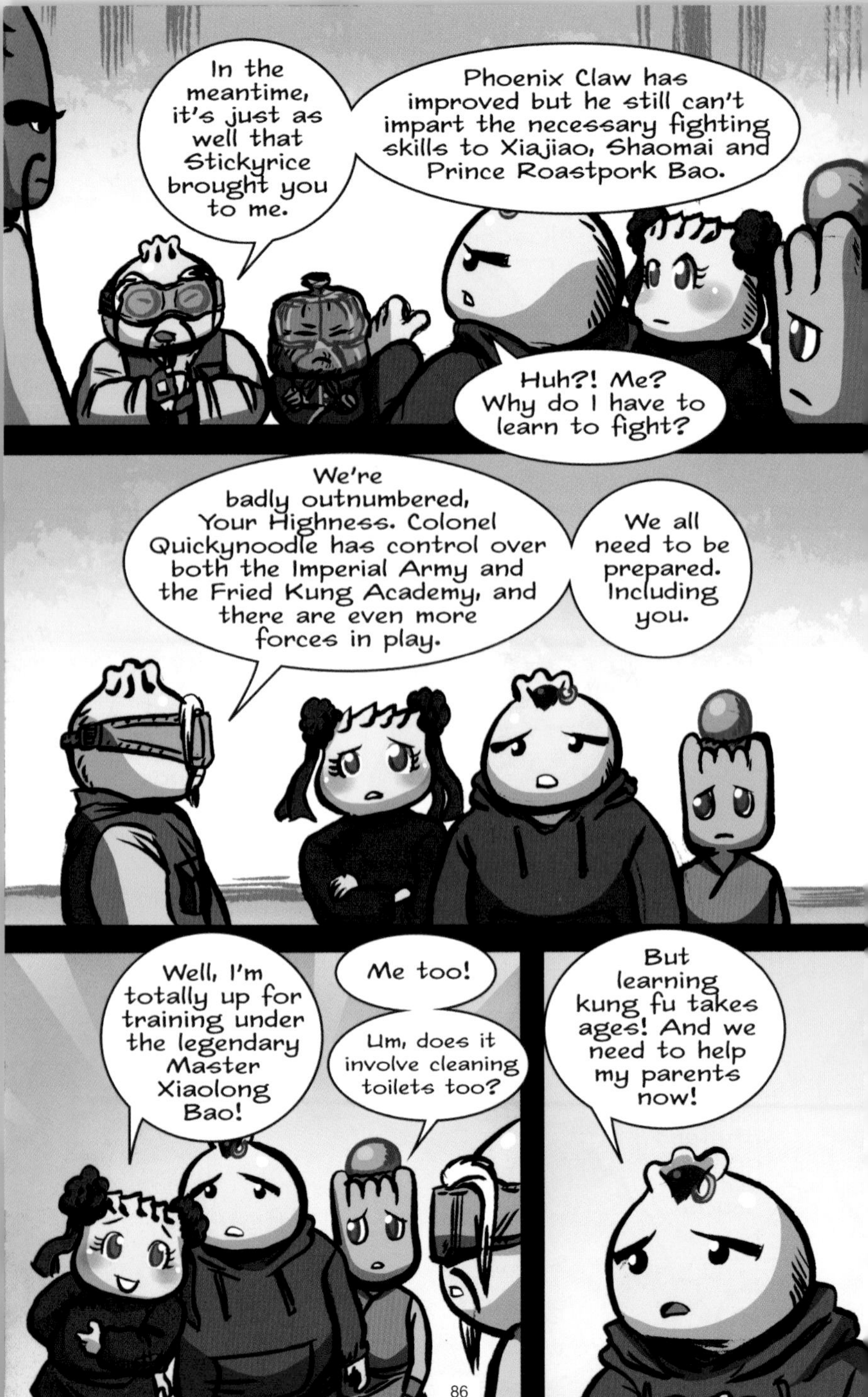
In the meantime, it's just as well that Stickyrice brought you to me.
Phoenix Claw has improved but he still can't impart the necessary fighting skills to Xiajiao, Shaomai and Prince Roastpork Bao.
Huh?! Me? Why do I have to learn to fight?
We're badly outnumbered, Your Highness. Colonel Quickynoodle has control over both the Imperial Army and the Fried Kung Academy, and there are even more forces in play.
We all need to be prepared. Including you.
Well, I'm totally up for training under the legendary Master Xiaolong Bao!
Me too!
Um, does it involve cleaning toilets too?
But learning kung fu takes ages! And we need to help my parents now!

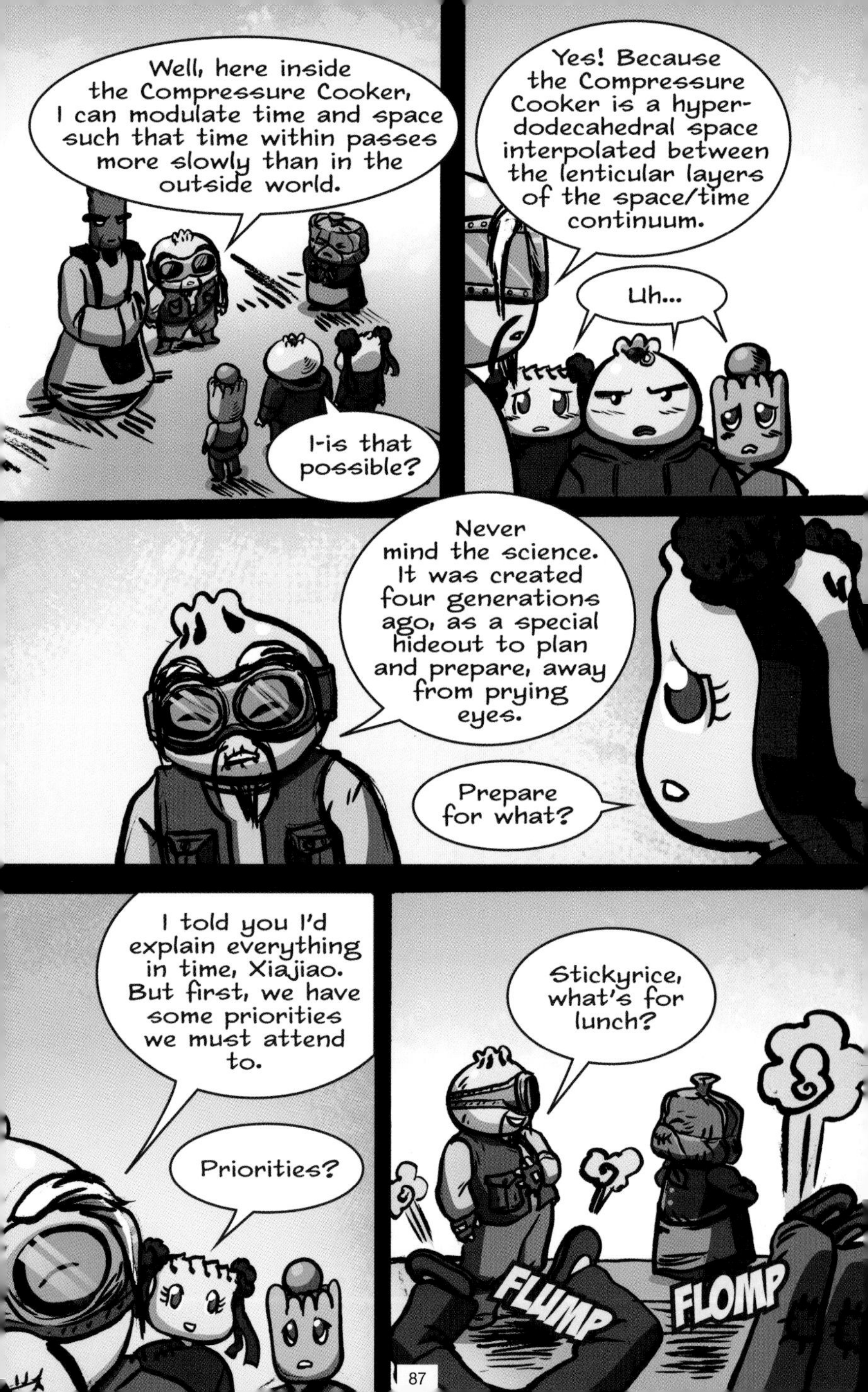
Well, here inside the Compressure Cooker, I can modulate time and space such that time within passes more slowly than in the outside world.
I-is that possible?
Yes! Because the Compressure Cooker is a hyper-dodecahedral space interpolated between the lenticular layers of the space/time continuum.
Uh...
Never mind the science. It was created four generations ago, as a special hideout to plan and prepare, away from prying eyes.
Prepare for what?
I told you I'd explain everything in time, Xiajiao. But first, we have some priorities we must attend to.
Priorities?
Stickyrice, what's for lunch?
FLUMP
FLOMP

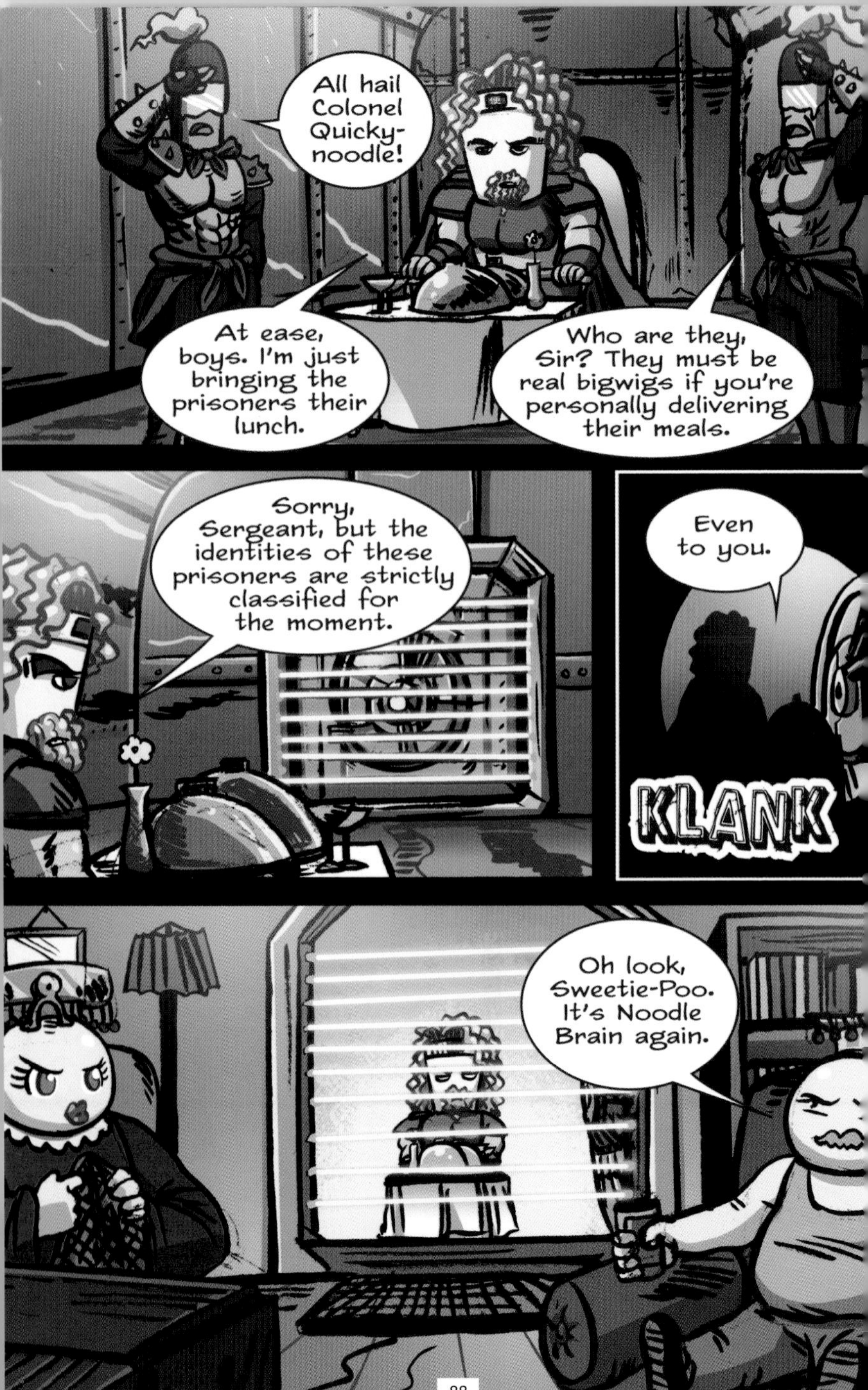
All hail Colonel Quicky-noodle!
At ease, boys. I'm just bringing the prisoners their lunch.
Who are they, Sir? They must be real bigwigs if you're personally delivering their meals.
Sorry, Sergeant, but the identities of these prisoners are strictly classified for the moment.
Even to you.
KLANK
Oh look, Sweetie-Poo. It's Noodle Brain again.

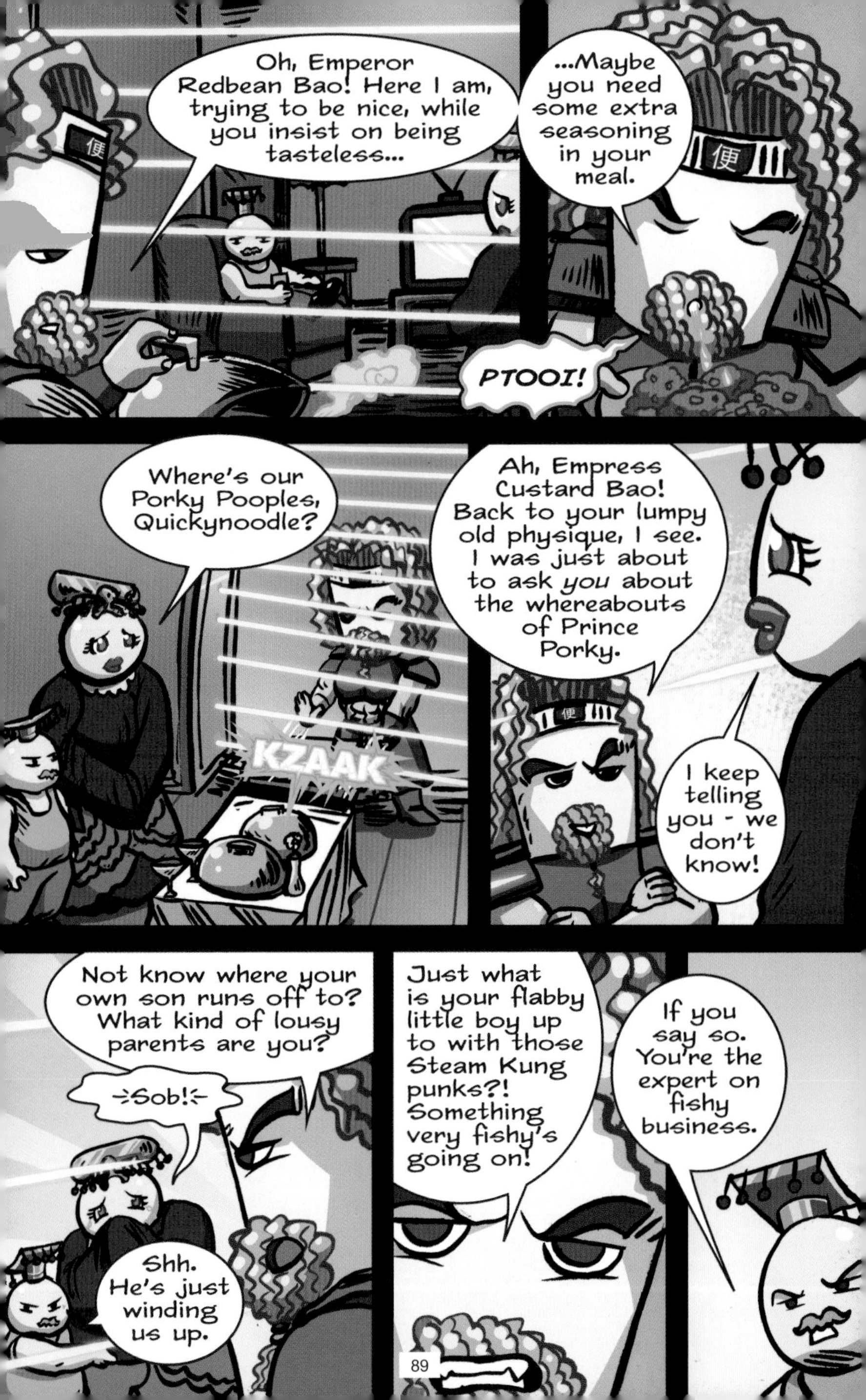
Oh, Emperor Redbean Bao! Here I am, trying to be nice, while you insist on being tasteless...
...Maybe you need some extra seasoning in your meal.
PTOOI!
Where's our Porky Pooples, Quickynoodle?
KZAAK
Ah, Empress Custard Bao! Back to your lumpy old physique, I see. I was just about to ask *you* about the whereabouts of Prince Porky.
I keep telling you - we don't know!
Not know where your own son runs off to? What kind of lousy parents are you?
Sob!
Shh. He's just winding us up.
Just what is your flabby little boy up to with those Steam Kung punks?! Something very fishy's going on!
If you say so. You're the expert on fishy business.

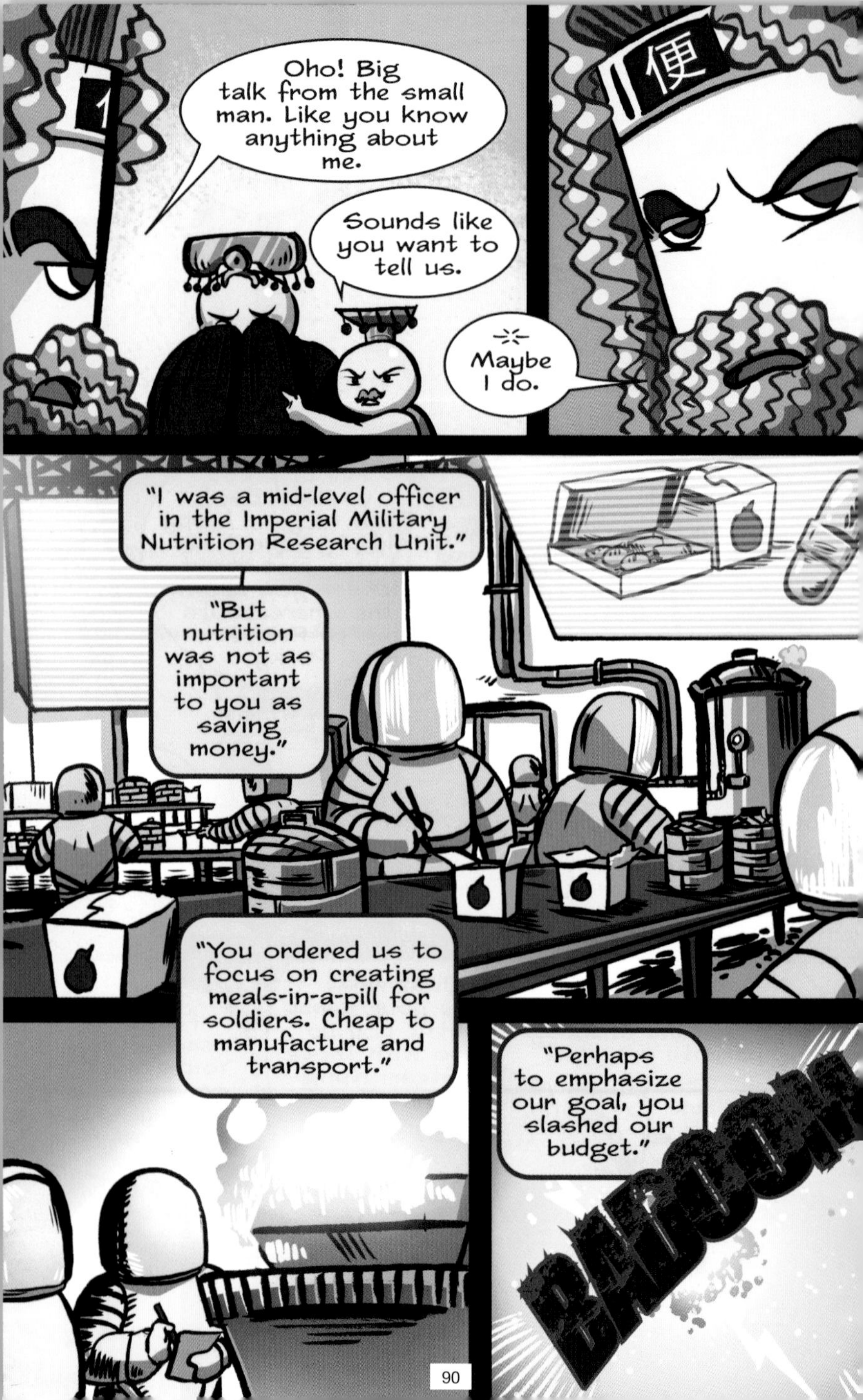

Oho! Big talk from the small man. Like you know anything about me.
Sounds like you want to tell us.
便
Maybe I do.
"I was a mid-level officer in the Imperial Military Nutrition Research Unit."
"But nutrition was not as important to you as saving money."
"You ordered us to focus on creating meals-in-a-pill for soldiers. Cheap to manufacture and transport."
"Perhaps to emphasize our goal, you slashed our budget."

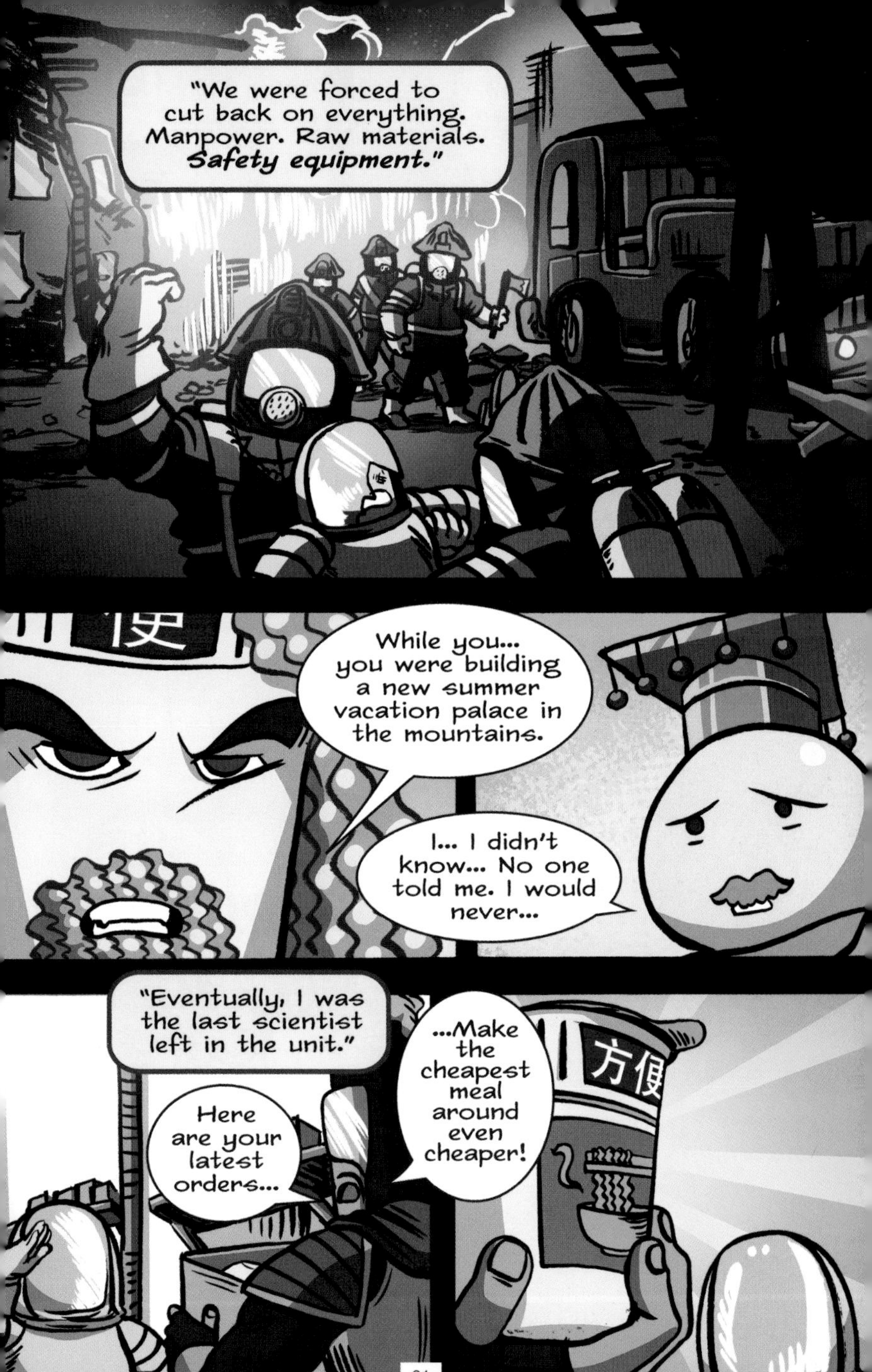
"We were forced to cut back on everything. Manpower. Raw materials. *Safety equipment.*"
While you... you were building a new summer vacation palace in the mountains.
I... I didn't know... No one told me. I would never...
"Eventually, I was the last scientist left in the unit."
Here are your latest orders...
...Make the cheapest meal around even cheaper!
方便

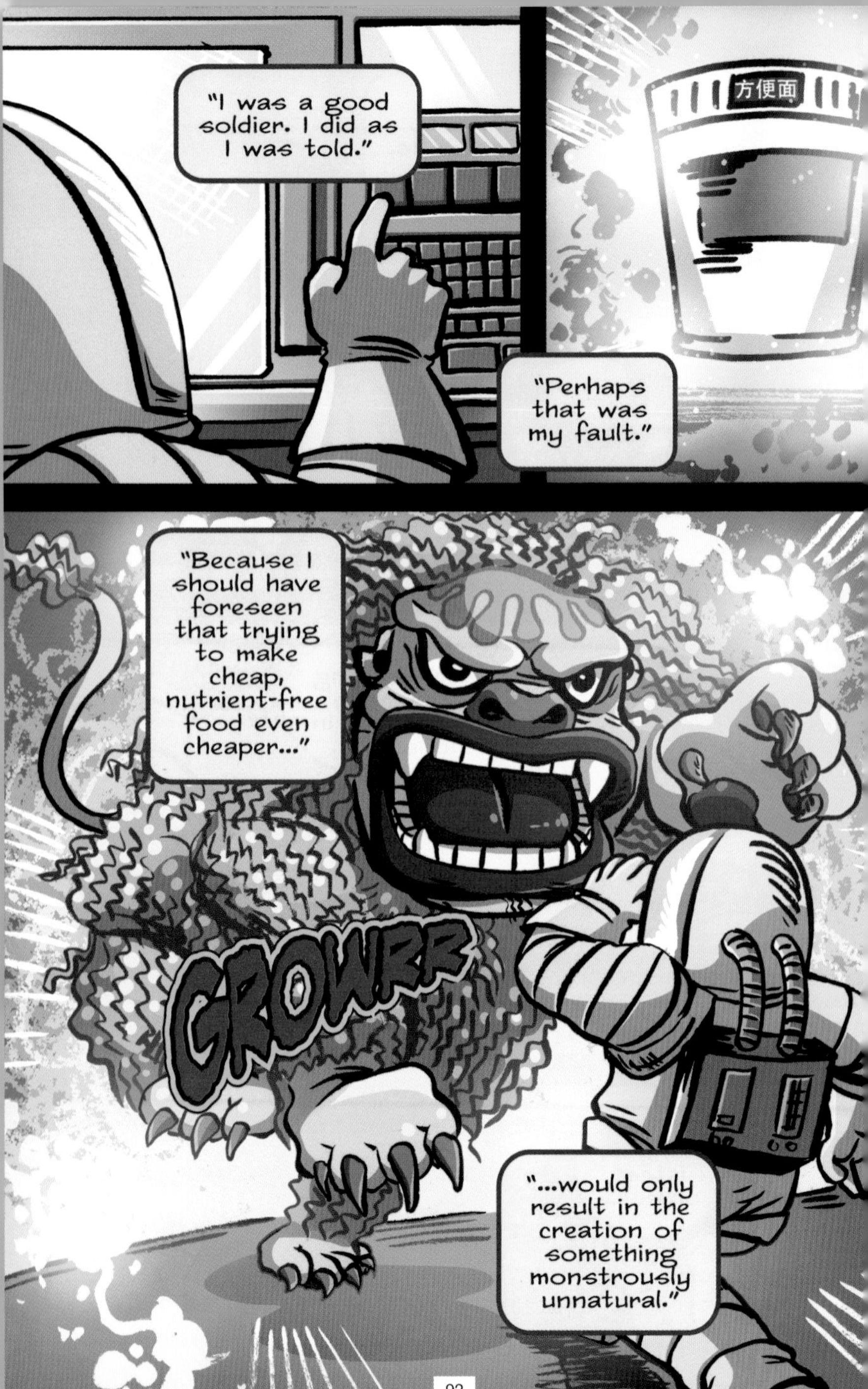
"I was a good soldier. I did as I was told."
方便面
"Perhaps that was my fault."
"Because I should have foreseen that trying to make cheap, nutrient-free food even cheaper..."
GROWRR
"...would only result in the creation of something monstrously unnatural."

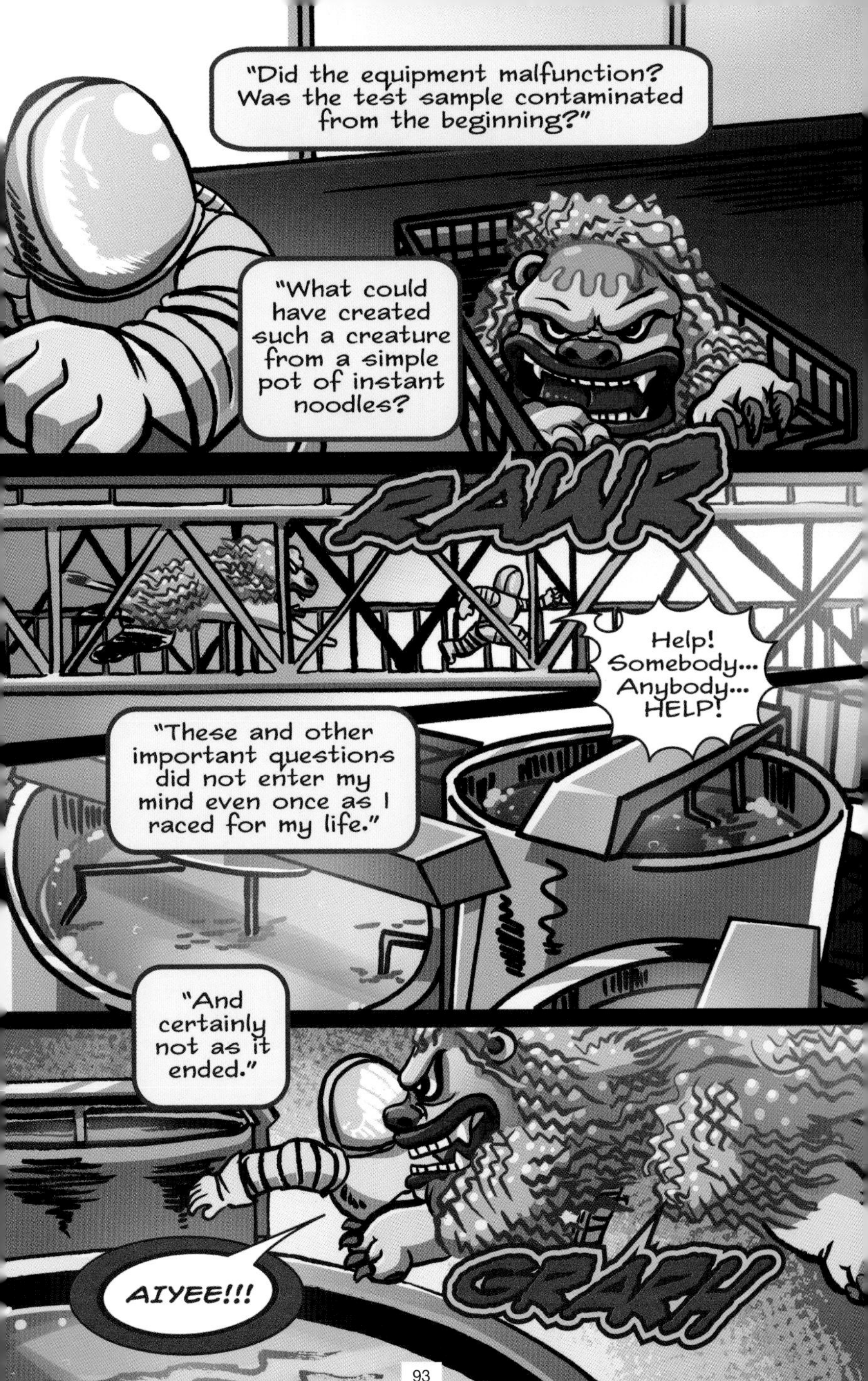
"Did the equipment malfunction? Was the test sample contaminated from the beginning?"
"What could have created such a creature from a simple pot of instant noodles?
RAWR
Help! Somebody... Anybody... HELP!
"These and other important questions did not enter my mind even once as I raced for my life."
"And certainly not as it ended."
AIYEE!!!
GRARH

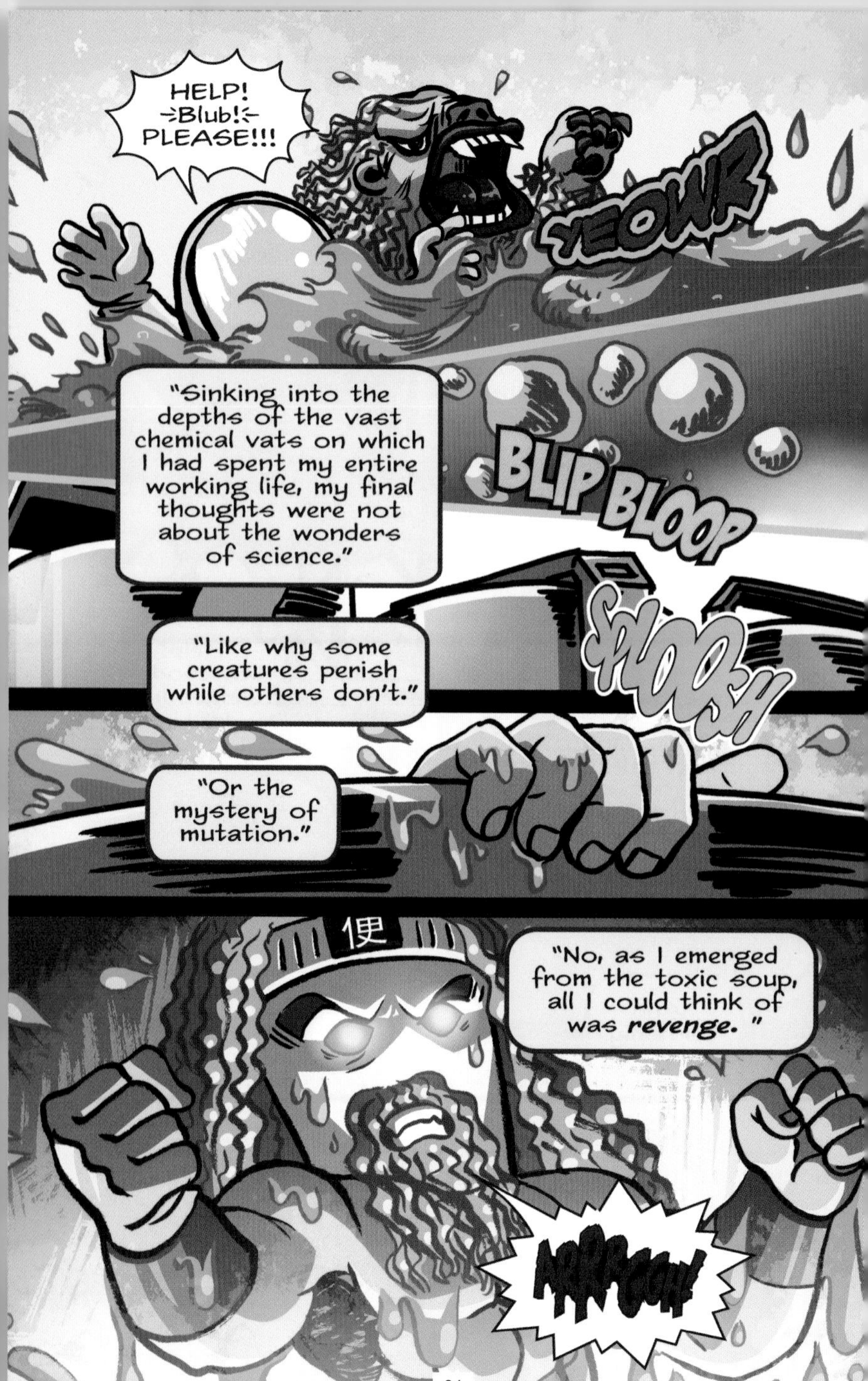
HELP! Blub! PLEASE!!!
YEOWR
"Sinking into the depths of the vast chemical vats on which I had spent my entire working life, my final thoughts were not about the wonders of science."
BLIP BLOOP
"Like why some creatures perish while others don't."
SPLOOSH
"Or the mystery of mutation."
便
"No, as I emerged from the toxic soup, all I could think of was ***revenge.***"

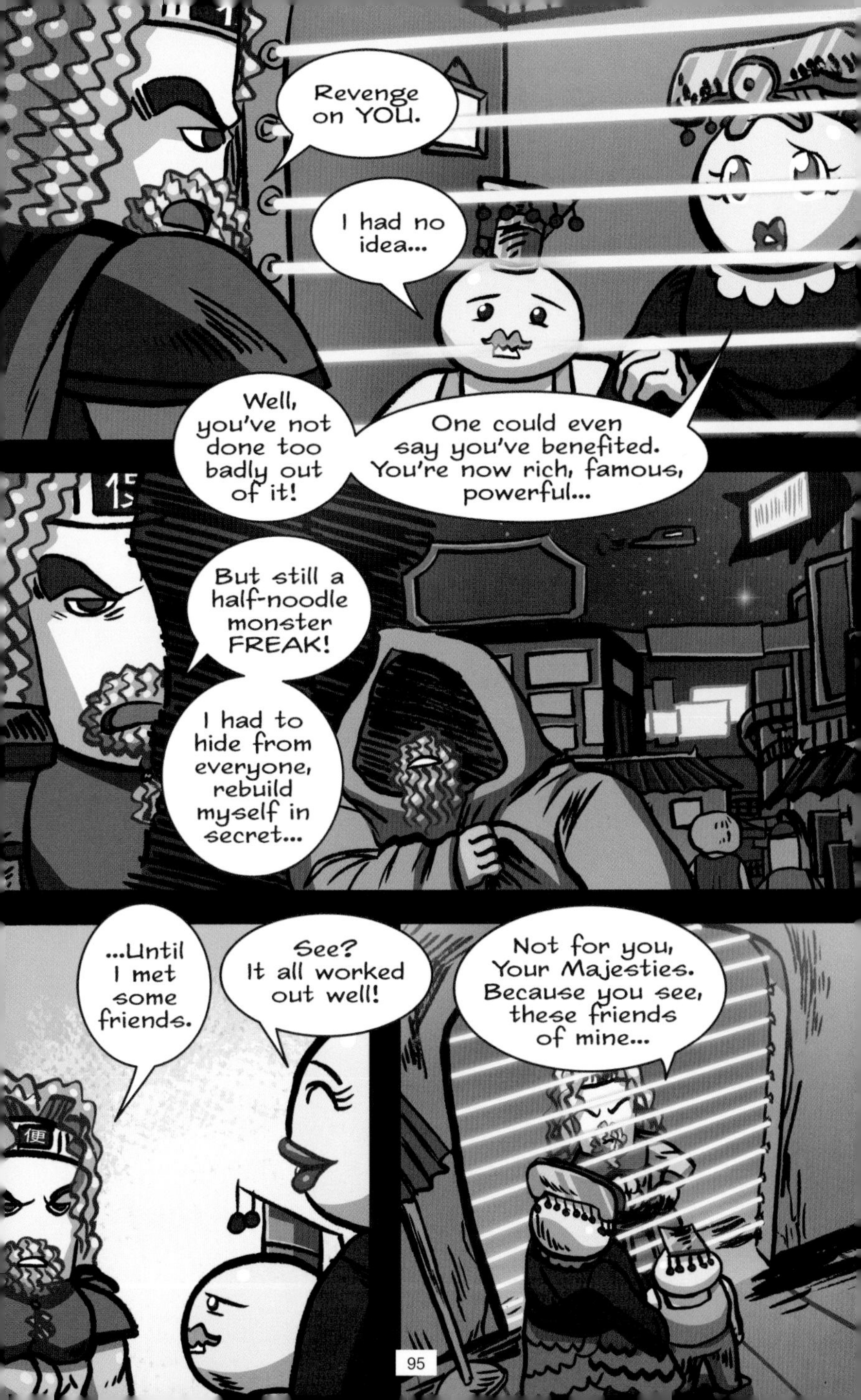
Revenge on YOU.
I had no idea...
Well, you've not done too badly out of it!
One could even say you've benefited. You're now rich, famous, powerful...
But still a half-noodle monster FREAK!
I had to hide from everyone, rebuild myself in secret...
...Until I met some friends.
See? It all worked out well!
Not for you, Your Majesties. Because you see, these friends of mine...

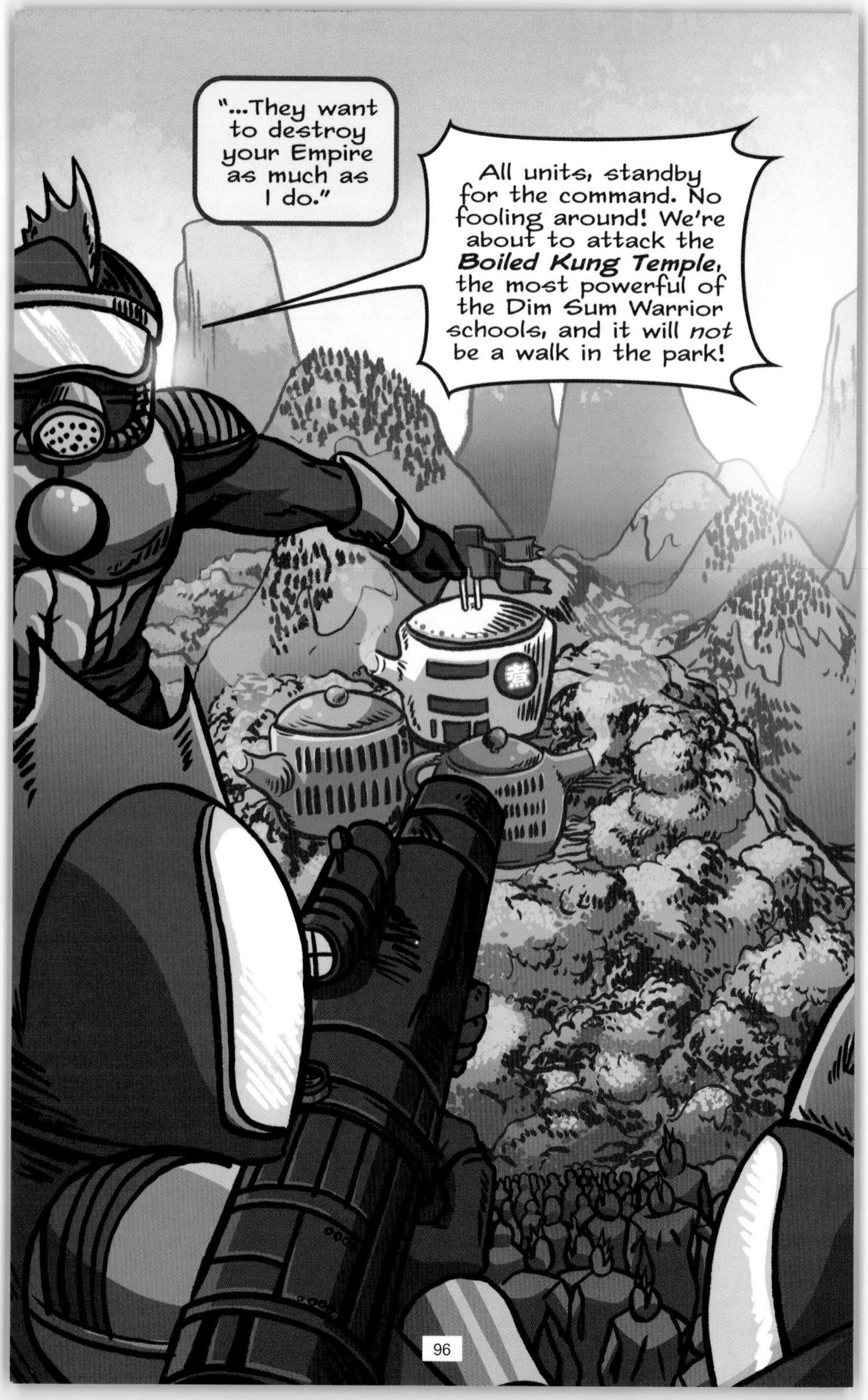
"...They want to destroy your Empire as much as I do."
All units, standby for the command. No fooling around! We're about to attack the ***Boiled Kung Temple***, the most powerful of the Dim Sum Warrior schools, and it will *not* be a walk in the park!
煮

# Chapter 11
# Boiling Point

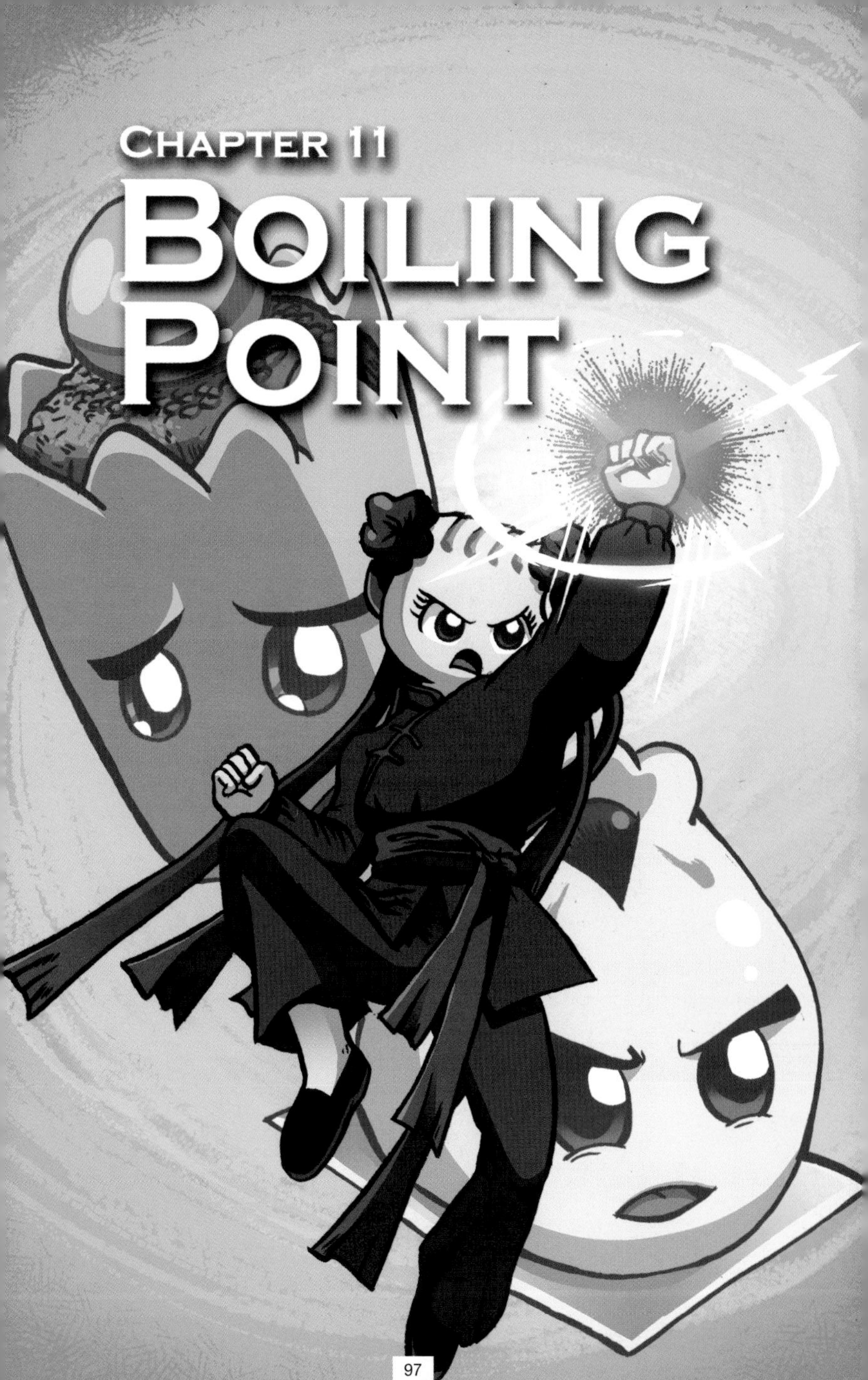

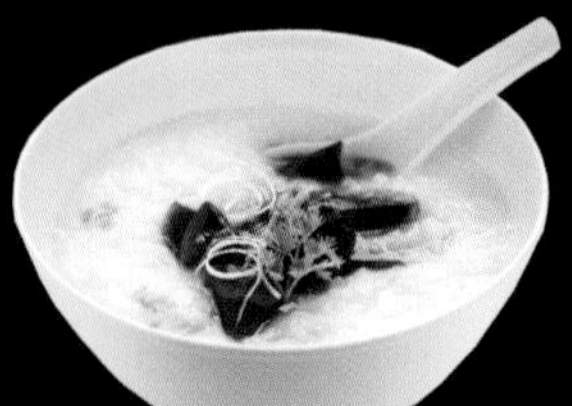

bonchan/ Shutterstock.com

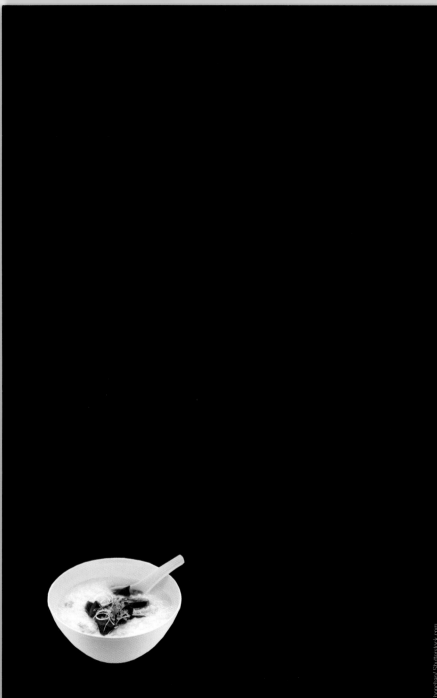

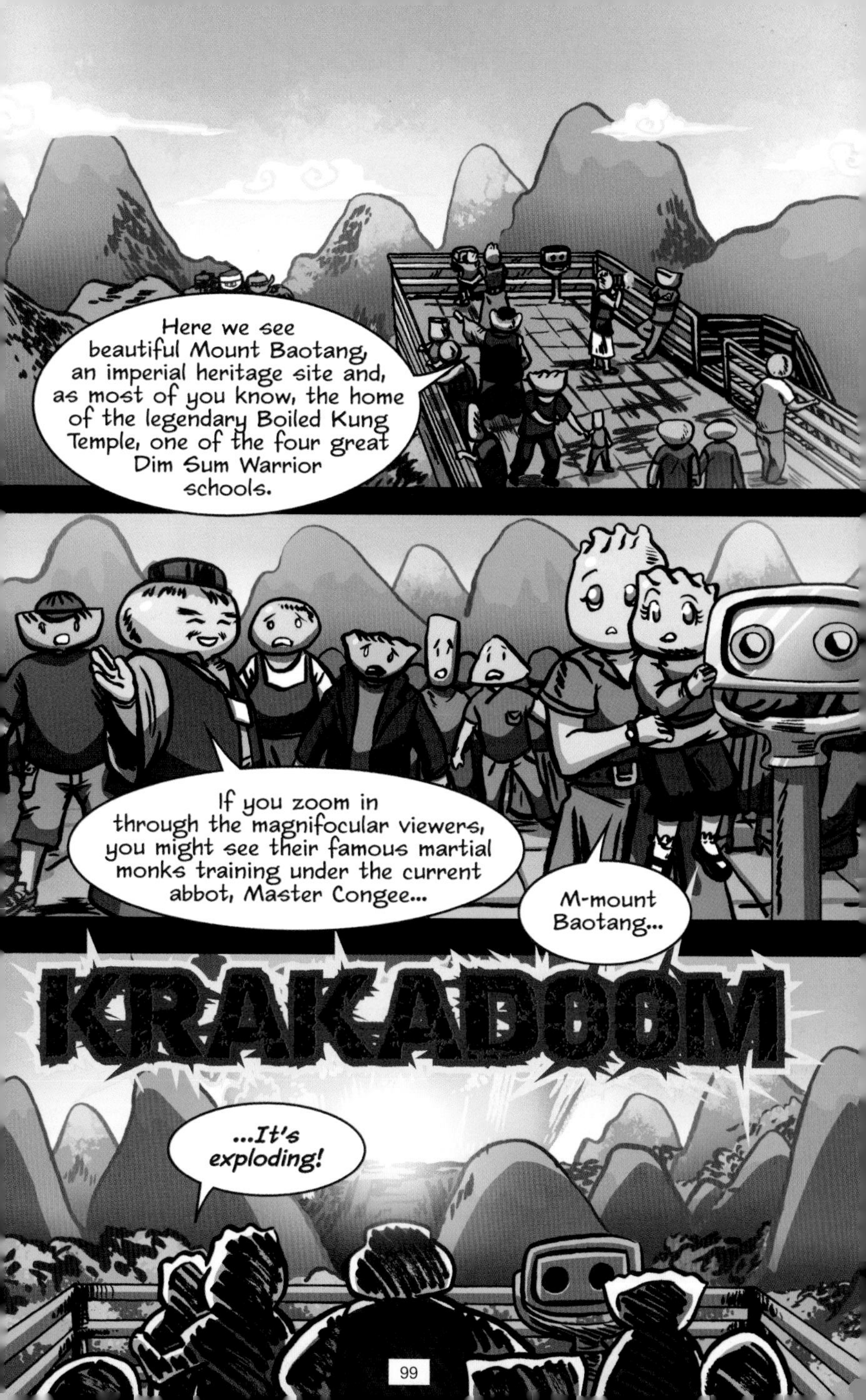
Here we see beautiful Mount Baotang, an imperial heritage site and, as most of you know, the home of the legendary Boiled Kung Temple, one of the four great Dim Sum Warrior schools.
If you zoom in through the magnifocular viewers, you might see their famous martial monks training under the current abbot, Master Congee...
M-mount Baotang...
KRAKABOOM
...It's exploding!

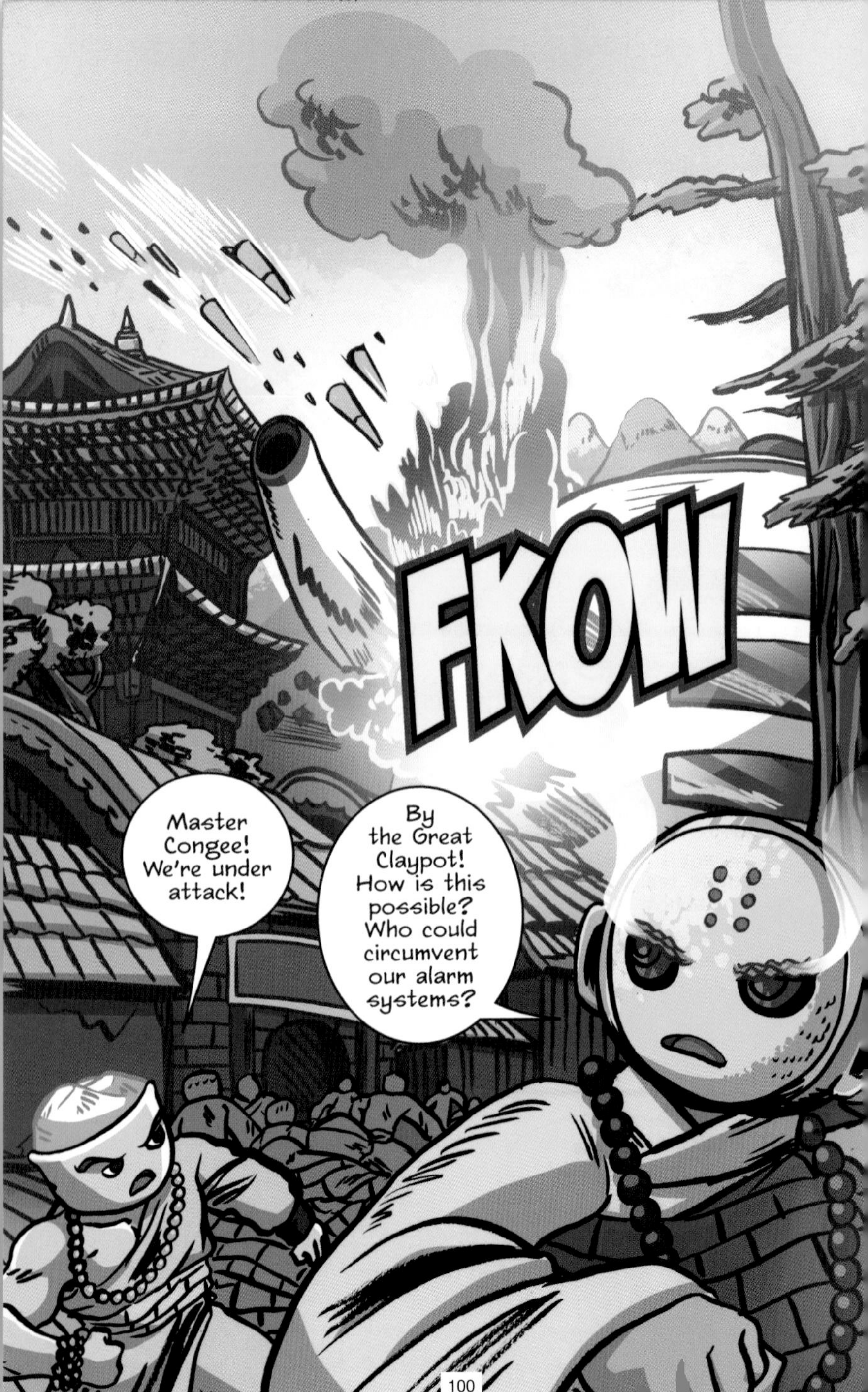
FKOW
Master Congee! We're under attack!
By the Great Claypot! How is this possible? Who could circumvent our alarm systems?

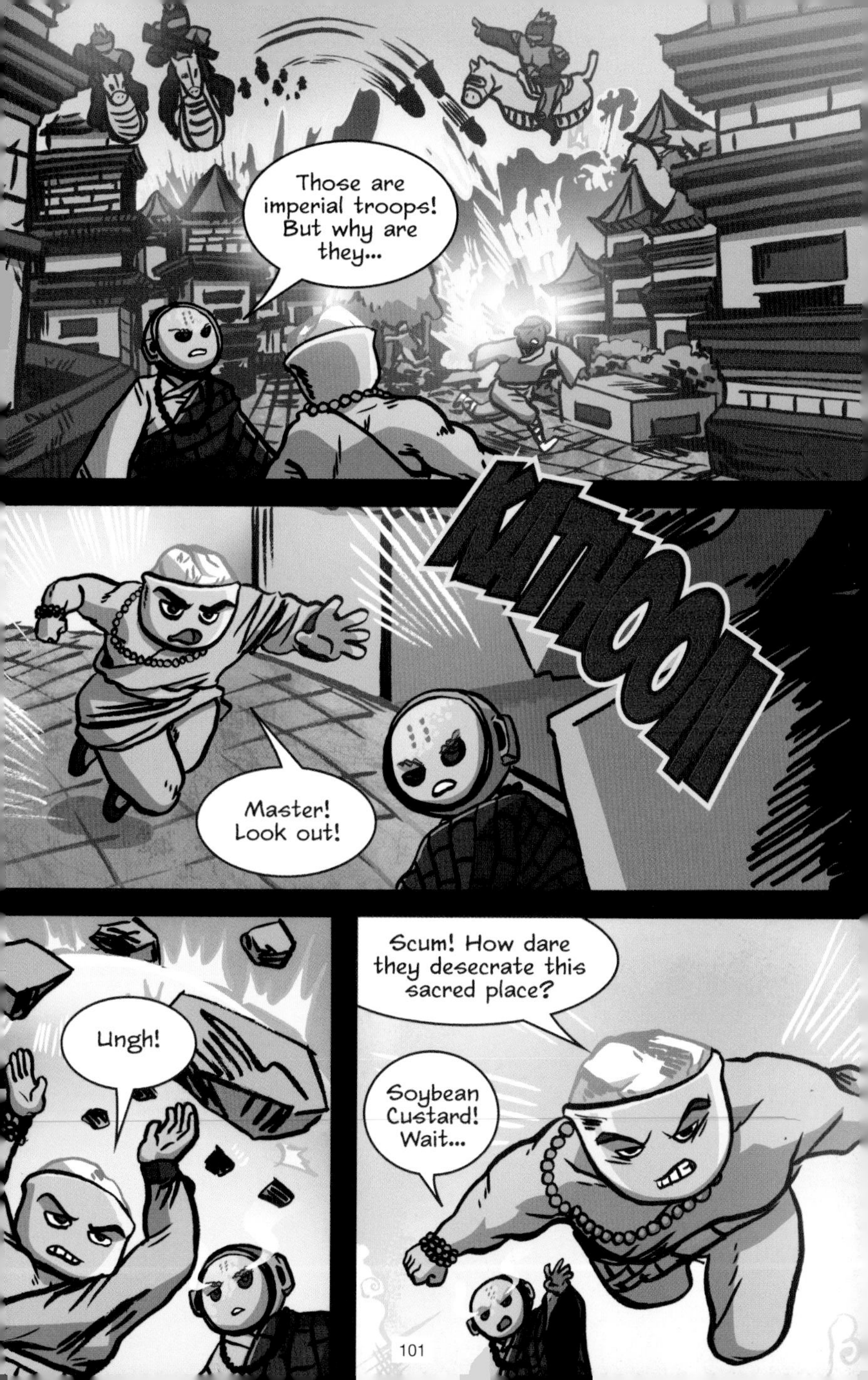
Those are imperial troops! But why are they...
KATHOOM
Master! Look out!
Ungh!
Scum! How dare they desecrate this sacred place?
Soybean Custard! Wait...

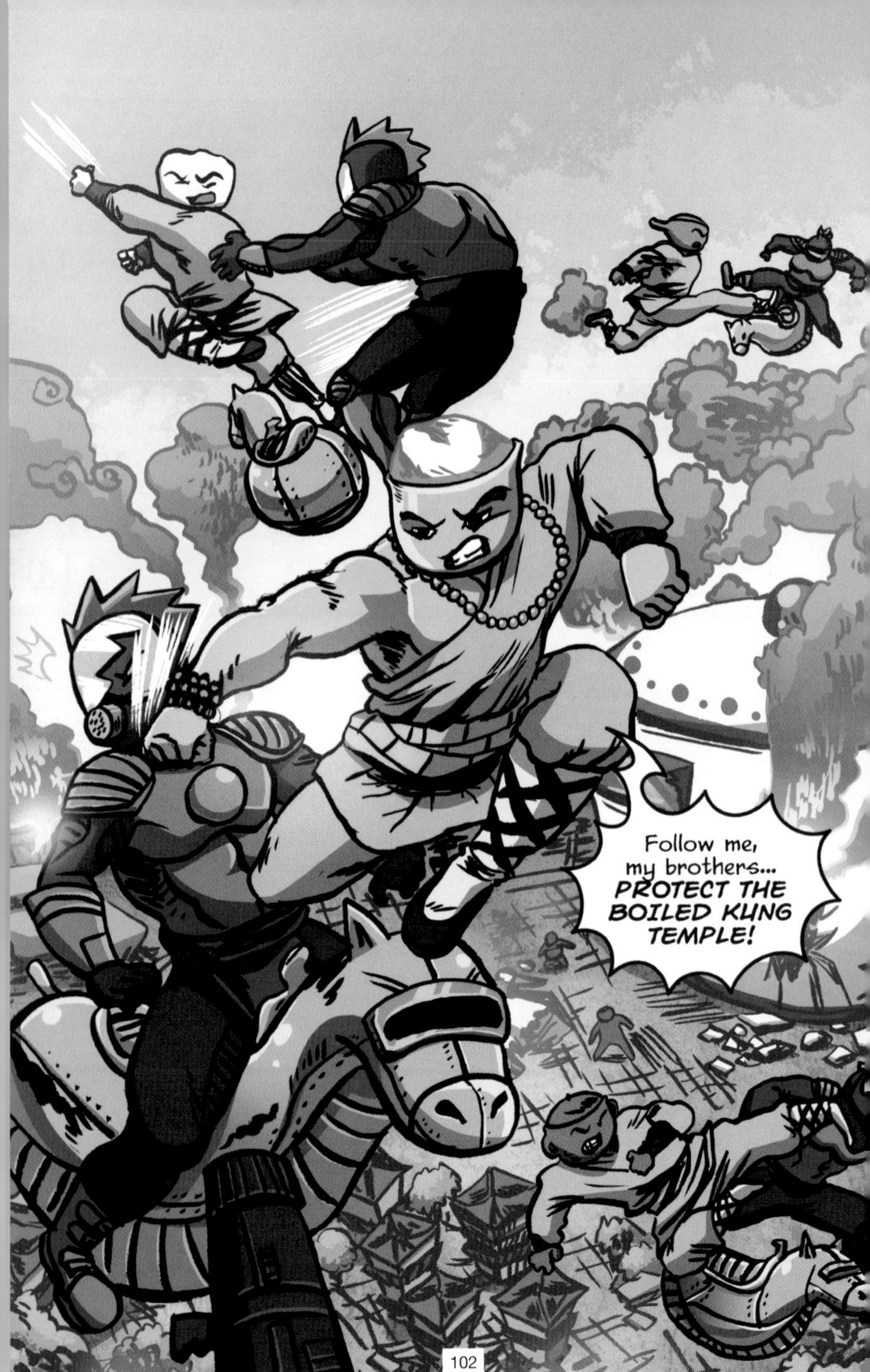
Follow me, my brothers... PROTECT THE BOILED KUNG TEMPLE!

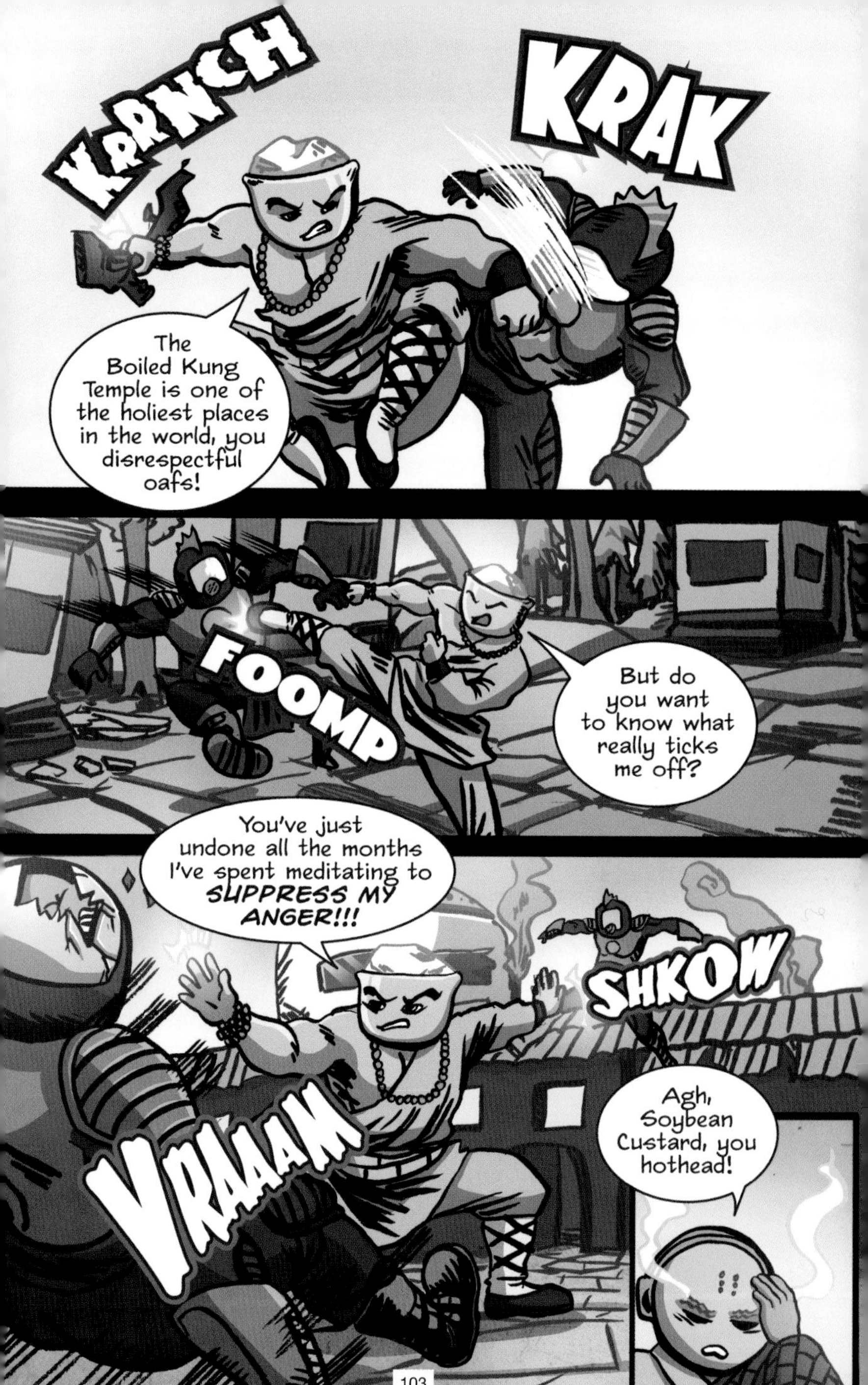
KRRNCH
KRAK
The Boiled Kung Temple is one of the holiest places in the world, you disrespectful oafs!
FOOMP
But do you want to know what really ticks me off?
You've just undone all the months I've spent meditating to SUPPRESS MY ANGER!!!
SHKOW
VRAAAM
Agh, Soybean Custard, you hothead!

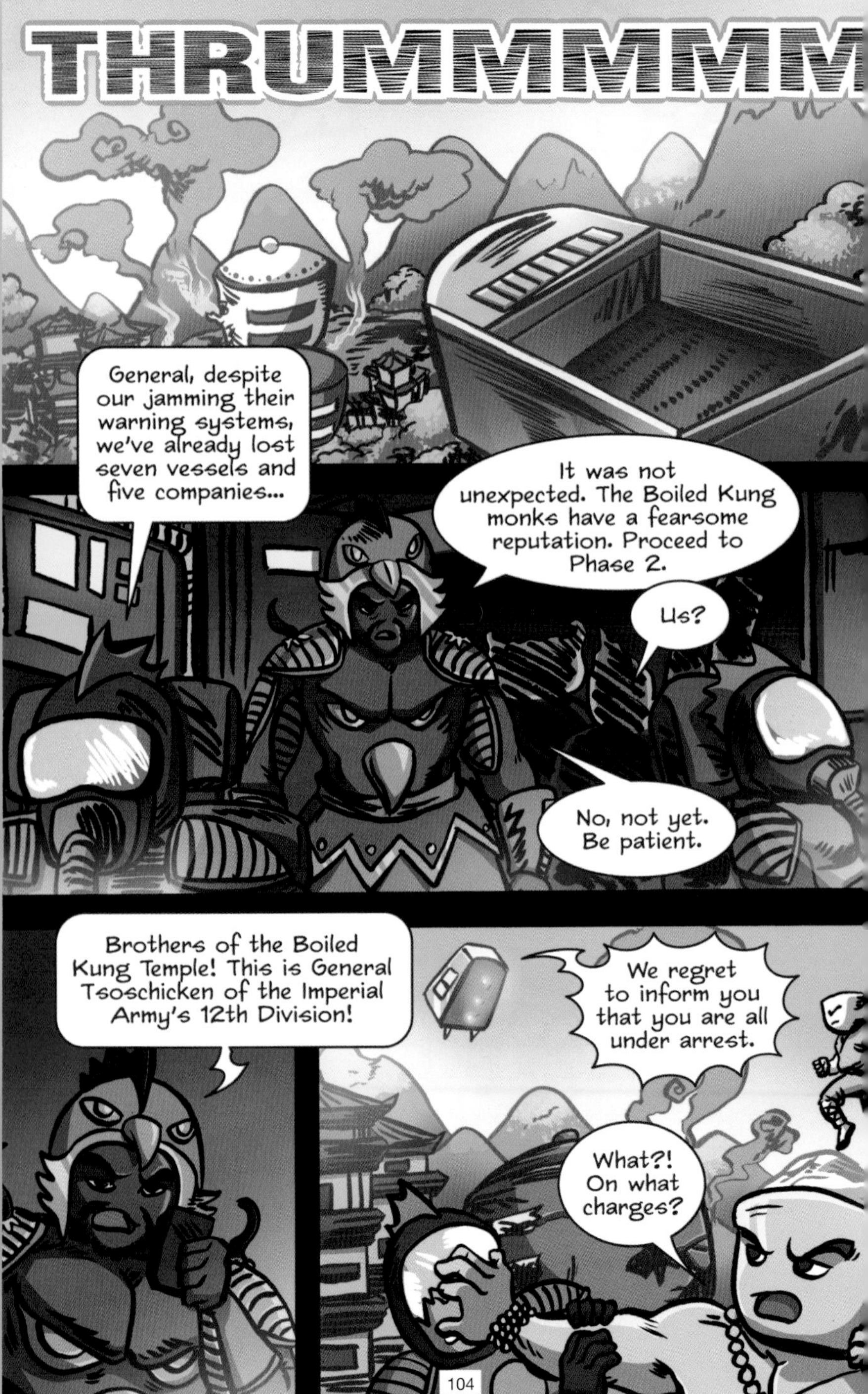
THRUMMMMMM
General, despite our jamming their warning systems, we've already lost seven vessels and five companies...
It was not unexpected. The Boiled Kung monks have a fearsome reputation. Proceed to Phase 2.
Us?
No, not yet. Be patient.
Brothers of the Boiled Kung Temple! This is General Tsoschicken of the Imperial Army's 12th Division!
We regret to inform you that you are all under arrest.
What?! On what charges?

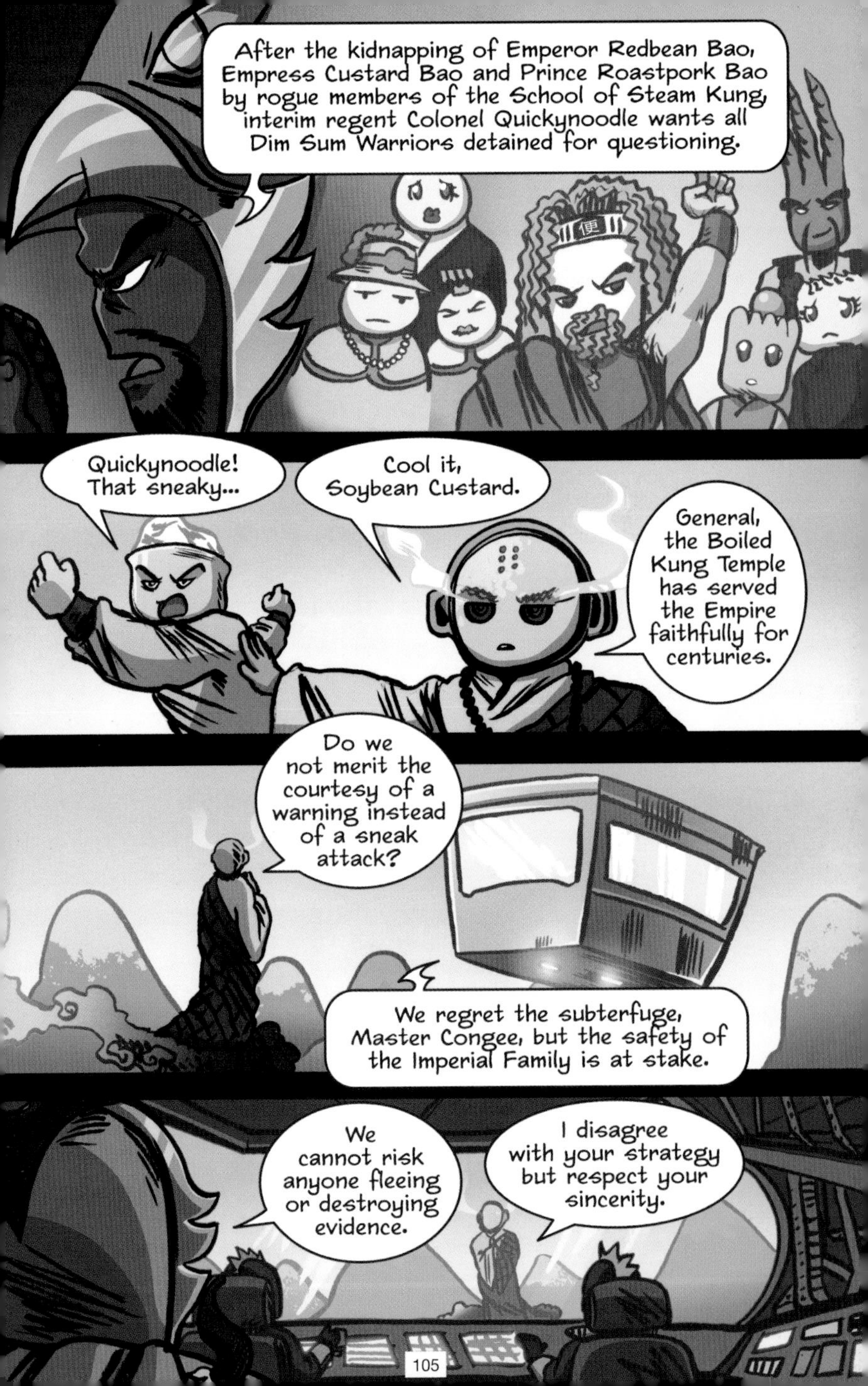
After the kidnapping of Emperor Redbean Bao, Empress Custard Bao and Prince Roastpork Bao by rogue members of the School of Steam Kung, interim regent Colonel Quickynoodle wants all Dim Sum Warriors detained for questioning.
Quickynoodle! That sneaky...
Cool it, Soybean Custard.
General, the Boiled Kung Temple has served the Empire faithfully for centuries.
Do we not merit the courtesy of a warning instead of a sneak attack?
We regret the subterfuge, Master Congee, but the safety of the Imperial Family is at stake.
We cannot risk anyone fleeing or destroying evidence.
I disagree with your strategy but respect your sincerity.

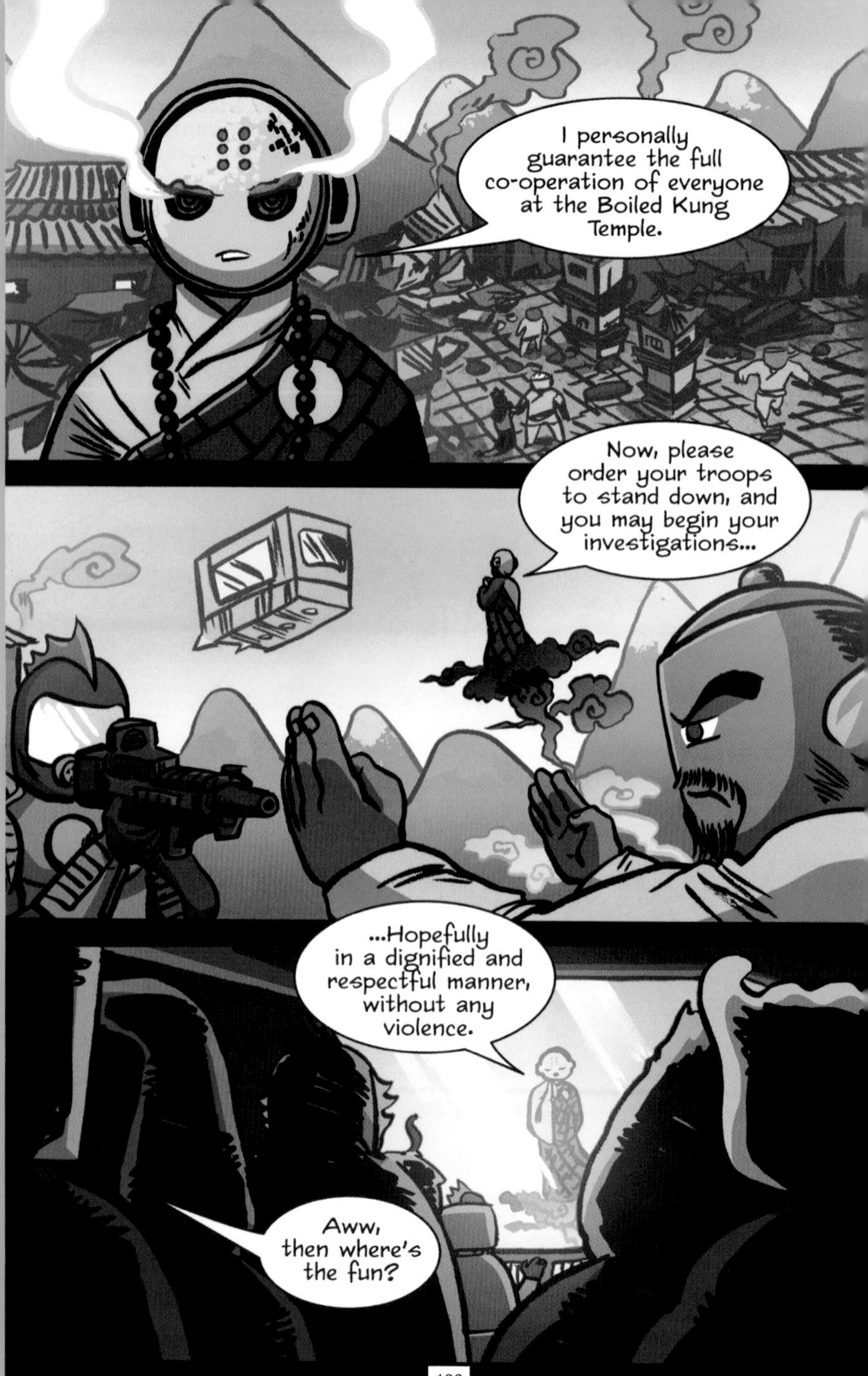
I personally guarantee the full co-operation of everyone at the Boiled Kung Temple.
Now, please order your troops to stand down, and you may begin your investigations...
...Hopefully in a dignified and respectful manner, without any violence.
Aww, then where's the fun?

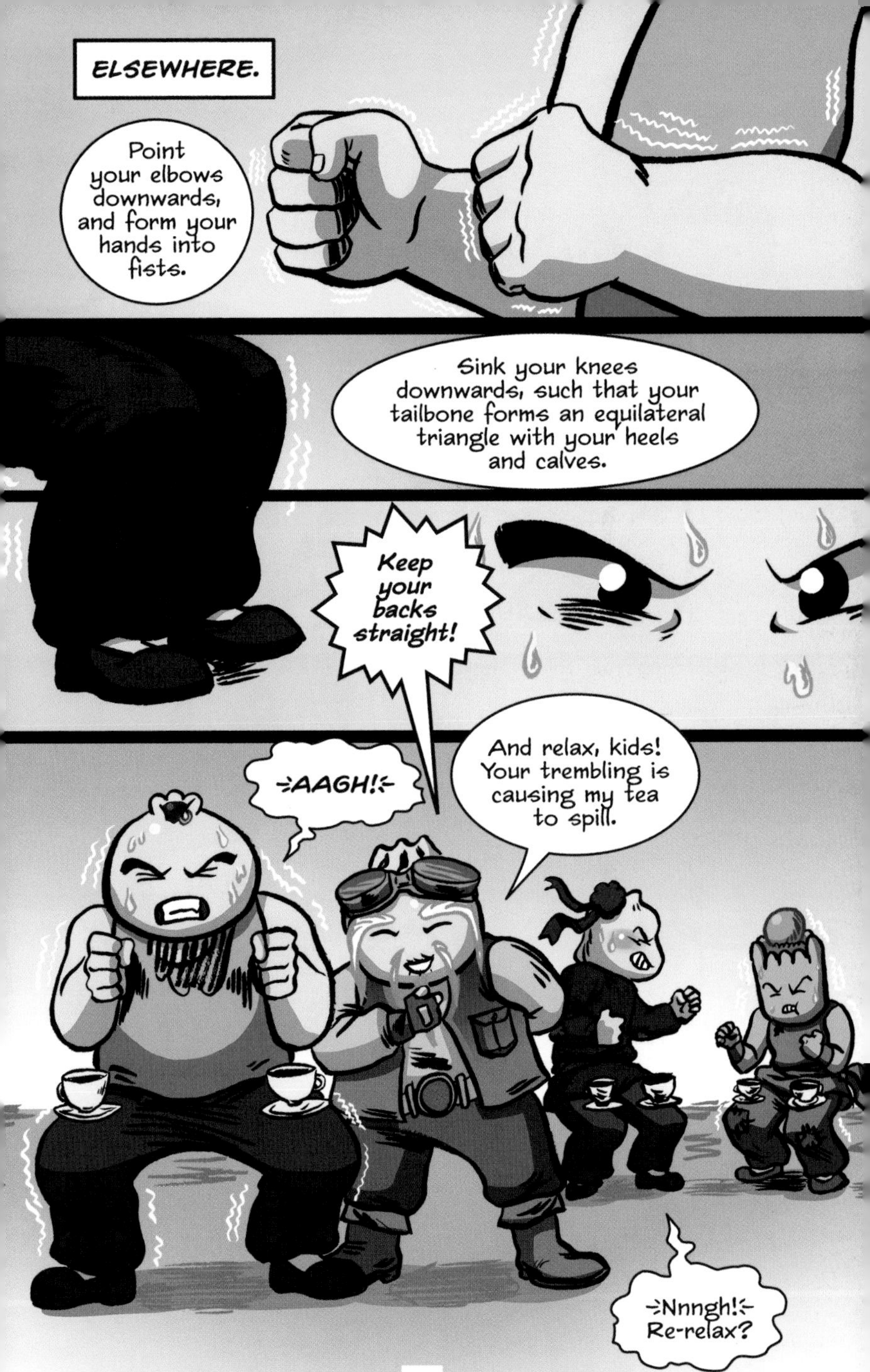
ELSEWHERE.
Point your elbows downwards, and form your hands into fists.
Sink your knees downwards, such that your tailbone forms an equilateral triangle with your heels and calves.
Keep your backs straight!
-AAGH!-
And relax, kids! Your trembling is causing my tea to spill.
-Nnngh!- Re-relax?

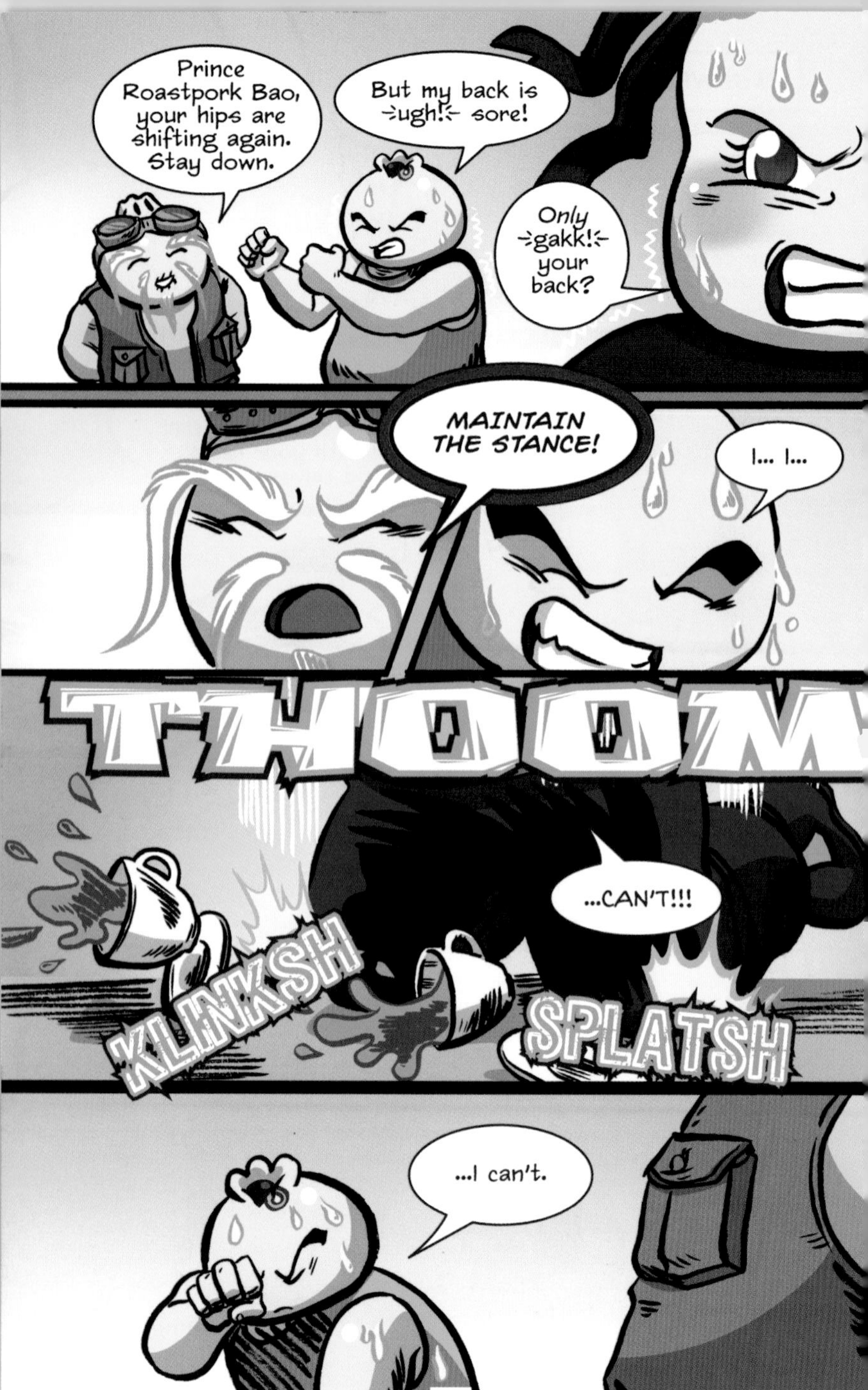
Prince Roastpork Bao, your hips are shifting again. Stay down.
But my back is -ugh!- sore!
Only -gakk!- your back?
MAINTAIN THE STANCE!
I... I...
THOOM
...CAN'T!!!
KLINKSH
SPLATSH
...I can't.

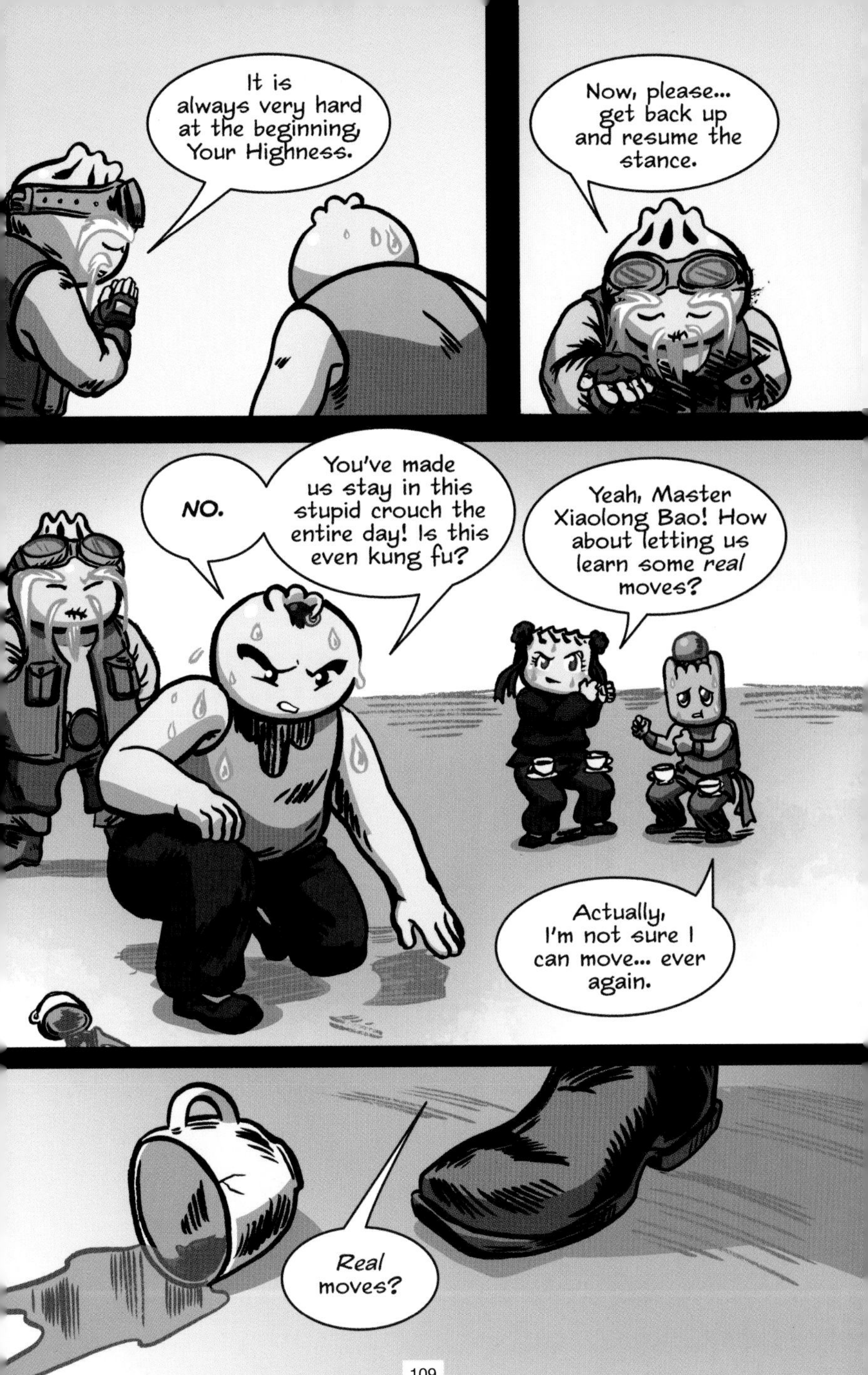
It is always very hard at the beginning, Your Highness.
Now, please... get back up and resume the stance.
NO.
You've made us stay in this stupid crouch the entire day! Is this even kung fu?
Yeah, Master Xiaolong Bao! How about letting us learn some *real* moves?
Actually, I'm not sure I can move... ever again.
*Real* moves?

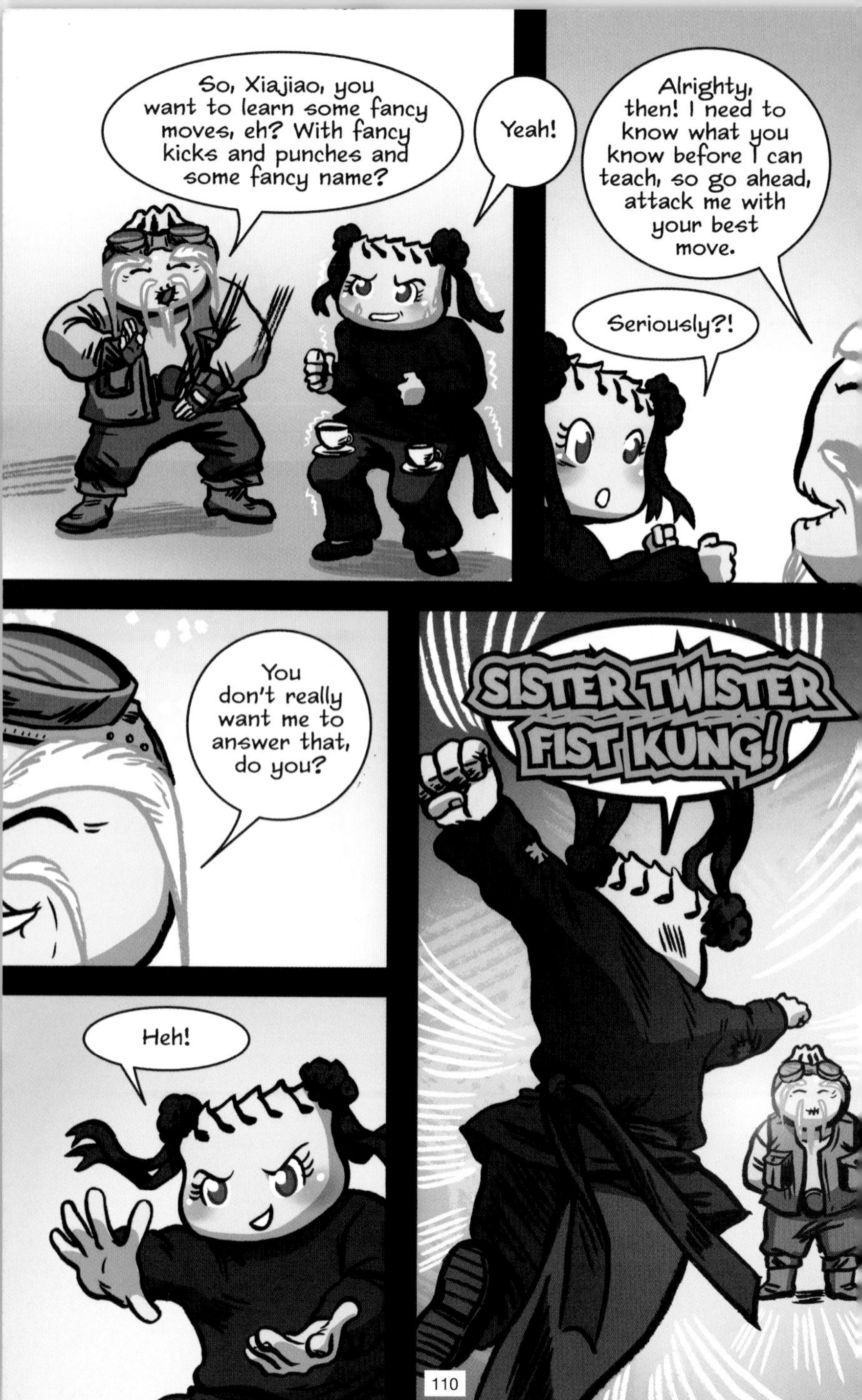
So, Xiajiao, you want to learn some fancy moves, eh? With fancy kicks and punches and some fancy name?
Yeah!
Alrighty, then! I need to know what you know before I can teach, so go ahead, attack me with your best move.
Seriously?!
You don't really want me to answer that, do you?
Heh!
SISTER TWISTER FIST KUNG!

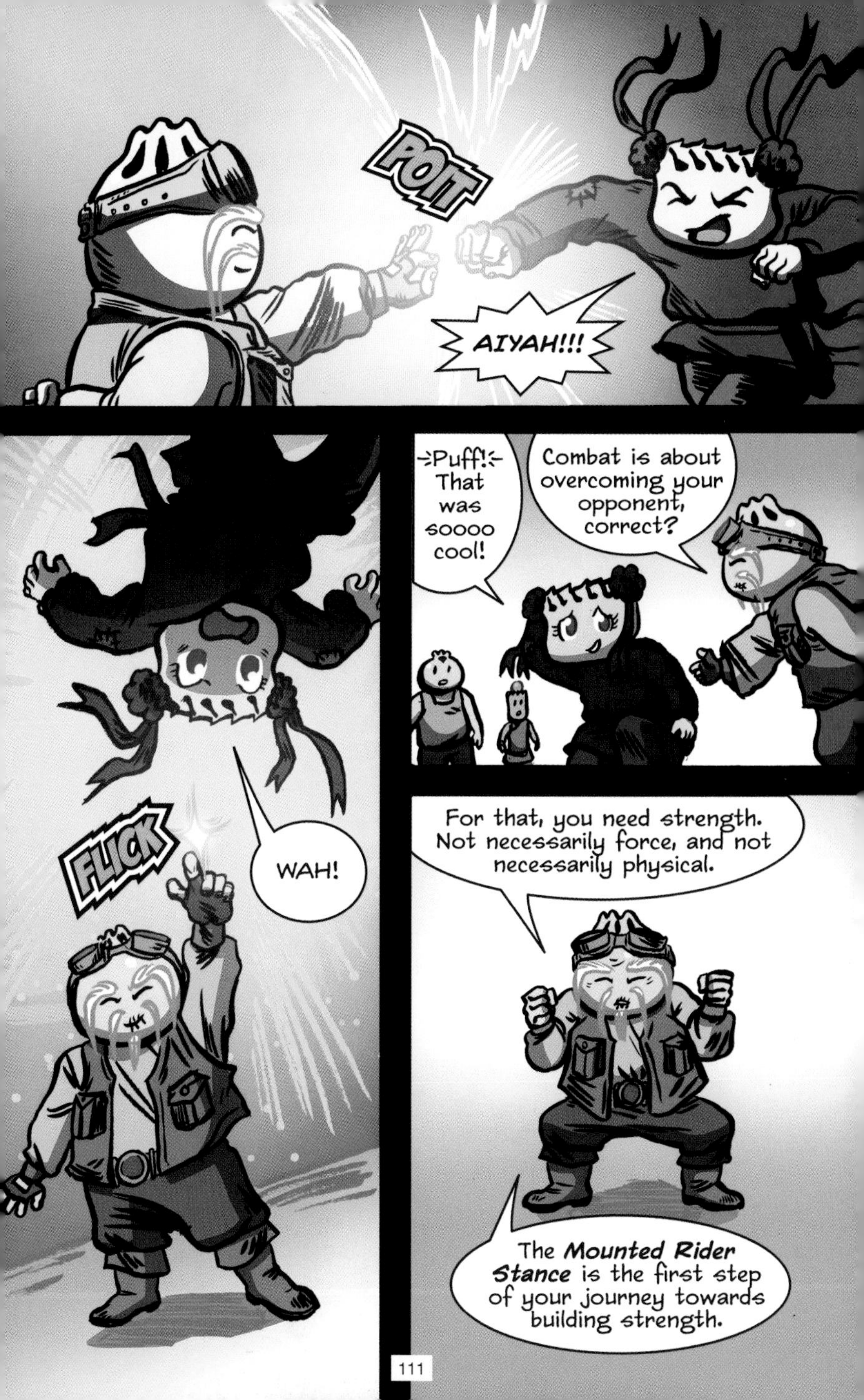
POIT
AIYAH!!!
FLICK
WAH!
-Puff!- That was soooo cool!
Combat is about overcoming your opponent, correct?
For that, you need strength. Not necessarily force, and not necessarily physical.
The **Mounted Rider Stance** is the first step of your journey towards building strength.

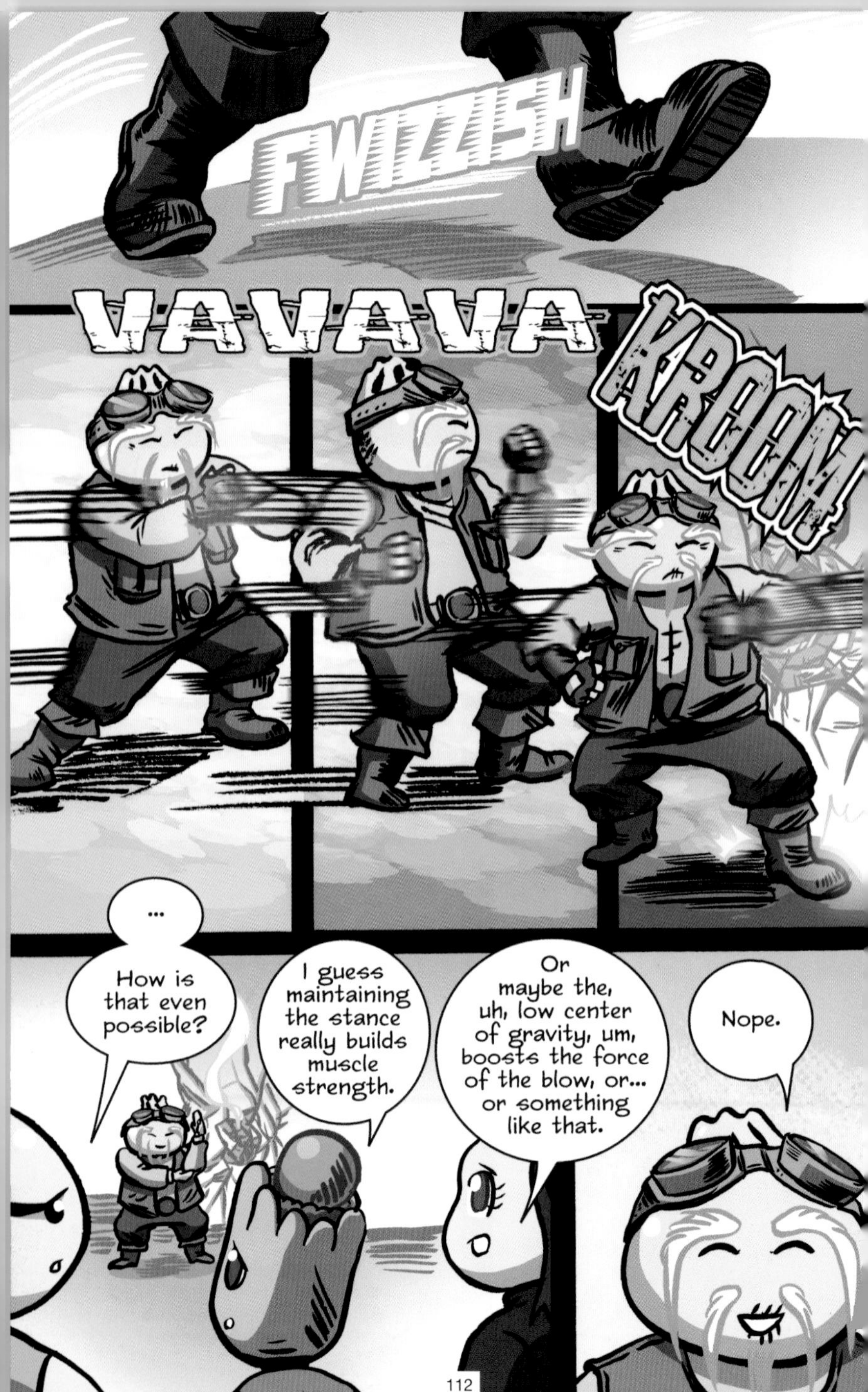

FWIZZISH
VAVAVAVA
KROOM
...
How is that even possible?
I guess maintaining the stance really builds muscle strength.
Or maybe the, uh, low center of gravity, um, boosts the force of the blow, or... or something like that.
Nope.

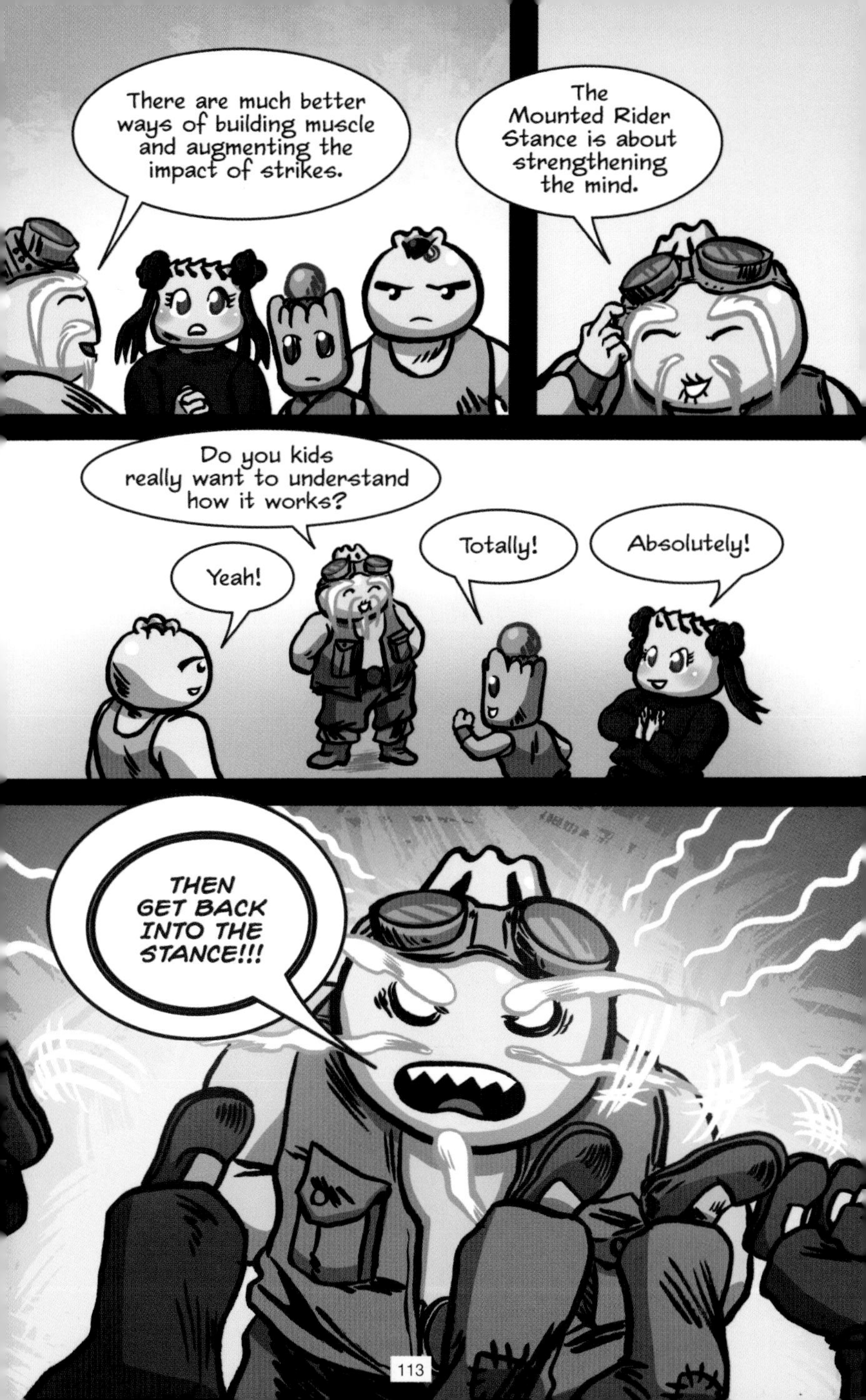
There are much better ways of building muscle and augmenting the impact of strikes.
The Mounted Rider Stance is about strengthening the mind.
Do you kids really want to understand how it works?
Yeah!
Totally!
Absolutely!
THEN GET BACK INTO THE STANCE!!!

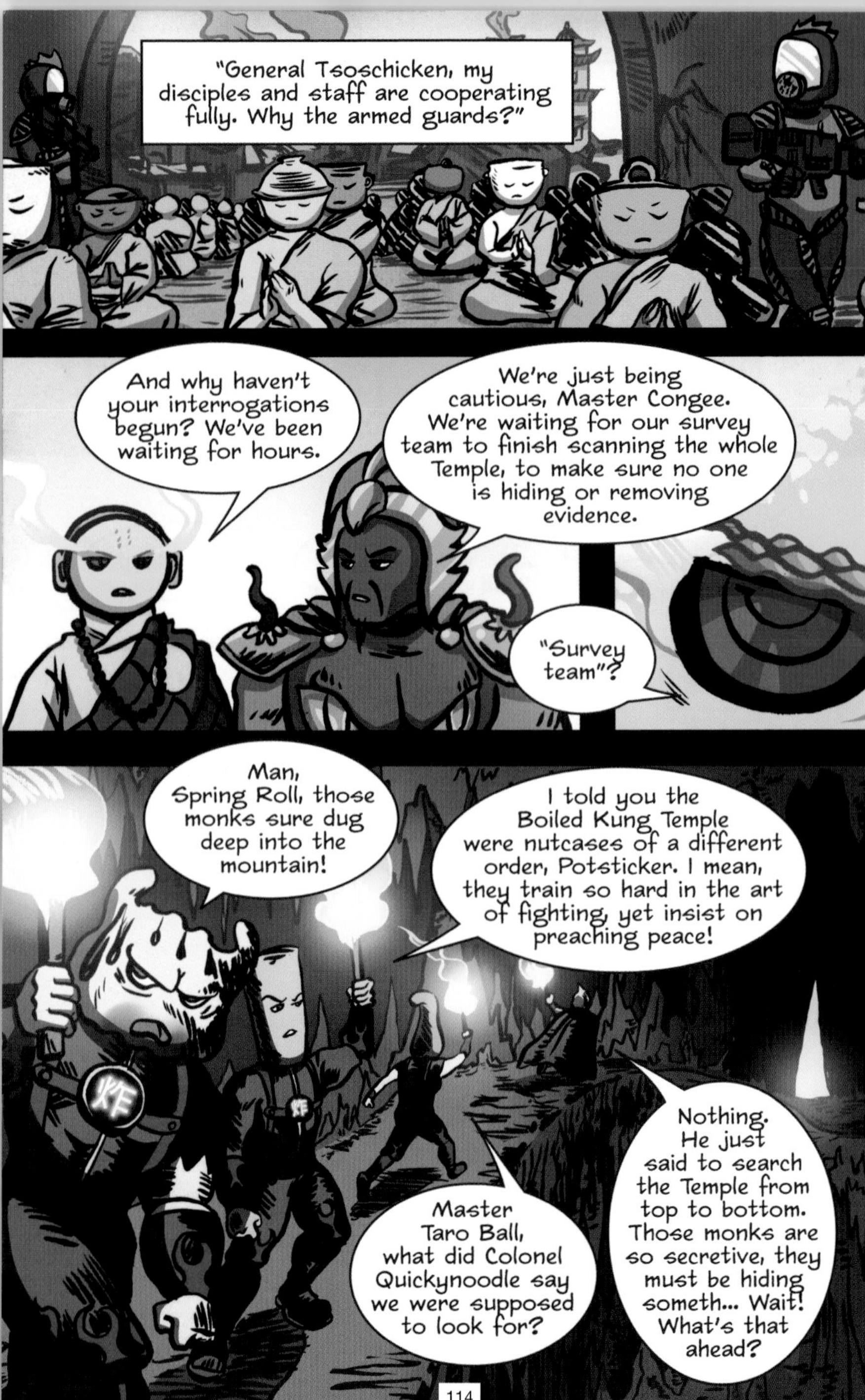
"General Tsoschicken, my disciples and staff are cooperating fully. Why the armed guards?"
And why haven't your interrogations begun? We've been waiting for hours.
We're just being cautious, Master Congee. We're waiting for our survey team to finish scanning the whole Temple, to make sure no one is hiding or removing evidence.
"Survey team"?
Man, Spring Roll, those monks sure dug deep into the mountain!
I told you the Boiled Kung Temple were nutcases of a different order, Potsticker. I mean, they train so hard in the art of fighting, yet insist on preaching peace!
Master Taro Ball, what did Colonel Quickynoodle say we were supposed to look for?
Nothing. He just said to search the Temple from top to bottom. Those monks are so secretive, they must be hiding someth... Wait! What's that ahead?

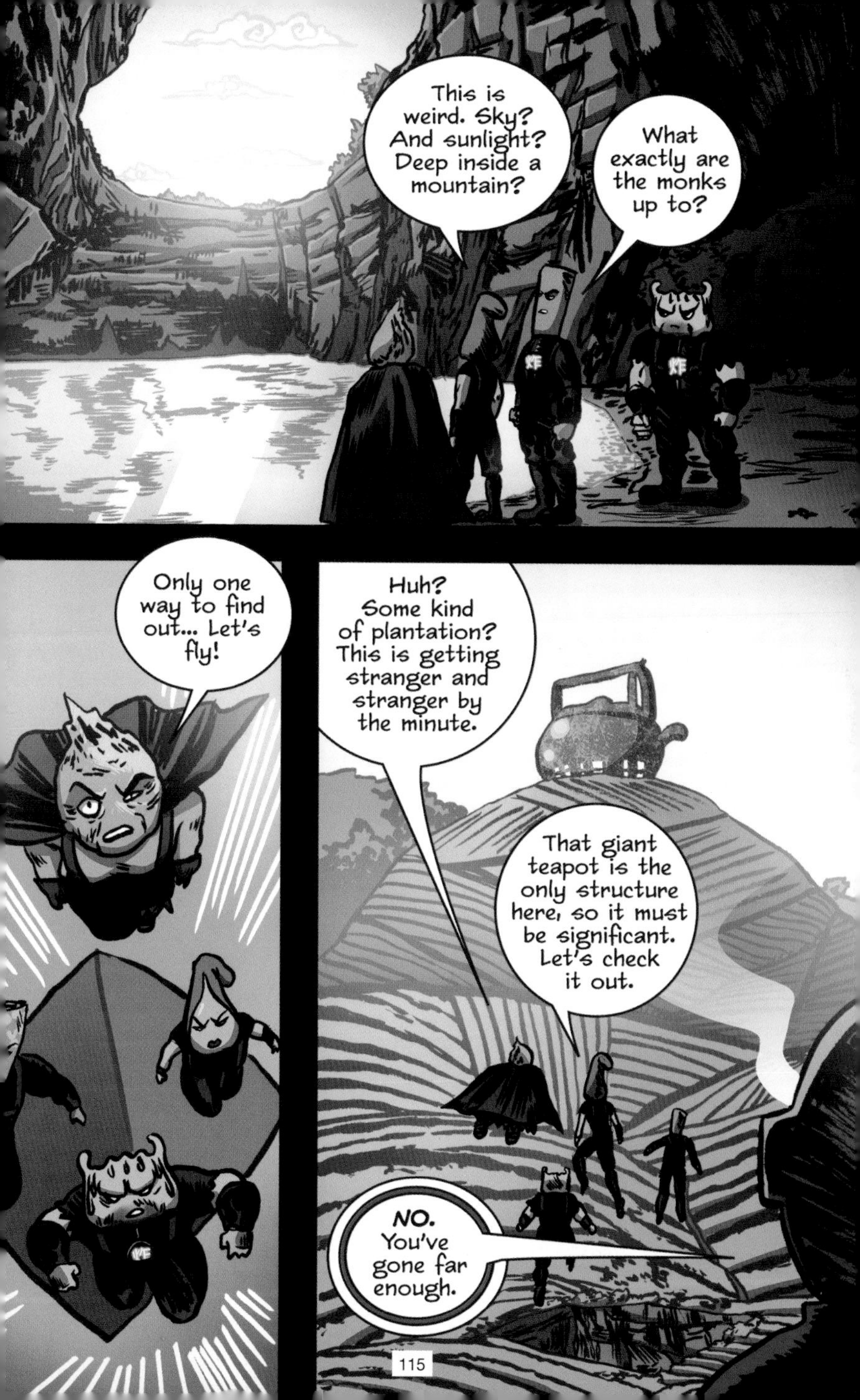

This is weird. Sky? And sunlight? Deep inside a mountain?
What exactly are the monks up to?
Only one way to find out... Let's fly!
Huh? Some kind of plantation? This is getting stranger and stranger by the minute.
That giant teapot is the only structure here, so it must be significant. Let's check it out.
NO. You've gone far enough.

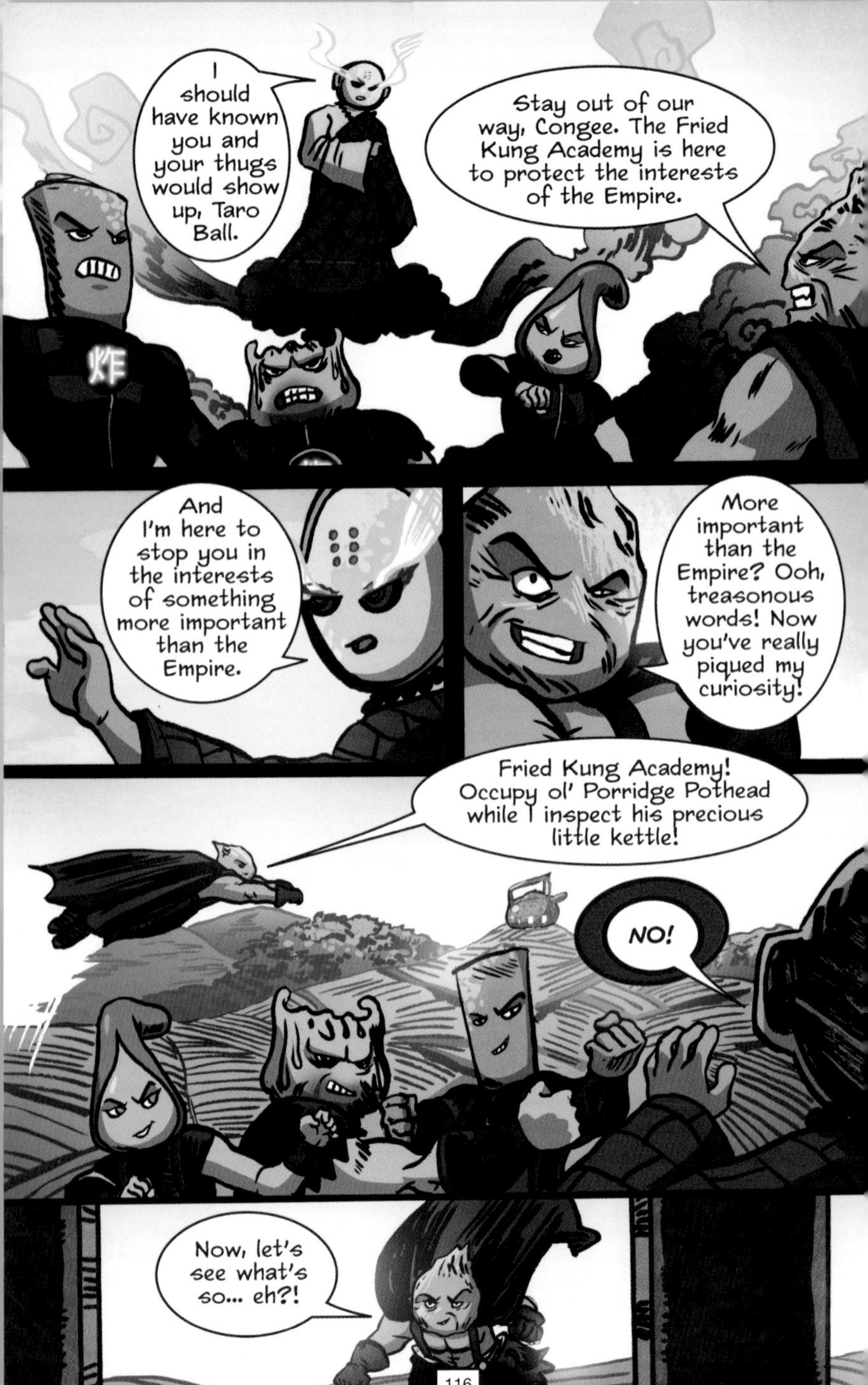
I should have known you and your thugs would show up, Taro Ball.
Stay out of our way, Congee. The Fried Kung Academy is here to protect the interests of the Empire.
And I'm here to stop you in the interests of something more important than the Empire.
More important than the Empire? Ooh, treasonous words! Now you've really piqued my curiosity!
Fried Kung Academy! Occupy ol' Porridge Pothead while I inspect his precious little kettle!
NO!
Now, let's see what's so... eh?!

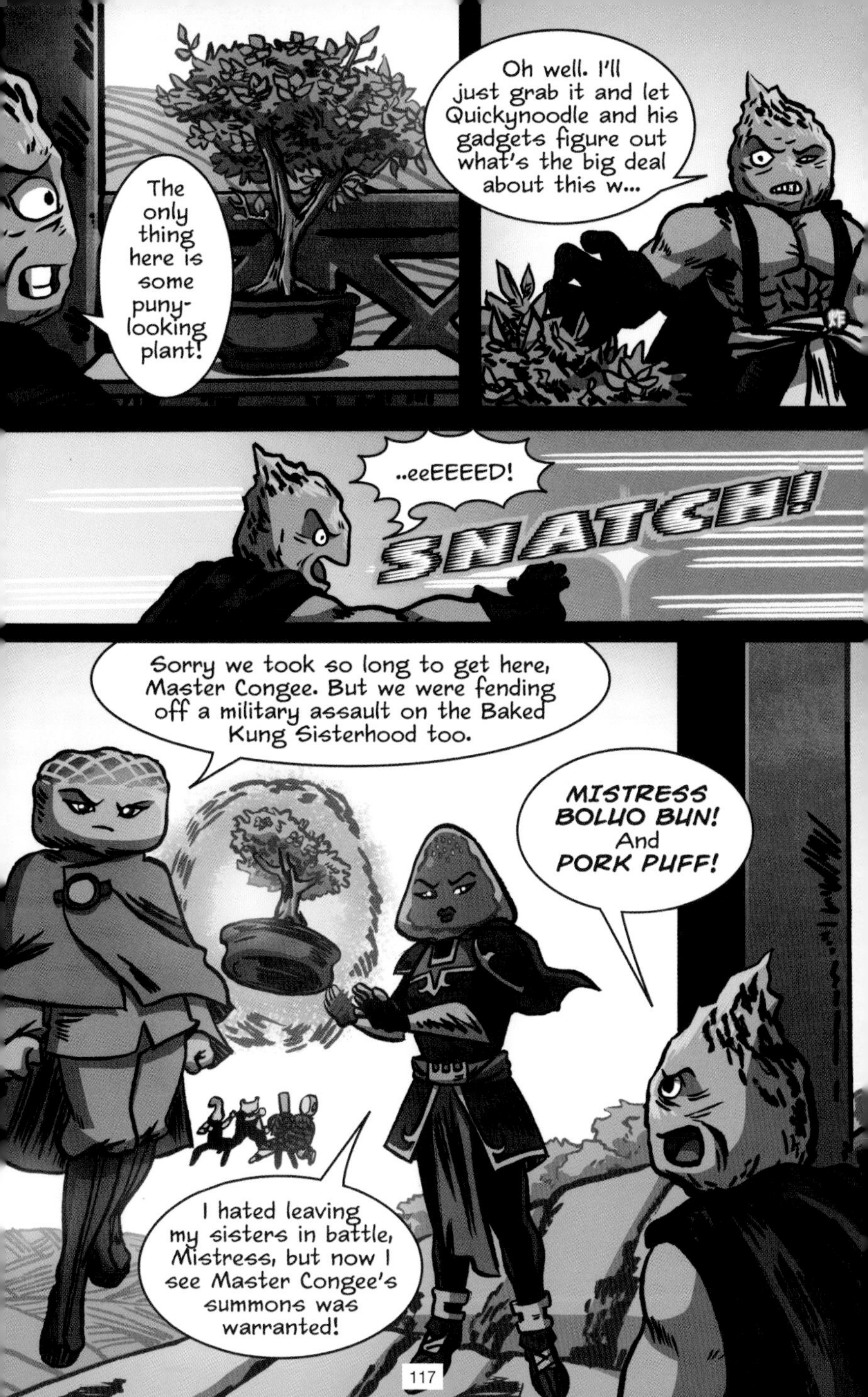
The only thing here is some puny-looking plant!
Oh well. I'll just grab it and let Quickynoodle and his gadgets figure out what's the big deal about this w...
..eeEEEED!
SNATCH!
Sorry we took so long to get here, Master Congee. But we were fending off a military assault on the Baked Kung Sisterhood too.
MISTRESS BOLUO BUN! And PORK PUFF!
I hated leaving my sisters in battle, Mistress, but now I see Master Congee's summons was warranted!

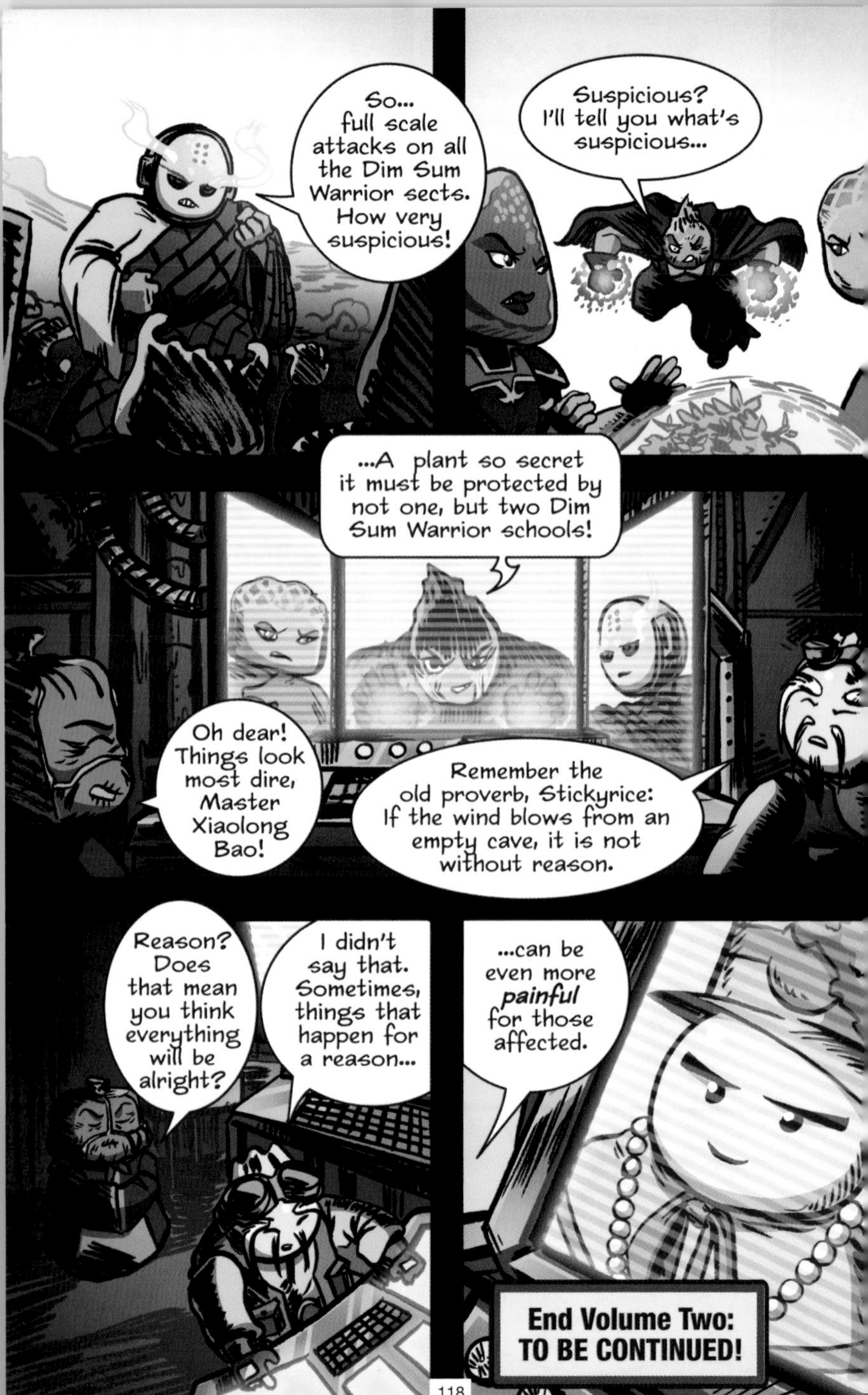
So... full scale attacks on all the Dim Sum Warrior sects. How very suspicious!
Suspicious? I'll tell you what's suspicious...
...A plant so secret it must be protected by not one, but two Dim Sum Warrior schools!
Oh dear! Things look most dire, Master Xiaolong Bao!
Remember the old proverb, Stickyrice: If the wind blows from an empty cave, it is not without reason.
Reason? Does that mean you think everything will be alright?
I didn't say that. Sometimes, things that happen for a reason...
...can be even more *painful* for those affected.
End Volume Two: TO BE CONTINUED!

# BIOGRAPHIES

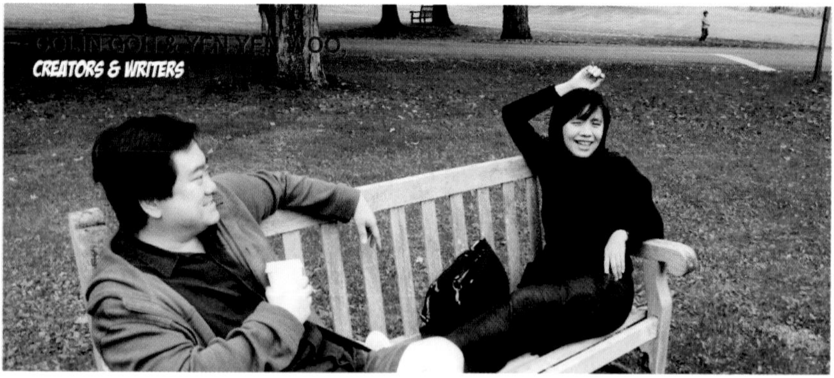
COLIN GOH & YEN YEN WOO
CREATORS & WRITERS

**Colin and Yen Yen are the creators and writers of Dim Sum Warriors.**

Together, they are also international award-winning filmmakers. Their feature film 'Singapore Dreaming' (2006) won the Montblanc New Screenwriters Award at the San Sebastian International Film Festival, the Audience Award for Narrative Feature at the Asian American International Film Festival in New York, and the Best Asian/Middle Eastern Film Award at the Tokyo International Film Festival. The film has since been sold to multiple territories worldwide, and has also been screened at the Brooklyn Museum of Art and the Smithsonian Institution.

They also founded TalkingCock.com, an award-winning satirical website about their home country of Singapore, which has been featured by the BBC, the Economist and Wired, amongst many other international media. The website also spawned the bestselling Coxford Singlish Dictionary, a lexicon of vernacular Singapore English which the Times of London has pronounced 'invaluable'.

Colin graduated from the Faculty of Laws in University College London and obtained his Masters from Columbia University's School of Law, where he was named a Harlan Fiske Stone Scholar. At 17, he became the very first Singaporean to write and draw a daily comic strip for the Singaporean newspapers, which he continued to do for over 20 years, even while practising as a commercial litigator. His cartoons have also been published in England, the USA, Japan and Malaysia. In 2012, he wrote and drew all the cartoons for the New York Times bestseller 'Search Inside Yourself' (HarperOne) by Google's Chade-Meng Tan. A short story he wrote, 'Last Time', was also selected for 'Singapore Noir' (2014), part of Akashic Books' internationally-acclaimed 'Noir' series.

Yen Yen received her doctorate from Teachers College, Columbia University in New York, where she was awarded the prestigious Spencer Research Fellowship. She is now an Associate Professor at the College of Education and Information Sciences at Long Island University, C.W. Post, teaching courses in Curriculum Development and Social Foundations of Education. She has also worked as an educational consultant for UNICEF to help the Education Ministry in Afghanistan design their new curriculum, as well as an instructional designer with a leading education software and animation company in Singapore. Her work has been published in journals such as Educational Researcher, Discourse, the Asia-Pacific Journal of Education and Teachers College Record. As if she wasn't busy enough, she recently started Yumcha Yoga, a specialist yoga studio in the bustling town of Flushing in New York City, where Colin and Yen Yen live together with their daughter.

## SOO LEE, *ARTIST*

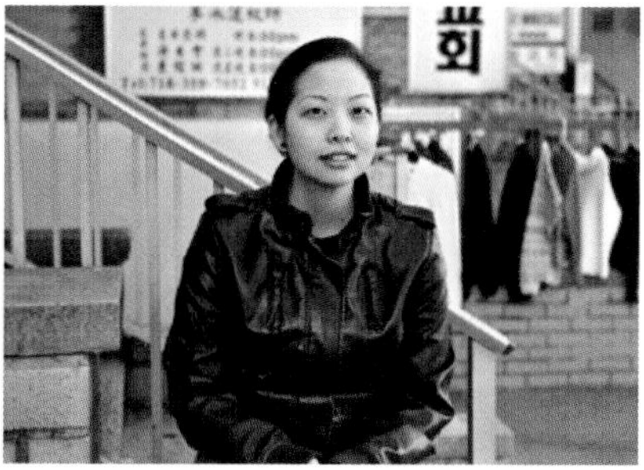

The winner of the Art Spiegelman Alumni Award during her time at the High School of Art and Design, Soo is a graduate of the School of Visual Art in New York. Dim Sum Warriors is her first published comic. She recenty illustrated 'The End of History and the Last Man', a short story written by Colin Goh for Volume 3 of Image Comics' Liquid City anthology series.

## MIKE LUCKAS, *COLORIST*

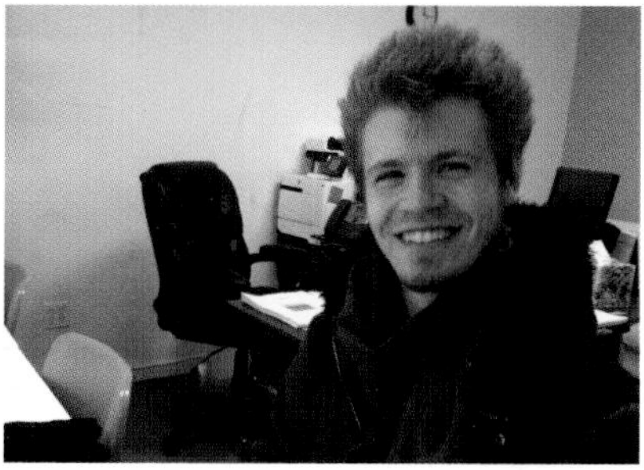

Mike Luckas is a freelance comic artist and illustrator with a BFA in Cartooning/ Illustration from the School of Visual Arts. Aside from self-publishing his own titles, he has worked as a professional colorist on Image Comics' 'Skullkickers'. He also illustrated their 12th issue, 'Four More Tavern Tales'. He is currently working on his own webcomics, 'Conquistas' and 'Das Moustache'.

## *YUMCHA STUDIOS LLC*

We're a New York-based multimedia company that's combining everything we've learned in the disciplines of comics, filmmaking, education, martial arts and interactive content—and also parenting!—to bring you exciting and meaningful cross-cultural stories for all ages. Dim Sum Warriors is our inaugural project.
Join us on our journey!

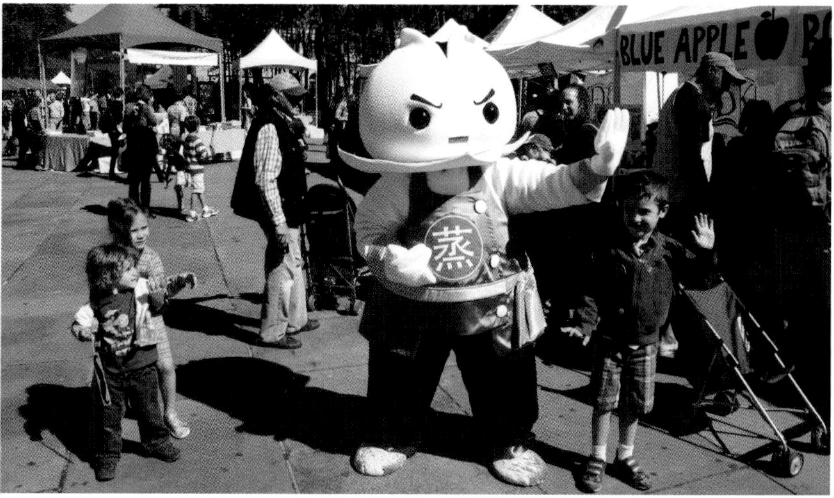
BLUE APPLE
蒸

*Special Presentation*

# BEHIND THE STEAM

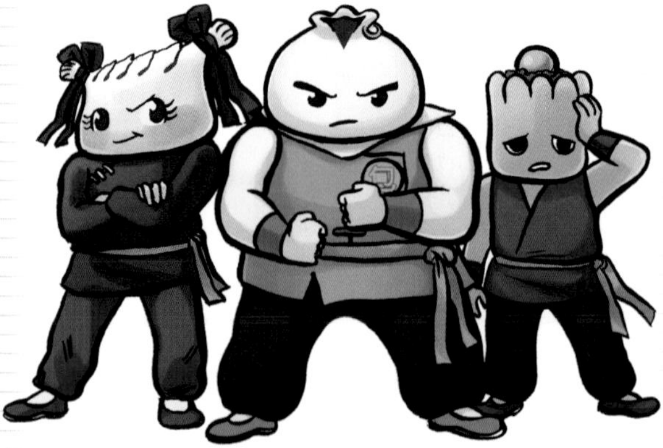

**Once upon a time, the guys above looked like the guys below:**

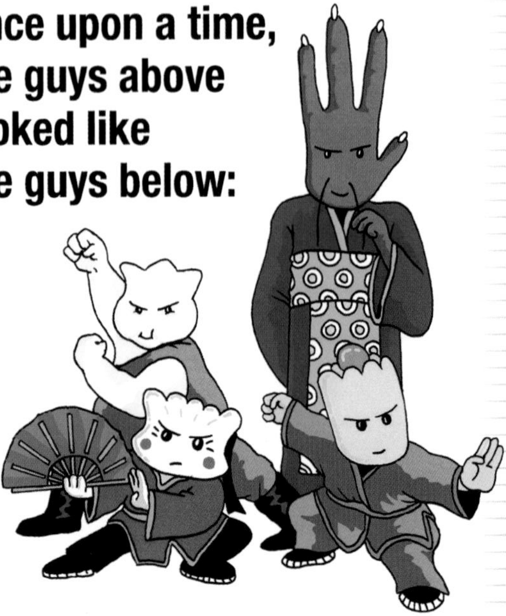

## STEAMY ORIGINS

Although we launched *Dim Sum Warriors* through Apple's App Store in April 2012, Yen Yen and I had been kicking the idea of a kids' series featuring anthropomorphic kung fu-fighting dim sum around for quite a while, even before we'd made our feature film, *Singapore Dreaming* (2006).

Its first incarnation was as a comic strip, which made sense since I'd been doing comic strips for The New Paper, a Singapore tabloid, for over 20 years. Here are some test strips which I actually submitted to several American comic strip syndicates:

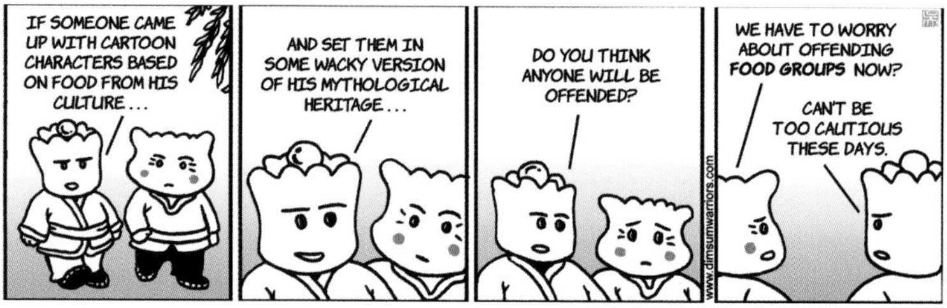
IF SOMEONE CAME UP WITH CARTOON CHARACTERS BASED ON FOOD FROM HIS CULTURE...
AND SET THEM IN SOME WACKY VERSION OF HIS MYTHOLOGICAL HERITAGE...
DO YOU THINK ANYONE WILL BE OFFENDED?
www.dimsumwarriors.com
WE HAVE TO WORRY ABOUT OFFENDING FOOD GROUPS NOW?
CAN'T BE TOO CAUTIOUS THESE DAYS.

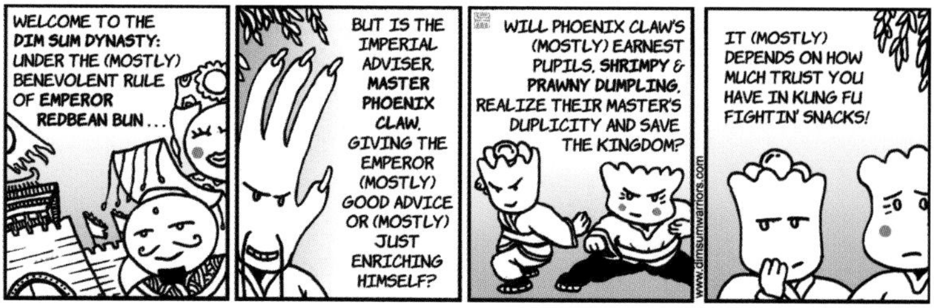
WELCOME TO THE DIM SUM DYNASTY: UNDER THE (MOSTLY) BENEVOLENT RULE OF EMPEROR REDBEAN BUN...
BUT IS THE IMPERIAL ADVISER, MASTER PHOENIX CLAW, GIVING THE EMPEROR (MOSTLY) GOOD ADVICE OR (MOSTLY) JUST ENRICHING HIMSELF?
WILL PHOENIX CLAW'S (MOSTLY) EARNEST PUPILS, SHRIMPY & PRAWNY DUMPLING, REALIZE THEIR MASTER'S DUPLICITY AND SAVE THE KINGDOM?
www.dimsumwarriors.com
IT (MOSTLY) DEPENDS ON HOW MUCH TRUST YOU HAVE IN KUNG FU FIGHTIN' SNACKS!

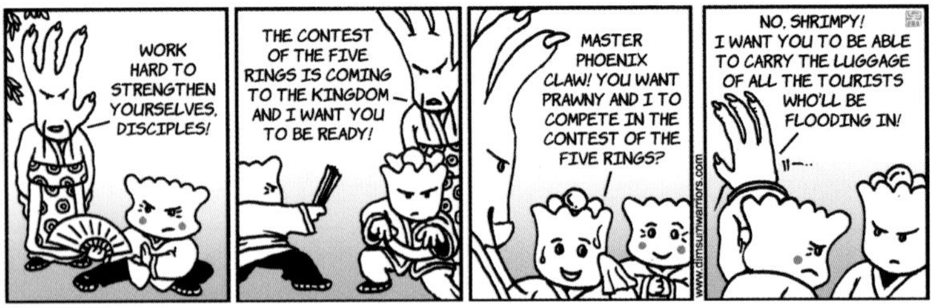
WORK HARD TO STRENGTHEN YOURSELVES, DISCIPLES!
THE CONTEST OF THE FIVE RINGS IS COMING TO THE KINGDOM AND I WANT YOU TO BE READY!
MASTER PHOENIX CLAW! YOU WANT PRAWNY AND I TO COMPETE IN THE CONTEST OF THE FIVE RINGS?
www.dimsumwarriors.com
NO, SHRIMPY! I WANT YOU TO BE ABLE TO CARRY THE LUGGAGE OF ALL THE TOURISTS WHO'LL BE FLOODING IN!
"—..

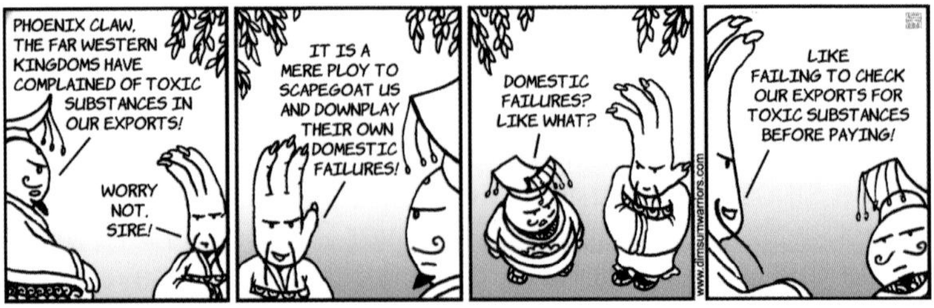
PHOENIX CLAW, THE FAR WESTERN KINGDOMS HAVE COMPLAINED OF TOXIC SUBSTANCES IN OUR EXPORTS!
WORRY NOT, SIRE!
IT IS A MERE PLOY TO SCAPEGOAT US AND DOWNPLAY THEIR OWN DOMESTIC FAILURES!
DOMESTIC FAILURES? LIKE WHAT?
www.dimsumwarriors.com
LIKE FAILING TO CHECK OUR EXPORTS FOR TOXIC SUBSTANCES BEFORE PAYING!

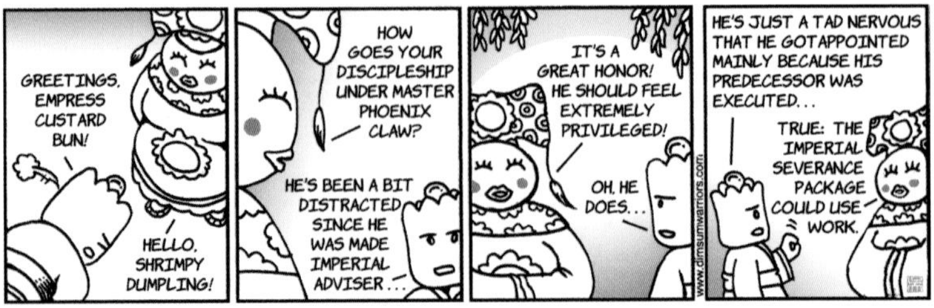
GREETINGS, EMPRESS CUSTARD BUN!
HELLO, SHRIMPY DUMPLING!
HOW GOES YOUR DISCIPLESHIP UNDER MASTER PHOENIX CLAW?
HE'S BEEN A BIT DISTRACTED SINCE HE WAS MADE IMPERIAL ADVISER...
IT'S A GREAT HONOR! HE SHOULD FEEL EXTREMELY PRIVILEGED!
OH, HE DOES...
www.dimsumwarriors.com
HE'S JUST A TAD NERVOUS THAT HE GOT APPOINTED MAINLY BECAUSE HIS PREDECESSOR WAS EXECUTED...
TRUE: THE IMPERIAL SEVERANCE PACKAGE COULD USE WORK.

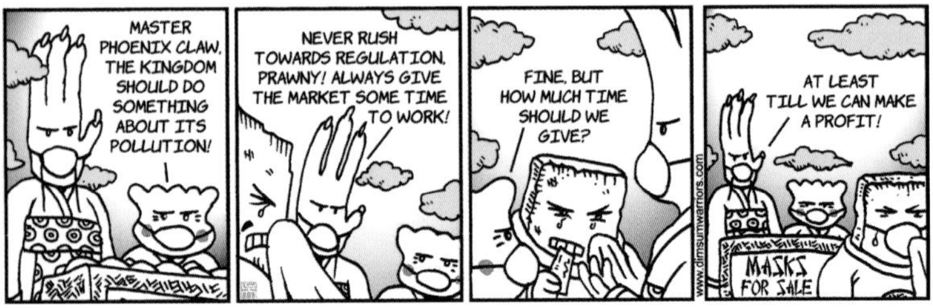
MASTER PHOENIX CLAW, THE KINGDOM SHOULD DO SOMETHING ABOUT ITS POLLUTION!
NEVER RUSH TOWARDS REGULATION, PRAWNY! ALWAYS GIVE THE MARKET SOME TIME TO WORK!
FINE, BUT HOW MUCH TIME SHOULD WE GIVE?
www.dimsumwarriors.com
AT LEAST TILL WE CAN MAKE A PROFIT!
MASKS FOR SALE

I wasn't surprised to be rejected by every single one of them. Quite apart from the newspaper business generally being on the decline, it was really hard for a new strip to displace the long-running ones - especially one with a comparatively exotic theme and cast of characters.

Still, it was worth a shot. We also toyed around with pitching a series of Dim Sum Warriors kids' books, but when things fell in place for *Singapore Dreaming*, we shelved everything else.

After *Singapore Dreaming* picked up several international awards and got sold to multiple territories, we thought we'd found our calling, and were all pumped up to do our next movie, working hard on the script, scouting for locations and production partners, etc, etc. - generally fulfilling Woody Allen's aphorism, "If you want to make God laugh, tell him your plans."

Because we - well, Yen - got pregnant. We expected disruption and workarounds, but didn't expect any major deviation from the overall plan. But when our daughter was born very suddenly and very prematurely at 30 weeks, all bets were off. I remember standing in the neonatal intensive care ward and seeing her tiny 2½ pound frame, looking for all the world like a skinned kitten, hooked up to all manner of tubes and wires, and knowing our life and career had just undergone an asteroid strike.

We'd read about all the risks that come with severe prematurity, so we knew our daughter's health and well-being had to be our top priority, and consequently, that moviemaking with its uncertainty and rollercoaster schedules had to be placed on a backburner.

Still, you can't suppress the creative urge. We started thinking about what we could still do under the circumstances. And so we dusted off *Dim Sum Warriors.* Now that we were raising a child with a jumbled heritage, telling a story about Chinese snacks in that most American of artforms, the comic book, seemed particularly apropos.

What you're about to see over the next 30 pages is an early draft. As you can see, we've retained some things with the eventual storyline, but there are also significant deviations, such as making Porky the main protagonist rather than Xiajiao and Shaomai (as Prawny and Shrimpy were renamed, along with many other characters). Also, as we were developing the story, the iPad debuted, and we decided to play with all the possibilities that the platform afforded us.

While there are some headscratching elements (Xiajiao/Prawny's Minnie Mouse-like ears, for example), I still think this early version has its crude charms, and I hope you'll enjoy this little snapshot of the evolution of Dim Sum Warriors.

**Colin Goh**
Flushing, New York
2013

# MEET THE DIM SUM WARRIORS

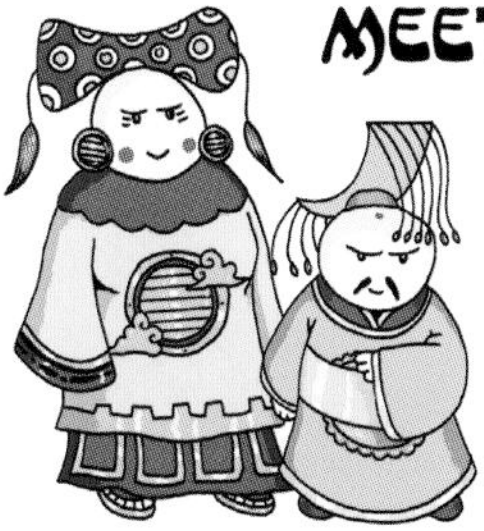

*Empress Custard Bao & Emperor Redbean Bao*

Welcome to Dim Sum Kingdom! It is the Bao Dynasty, and **Emperor Redbean Bao** and **Empress Custard Bao** preside over a court filled with intrigue and silliness.

The main source of this unruliness is the rivalry between the kingdom's four Dim Sum Warrior schools:
- The Fried Kung Academy;
- The Institute of Baked Kung;
- The Boiled Kung Temple;
- And last, and certainly least of the four:

**the School of Steam Kung**.

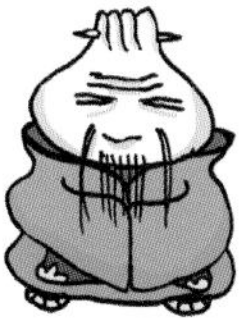

*Shifu Dragon Dumpling*

Under **Shifu Dragon Dumpling**, the School of Steam Kung was the kingdom's top martial arts institution. But Dragon Dumpling mysteriously disappeared, leaving the school in the care of his disciple, **Phoenix Claw**, who seems more interested in making a fast buck through dodgy business schemes rather than training the school's last two remaining pupils, **Prawny & Shrimpy Dumpling**.

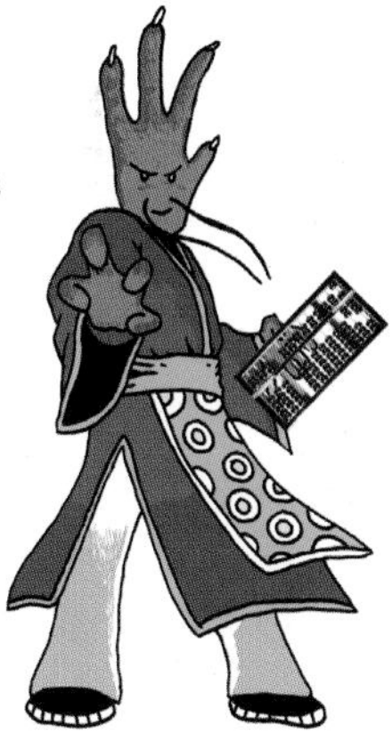

*Phoenix Claw*

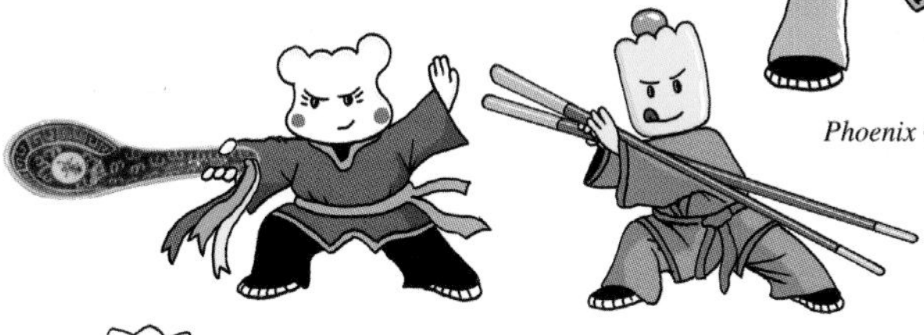

*Prawny & Shrimpy Dumpling*

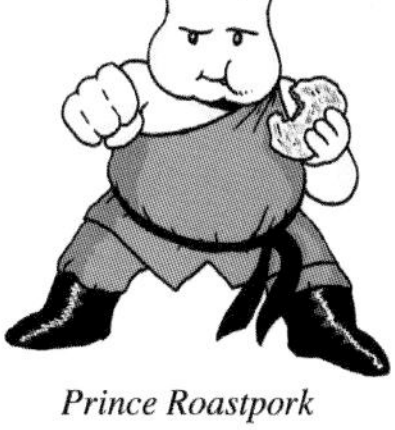

*Prince Roastpork 'Porky' Bao*

Recently, Emperor Bao has convened a massive martial arts tournament, making the four schools compete for the honor of enrolling his son, **Prince Roastpork Bao**, as a disciple.

**Meanwhile, other forces are stirring, that are about to change the kingdom forever...**

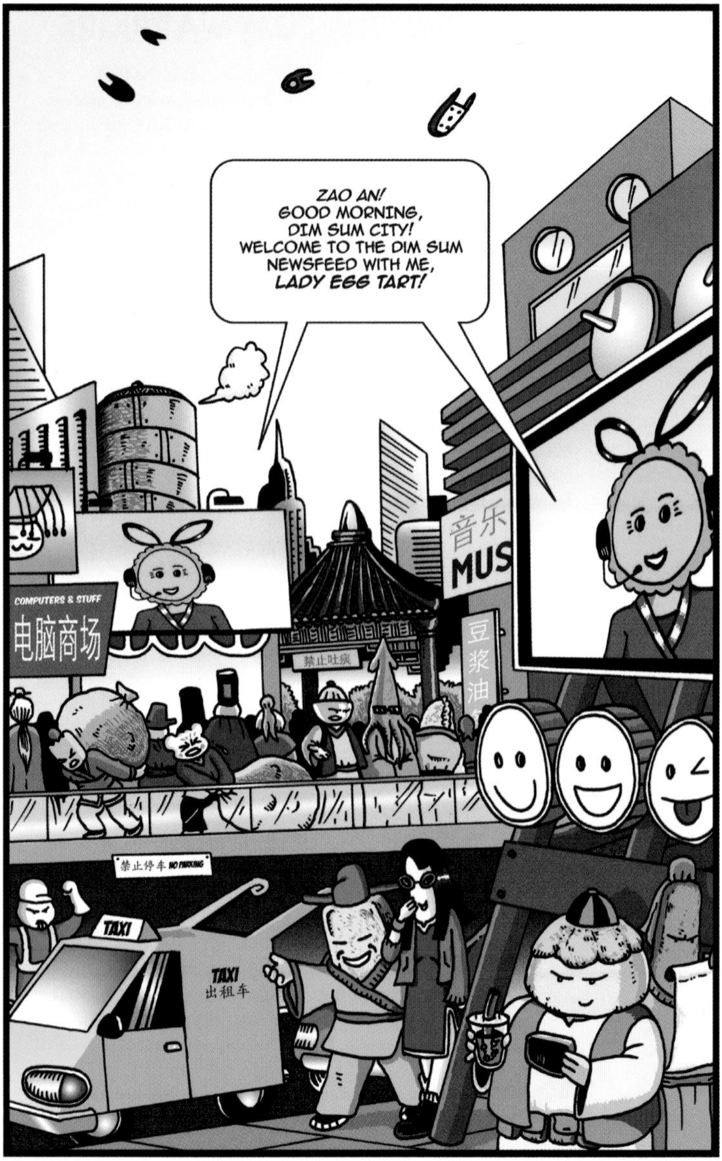
ZAO AN! GOOD MORNING, DIM SUM CITY! WELCOME TO THE DIM SUM NEWSFEED WITH ME, ***LADY EGG TART!***
COMPUTERS & STUFF
电脑商场
禁止吐痰
音乐
MUS
豆浆油
禁止停车 NO PARKING
TAXI
TAXI
出租车

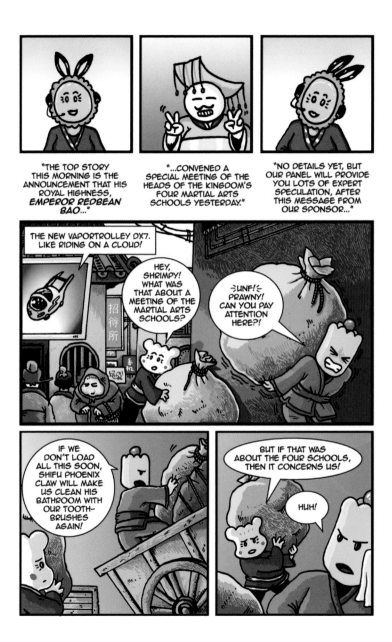

"THE TOP STORY THIS MORNING IS THE ANNOUNCEMENT THAT HIS ROYAL HIGHNESS, *EMPEROR REDBEAN BAO*..."

"...CONVENED A SPECIAL MEETING OF THE HEADS OF THE KINGDOM'S FOUR MARTIAL ARTS SCHOOLS YESTERDAY."

"NO DETAILS YET, BUT OUR PANEL WILL PROVIDE YOU LOTS OF EXPERT SPECULATION, AFTER THIS MESSAGE FROM OUR SPONSOR..."

THE NEW VAPORTROLLEY DX7. LIKE RIDING ON A *CLOUD!*

HEY, SHRIMPY! WHAT WAS THAT ABOUT A MEETING OF THE MARTIAL ARTS SCHOOLS?

‑UNF!‑ PRAWNY! CAN YOU PAY ATTENTION HERE?!

IF WE DON'T LOAD ALL THIS SOON, SHIFU PHOENIX CLAW WILL MAKE US CLEAN HIS BATHROOM WITH OUR TOOTH-BRUSHES AGAIN!

BUT IF THAT WAS ABOUT THE FOUR SCHOOLS, THEN IT CONCERNS US!

HUH!

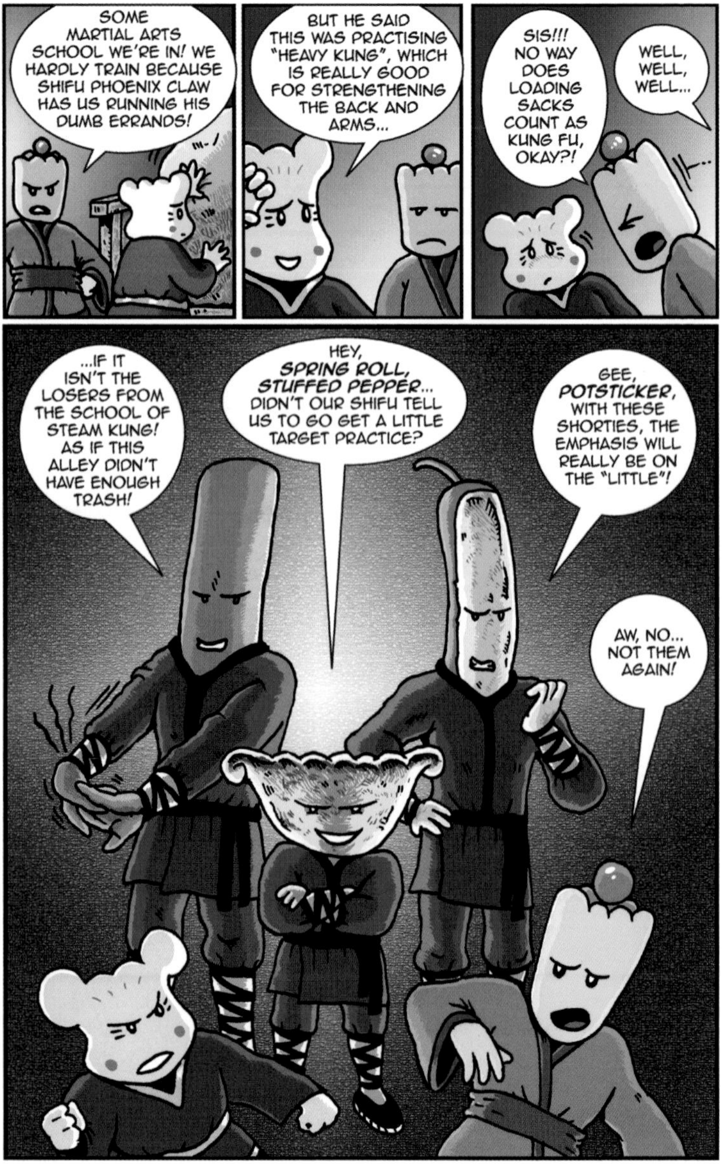
SOME MARTIAL ARTS SCHOOL WE'RE IN! WE HARDLY TRAIN BECAUSE SHIFU PHOENIX CLAW HAS US RUNNING HIS DUMB ERRANDS!
BUT HE SAID THIS WAS PRACTISING "HEAVY KUNG", WHICH IS REALLY GOOD FOR STRENGTHENING THE BACK AND ARMS...
SIS!!! NO WAY DOES LOADING SACKS COUNT AS KUNG FU, OKAY?!
WELL, WELL, WELL...
...IF IT ISN'T THE LOSERS FROM THE SCHOOL OF STEAM KUNG! AS IF THIS ALLEY DIDN'T HAVE ENOUGH TRASH!
HEY, *SPRING ROLL, STUFFED PEPPER*... DIDN'T OUR SHIFU TELL US TO GO GET A LITTLE TARGET PRACTICE?
GEE, *POTSTICKER,* WITH THESE SHORTIES, THE EMPHASIS WILL REALLY BE ON THE "LITTLE"!
AW, NO... NOT THEM AGAIN!

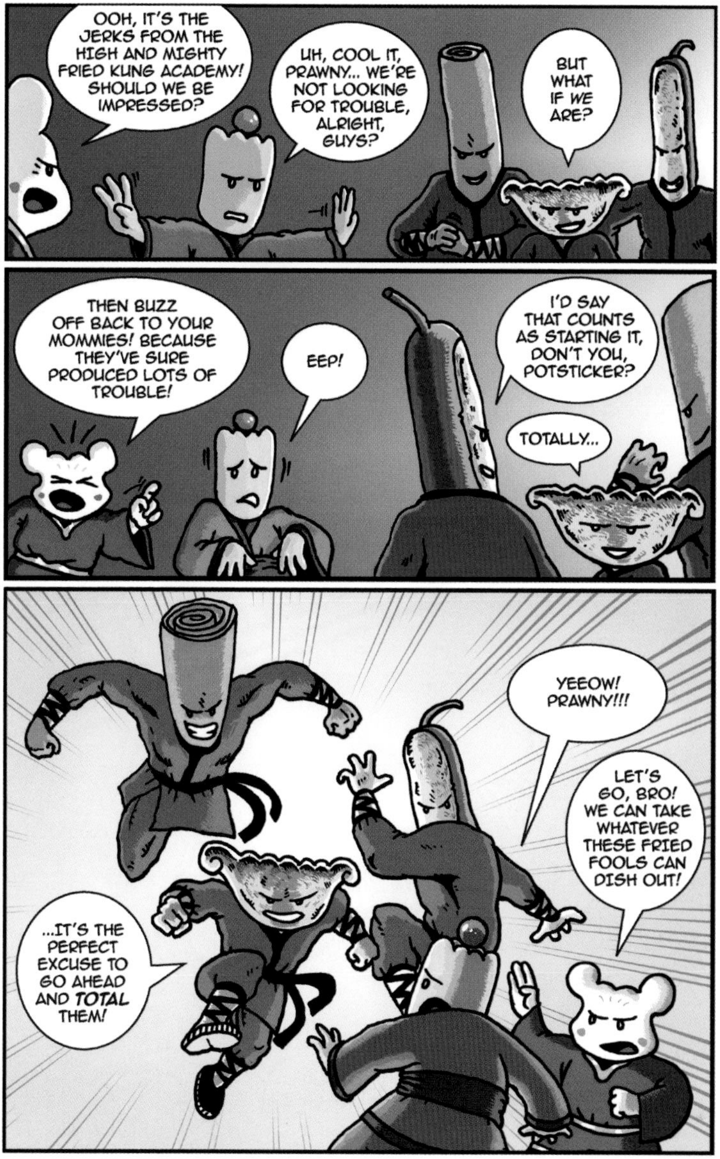
OOH, IT'S THE JERKS FROM THE HIGH AND MIGHTY FRIED KUNG ACADEMY! SHOULD WE BE IMPRESSED?
UH, COOL IT, PRAWNY... WE'RE NOT LOOKING FOR TROUBLE, ALRIGHT, GUYS?
BUT WHAT IF WE ARE?
THEN BUZZ OFF BACK TO YOUR MOMMIES! BECAUSE THEY'VE SURE PRODUCED LOTS OF TROUBLE!
EEP!
I'D SAY THAT COUNTS AS STARTING IT, DON'T YOU, POTSTICKER?
TOTALLY...
...IT'S THE PERFECT EXCUSE TO GO AHEAD AND *TOTAL* THEM!
YEEOW! PRAWNY!!!
LET'S GO, BRO! WE CAN TAKE WHATEVER THESE FRIED FOOLS CAN DISH OUT!

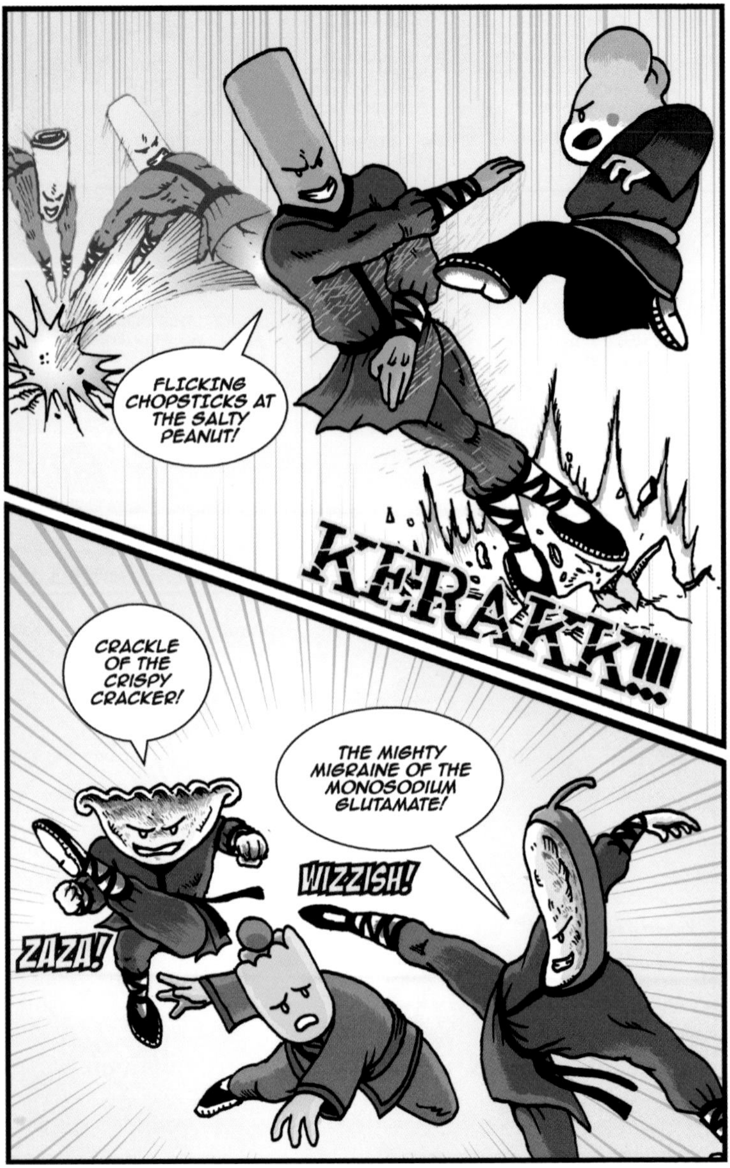
FLICKING CHOPSTICKS AT THE SALTY PEANUT!
KERAKK!!!
CRACKLE OF THE CRISPY CRACKER!
THE MIGHTY MIGRAINE OF THE MONOSODIUM GLUTAMATE!
WIZZISH!
ZAZA!

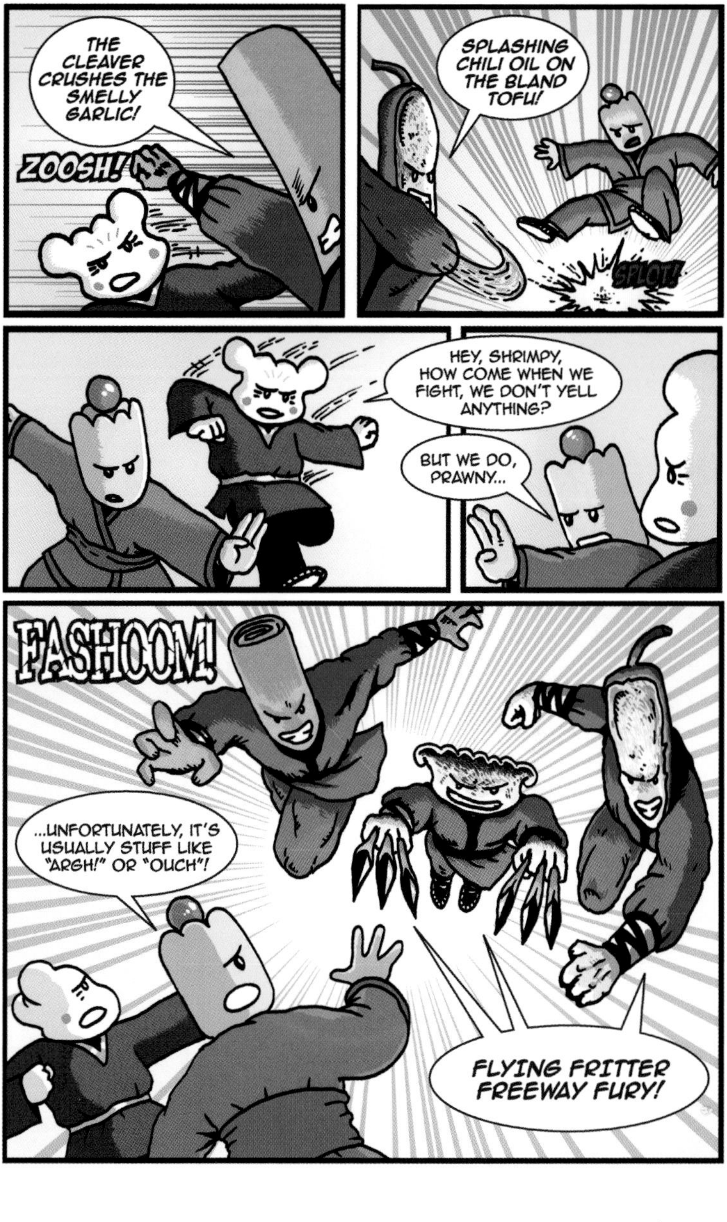
THE CLEAVER CRUSHES THE SMELLY GARLIC!
ZOOSH!
SPLASHING CHILI OIL ON THE BLAND TOFU!
SPLOT!
HEY, SHRIMPY, HOW COME WHEN WE FIGHT, WE DON'T YELL ANYTHING?
BUT WE DO, PRAWNY...
FASHOOM!
...UNFORTUNATELY, IT'S USUALLY STUFF LIKE "ARGH!" OR "OUCH"!
FLYING FRITTER FREEWAY FURY!

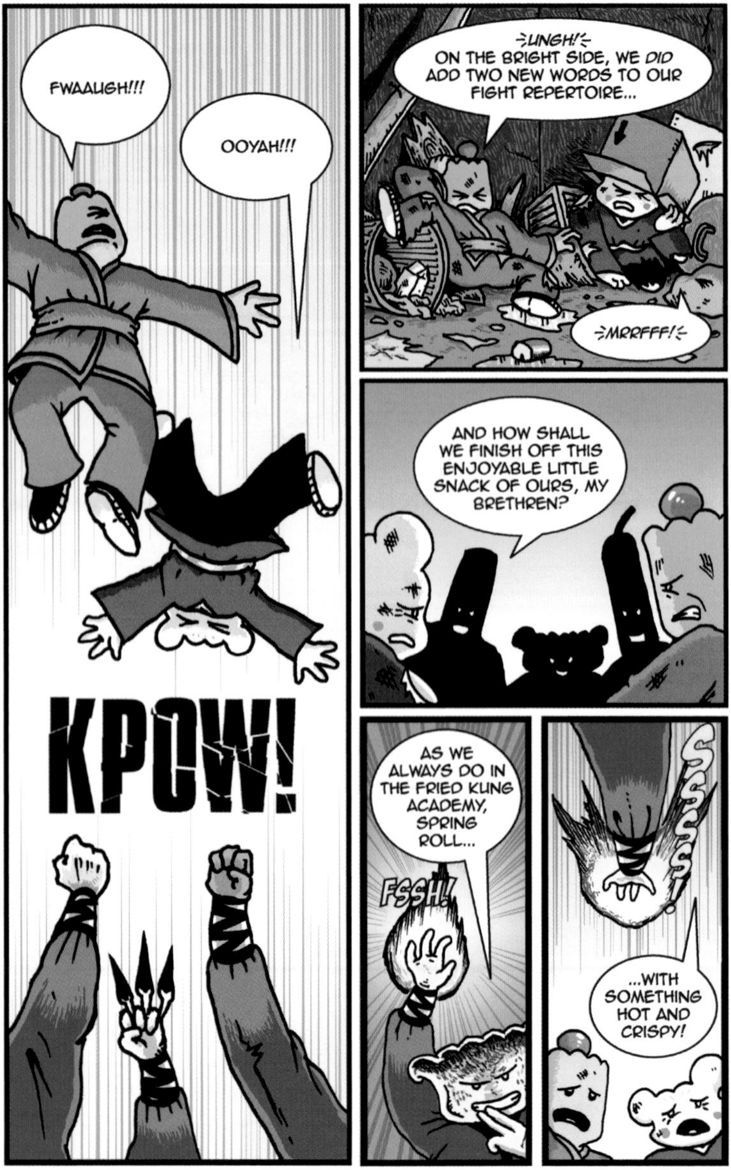
FWAAUGH!!!
OOYAH!!!
KPOW!
=UNGH!= ON THE BRIGHT SIDE, WE DID ADD TWO NEW WORDS TO OUR FIGHT REPERTOIRE...
=MRRFFF!=
AND HOW SHALL WE FINISH OFF THIS ENJOYABLE LITTLE SNACK OF OURS, MY BRETHREN?
AS WE ALWAYS DO IN THE FRIED KUNG ACADEMY, SPRING ROLL...
FSSH!
SSSSSS!
...WITH SOMETHING HOT AND CRISPY!

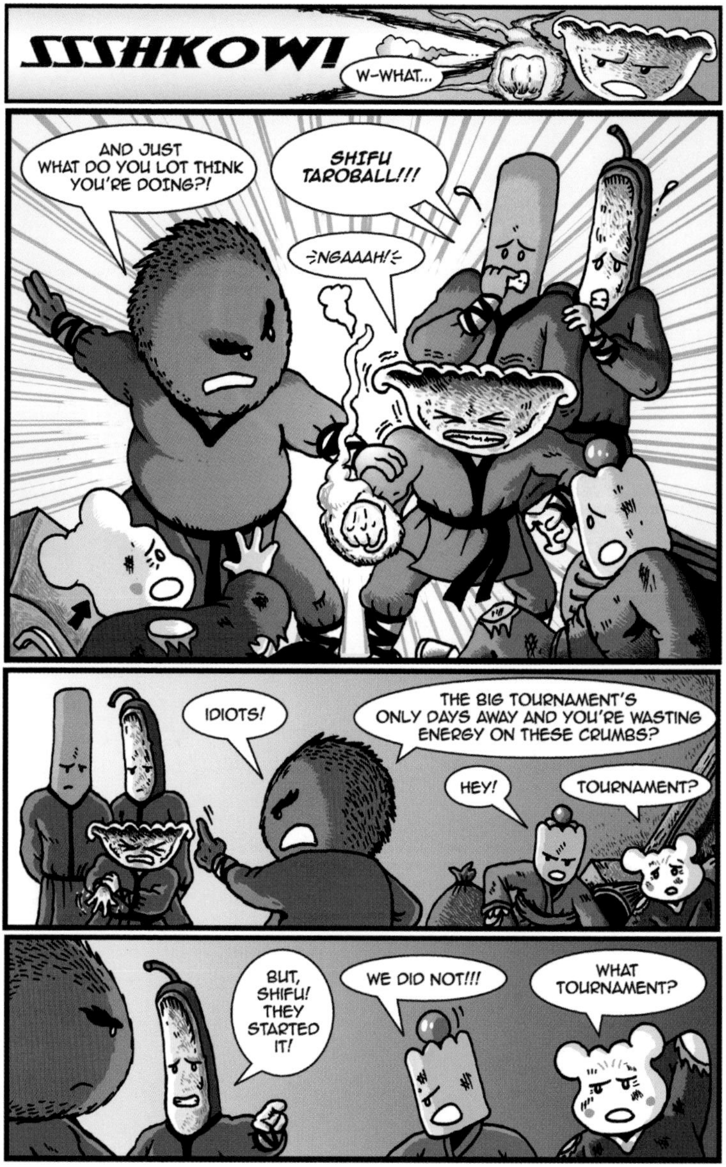
SSSHKOW!
W-WHAT...
AND JUST WHAT DO YOU LOT THINK YOU'RE DOING?!
SHIFU TAROBALL!!!
NGAAAH!
IDIOTS!
THE BIG TOURNAMENT'S ONLY DAYS AWAY AND YOU'RE WASTING ENERGY ON THESE CRUMBS?
HEY!
TOURNAMENT?
BUT, SHIFU! THEY STARTED IT!
WE DID NOT!!!
WHAT TOURNAMENT?

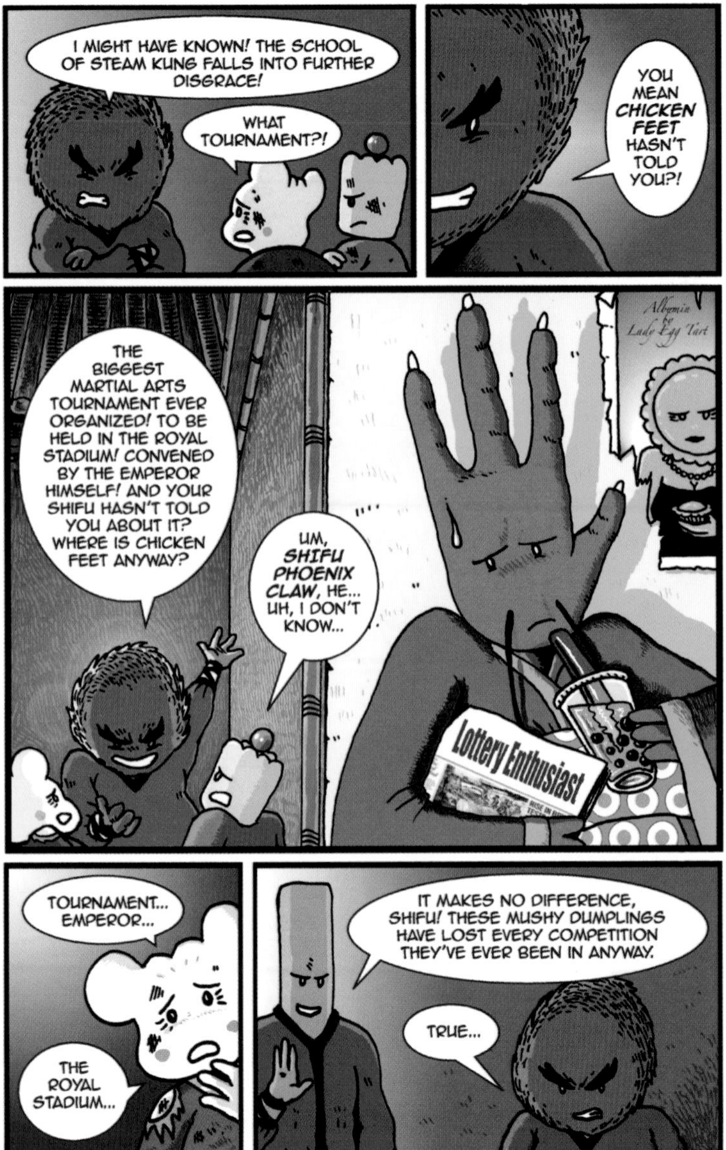
I MIGHT HAVE KNOWN! THE SCHOOL OF STEAM KUNG FALLS INTO FURTHER DISGRACE!
WHAT TOURNAMENT?!
YOU MEAN CHICKEN FEET HASN'T TOLD YOU?!
THE BIGGEST MARTIAL ARTS TOURNAMENT EVER ORGANIZED! TO BE HELD IN THE ROYAL STADIUM! CONVENED BY THE EMPEROR HIMSELF! AND YOUR SHIFU HASN'T TOLD YOU ABOUT IT? WHERE IS CHICKEN FEET ANYWAY?
UM, SHIFU PHOENIX CLAW, HE... UH, I DON'T KNOW...
Albumin by Lady Egg Tart
Lottery Enthusiast
TOURNAMENT... EMPEROR...
THE ROYAL STADIUM...
IT MAKES NO DIFFERENCE, SHIFU! THESE MUSHY DUMPLINGS HAVE LOST EVERY COMPETITION THEY'VE EVER BEEN IN ANYWAY.
TRUE...

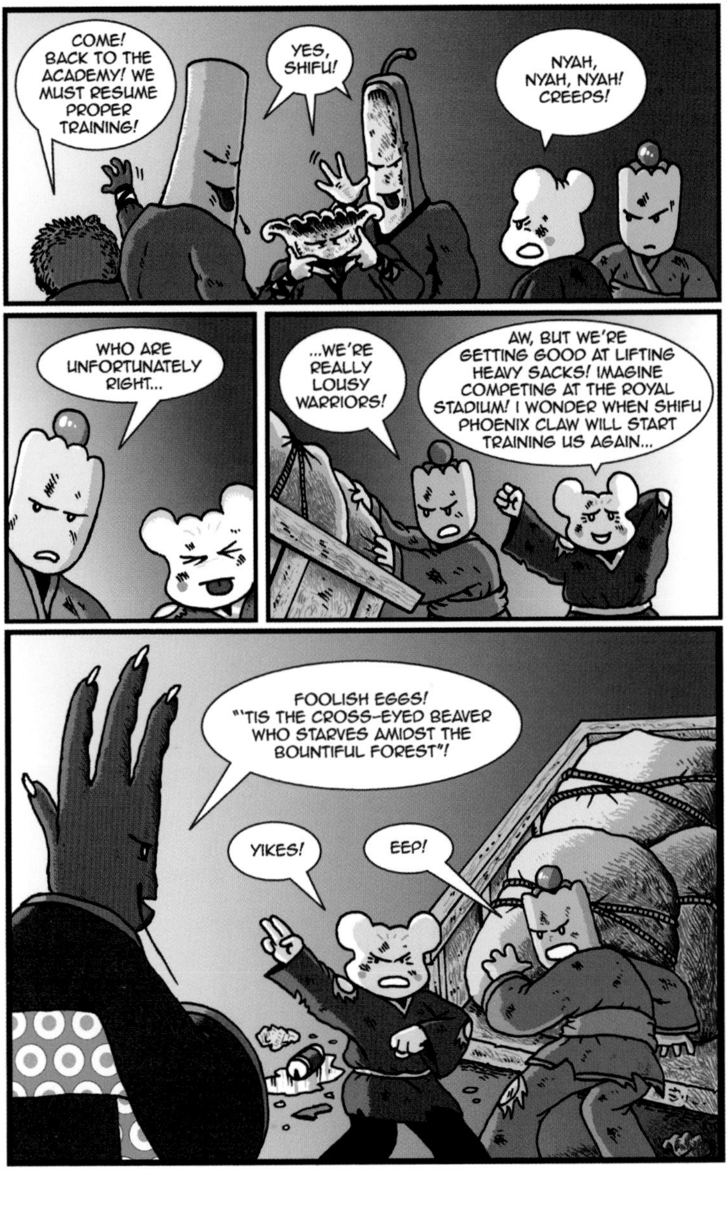
COME! BACK TO THE ACADEMY! WE MUST RESUME PROPER TRAINING!
YES, SHIFU!
NYAH, NYAH, NYAH! CREEPS!
WHO ARE UNFORTUNATELY RIGHT...
...WE'RE REALLY LOUSY WARRIORS!
AW, BUT WE'RE GETTING GOOD AT LIFTING HEAVY SACKS! IMAGINE COMPETING AT THE ROYAL STADIUM! I WONDER WHEN SHIFU PHOENIX CLAW WILL START TRAINING US AGAIN...
FOOLISH EGGS! "'TIS THE CROSS-EYED BEAVER WHO STARVES AMIDST THE BOUNTIFUL FOREST"!
YIKES!
EEP!

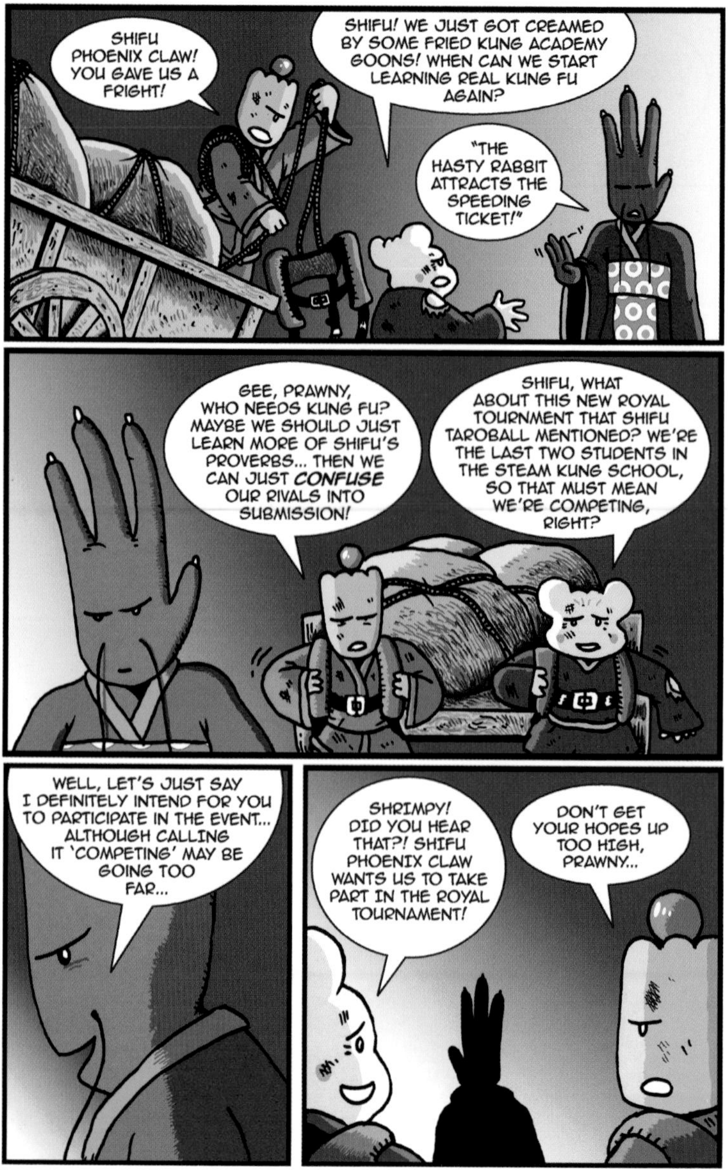
SHIFU PHOENIX CLAW! YOU GAVE US A FRIGHT!
SHIFU! WE JUST GOT CREAMED BY SOME FRIED KUNG ACADEMY GOONS! WHEN CAN WE START LEARNING REAL KUNG FU AGAIN?
"THE HASTY RABBIT ATTRACTS THE SPEEDING TICKET!"
GEE, PRAWNY, WHO NEEDS KUNG FU? MAYBE WE SHOULD JUST LEARN MORE OF SHIFU'S PROVERBS... THEN WE CAN JUST *CONFUSE* OUR RIVALS INTO SUBMISSION!
SHIFU, WHAT ABOUT THIS NEW ROYAL TOURNMENT THAT SHIFU TAROBALL MENTIONED? WE'RE THE LAST TWO STUDENTS IN THE STEAM KUNG SCHOOL, SO THAT MUST MEAN WE'RE COMPETING, RIGHT?
WELL, LET'S JUST SAY I DEFINITELY INTEND FOR YOU TO PARTICIPATE IN THE EVENT... ALTHOUGH CALLING IT 'COMPETING' MAY BE GOING TOO FAR...
SHRIMPY! DID YOU HEAR THAT?! SHIFU PHOENIX CLAW WANTS US TO TAKE PART IN THE ROYAL TOURNAMENT!
DON'T GET YOUR HOPES UP TOO HIGH, PRAWNY...

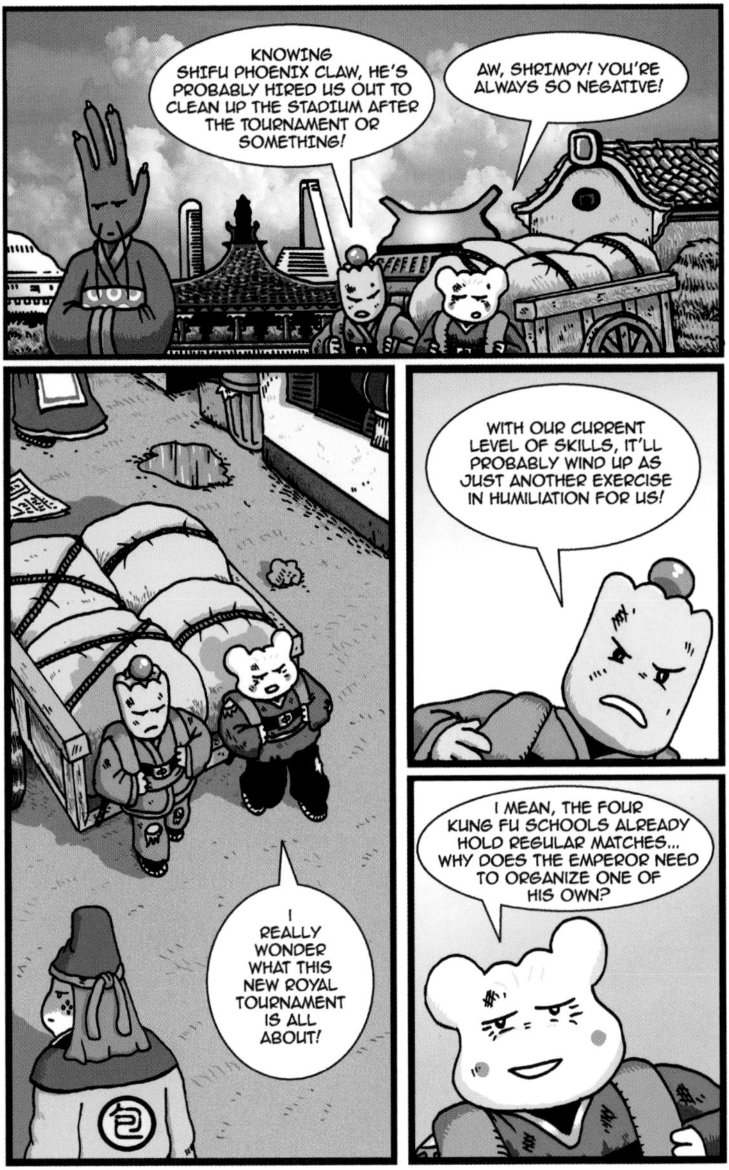
KNOWING SHIFU PHOENIX CLAW, HE'S PROBABLY HIRED US OUT TO CLEAN UP THE STADIUM AFTER THE TOURNAMENT OR SOMETHING!
AW, SHRIMPY! YOU'RE ALWAYS SO NEGATIVE!
I REALLY WONDER WHAT THIS NEW ROYAL TOURNAMENT IS ALL ABOUT!
WITH OUR CURRENT LEVEL OF SKILLS, IT'LL PROBABLY WIND UP AS JUST ANOTHER EXERCISE IN HUMILIATION FOR US!
I MEAN, THE FOUR KUNG FU SCHOOLS ALREADY HOLD REGULAR MATCHES... WHY DOES THE EMPEROR NEED TO ORGANIZE ONE OF HIS OWN?

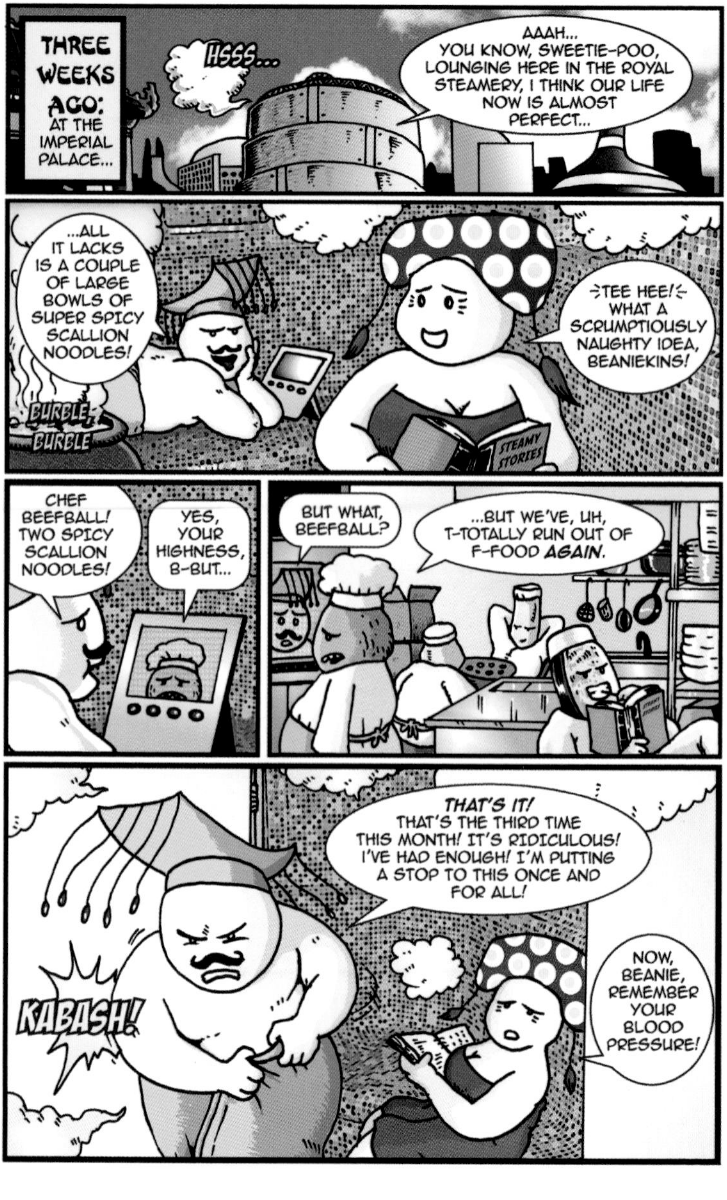
THREE WEEKS AGO: AT THE IMPERIAL PALACE...
HSSS...
AAAH... YOU KNOW, SWEETIE-POO, LOUNGING HERE IN THE ROYAL STEAMERY, I THINK OUR LIFE NOW IS ALMOST PERFECT...
...ALL IT LACKS IS A COUPLE OF LARGE BOWLS OF SUPER SPICY SCALLION NOODLES!
BURBLE BURBLE
TEE HEE! WHAT A SCRUMPTIOUSLY NAUGHTY IDEA, BEANIEKINS!
STEAMY STORIES
CHEF BEEFBALL! TWO SPICY SCALLION NOODLES!
YES, YOUR HIGHNESS, B-BUT...
BUT WHAT, BEEFBALL?
...BUT WE'VE, UH, T-TOTALLY RUN OUT OF F-FOOD AGAIN.
THAT'S IT! THAT'S THE THIRD TIME THIS MONTH! IT'S RIDICULOUS! I'VE HAD ENOUGH! I'M PUTTING A STOP TO THIS ONCE AND FOR ALL!
KABASH!
NOW, BEANIE, REMEMBER YOUR BLOOD PRESSURE!

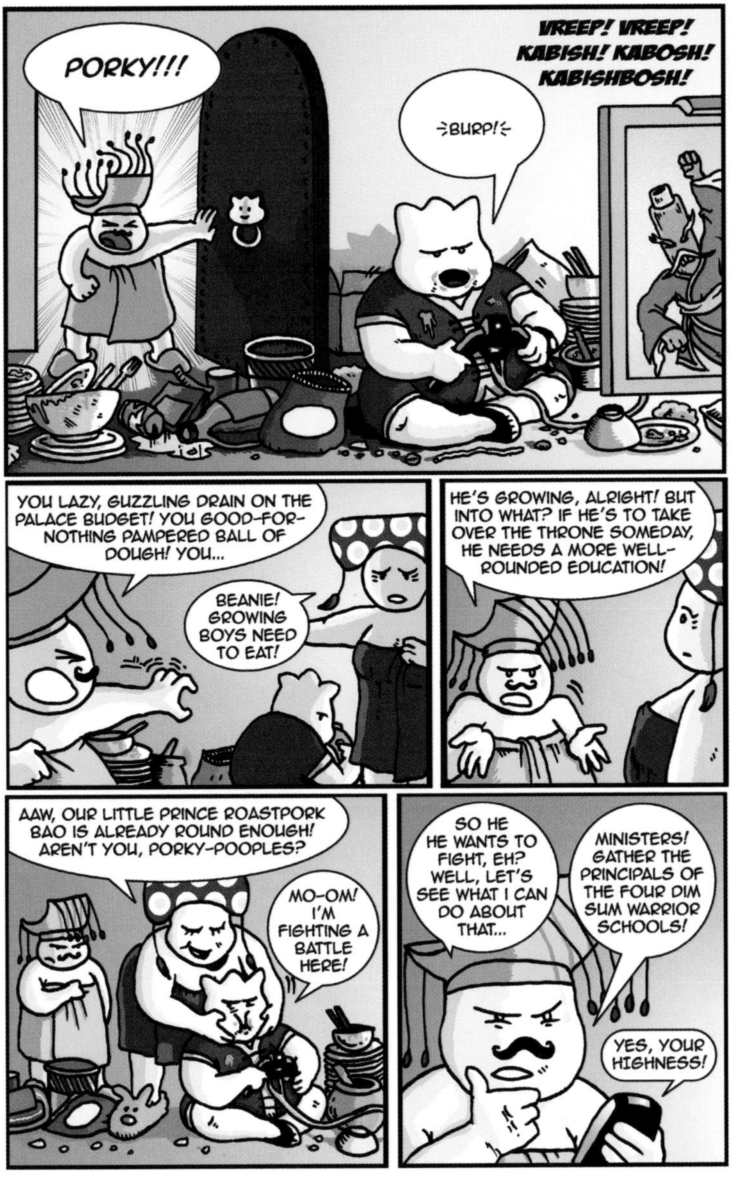
PORKY!!!
VREEP! VREEP! KABISH! KABOSH! KABISHBOSH!
BURP!
YOU LAZY, GUZZLING DRAIN ON THE PALACE BUDGET! YOU GOOD-FOR-NOTHING PAMPERED BALL OF DOUGH! YOU...
BEANIE! GROWING BOYS NEED TO EAT!
HE'S GROWING, ALRIGHT! BUT INTO WHAT? IF HE'S TO TAKE OVER THE THRONE SOMEDAY, HE NEEDS A MORE WELL-ROUNDED EDUCATION!
AAW, OUR LITTLE PRINCE ROASTPORK BAO IS ALREADY ROUND ENOUGH! AREN'T YOU, PORKY-POOPLES?
MO-OM! I'M FIGHTING A BATTLE HERE!
SO HE HE WANTS TO FIGHT, EH? WELL, LET'S SEE WHAT I CAN DO ABOUT THAT...
MINISTERS! GATHER THE PRINCIPALS OF THE FOUR DIM SUM WARRIOR SCHOOLS!
YES, YOUR HIGHNESS!

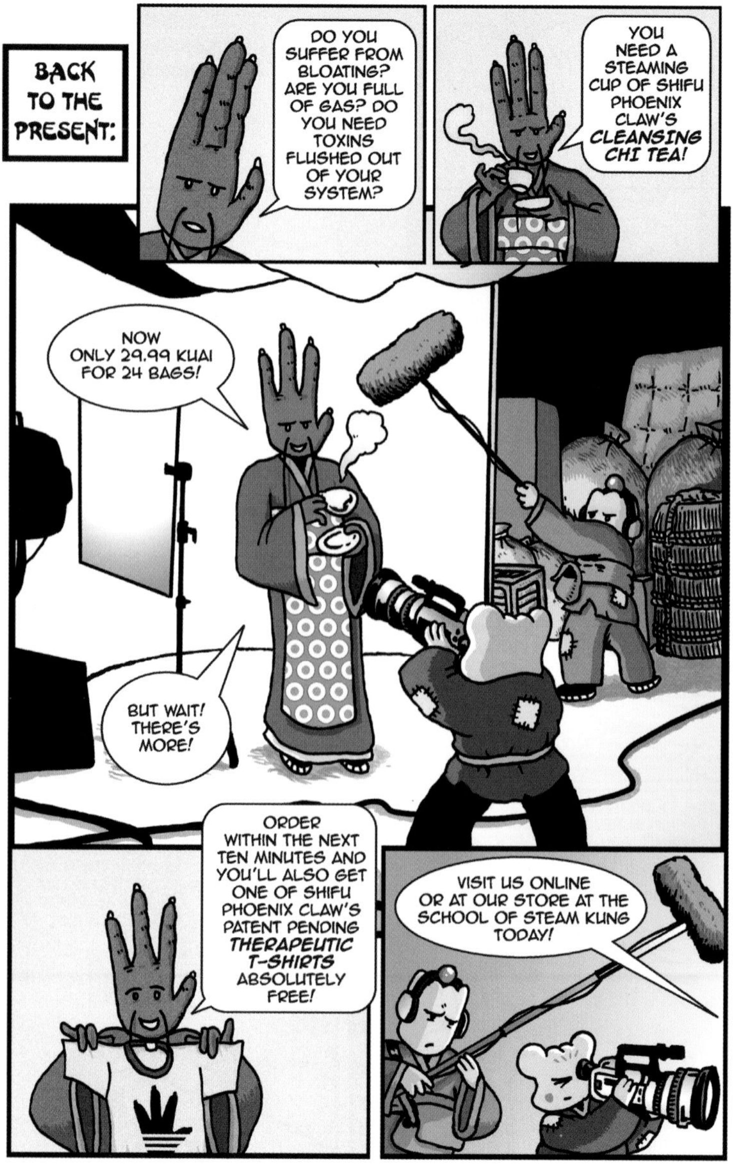
BACK TO THE PRESENT:
DO YOU SUFFER FROM BLOATING? ARE YOU FULL OF GAS? DO YOU NEED TOXINS FLUSHED OUT OF YOUR SYSTEM?
YOU NEED A STEAMING CUP OF SHIFU PHOENIX CLAW'S ***CLEANSING CHI TEA!***
NOW ONLY 29.99 KUAI FOR 24 BAGS!
BUT WAIT! THERE'S MORE!
ORDER WITHIN THE NEXT TEN MINUTES AND YOU'LL ALSO GET ONE OF SHIFU PHOENIX CLAW'S PATENT PENDING ***THERAPEUTIC T-SHIRTS*** ABSOLUTELY FREE!
VISIT US ONLINE OR AT OUR STORE AT THE SCHOOL OF STEAM KUNG TODAY!

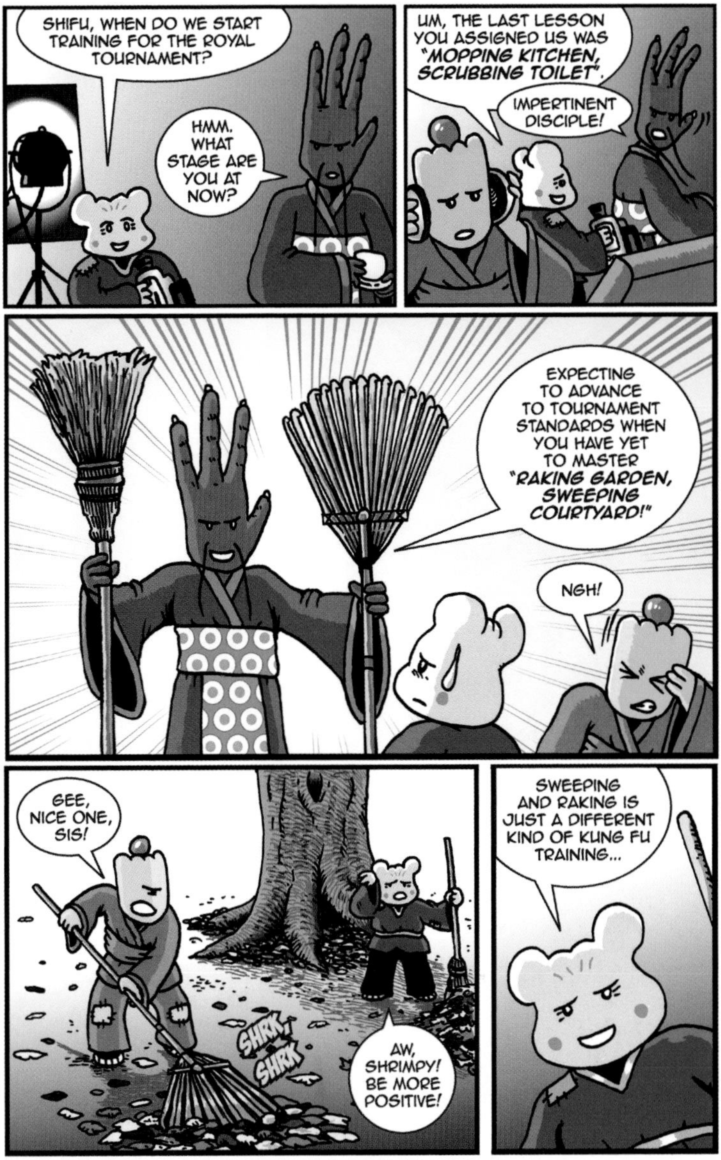
SHIFU, WHEN DO WE START TRAINING FOR THE ROYAL TOURNAMENT?
HMM. WHAT STAGE ARE YOU AT NOW?
UM, THE LAST LESSON YOU ASSIGNED US WAS "MOPPING KITCHEN, SCRUBBING TOILET".
IMPERTINENT DISCIPLE!
EXPECTING TO ADVANCE TO TOURNAMENT STANDARDS WHEN YOU HAVE YET TO MASTER "RAKING GARDEN, SWEEPING COURTYARD!"
NGH!
GEE, NICE ONE, SIS!
SHRK SHRK
AW, SHRIMPY! BE MORE POSITIVE!
SWEEPING AND RAKING IS JUST A DIFFERENT KIND OF KUNG FU TRAINING...

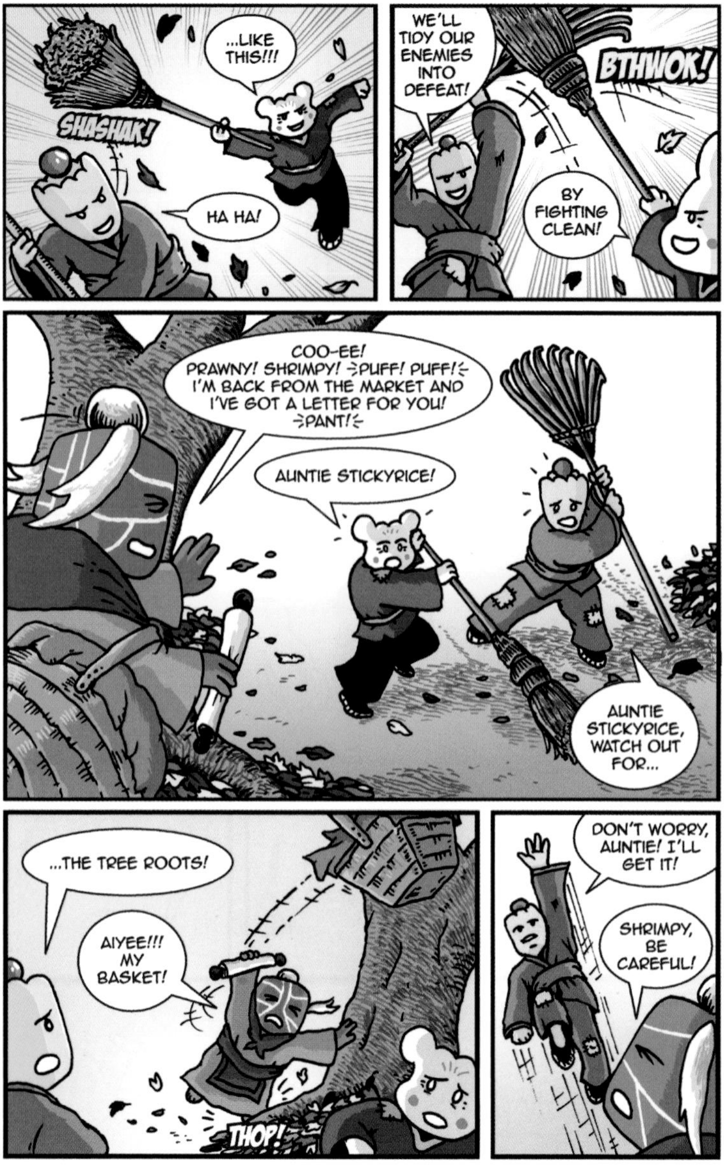
...LIKE THIS!!!
SHASHAK!
HA HA!
WE'LL TIDY OUR ENEMIES INTO DEFEAT!
BTHWOK!
BY FIGHTING CLEAN!
COO-EE! PRAWNY! SHRIMPY! ⪢PUFF! PUFF!⪡ I'M BACK FROM THE MARKET AND I'VE GOT A LETTER FOR YOU! ⪢PANT!⪡
AUNTIE STICKYRICE!
AUNTIE STICKYRICE, WATCH OUT FOR...
...THE TREE ROOTS!
AIYEE!!! MY BASKET!
THOP!
DON'T WORRY, AUNTIE! I'LL GET IT!
SHRIMPY, BE CAREFUL!

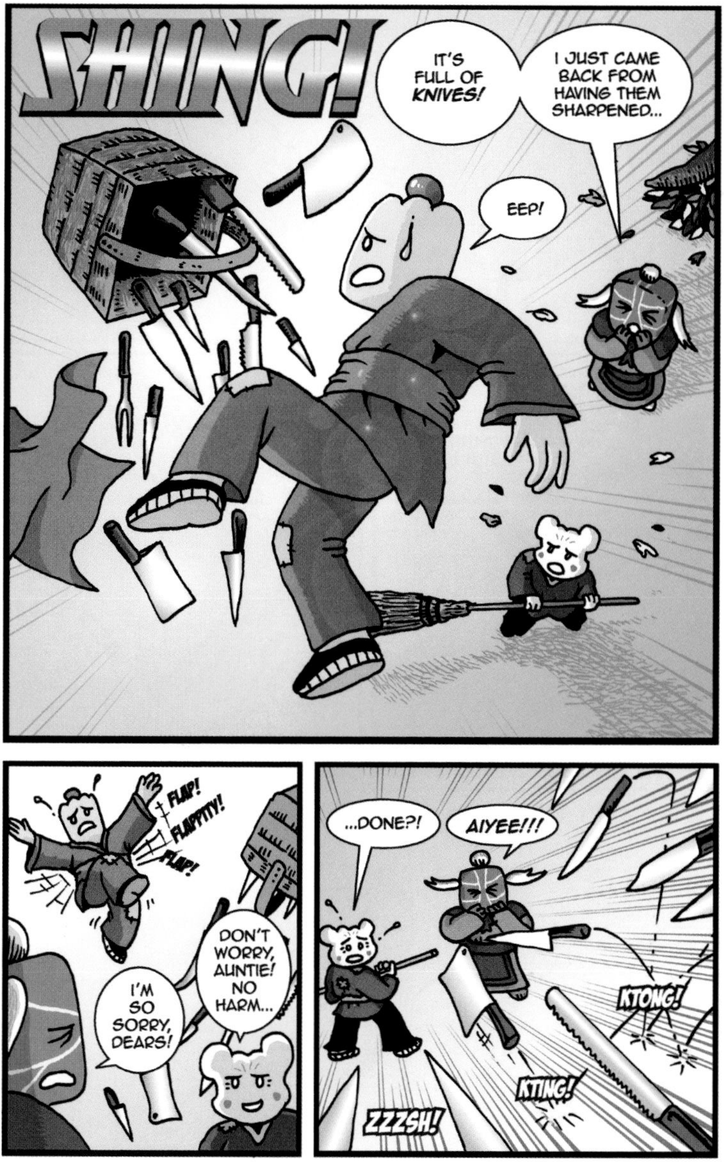
SHING!
IT'S FULL OF KNIVES!
I JUST CAME BACK FROM HAVING THEM SHARPENED...
EEP!
FLAP!
FLAPPITY!
FLAP!
I'M SO SORRY, DEARS!
DON'T WORRY, AUNTIE! NO HARM...
...DONE?!
AIYEE!!!
KTONG!
KTING!
ZZZSH!

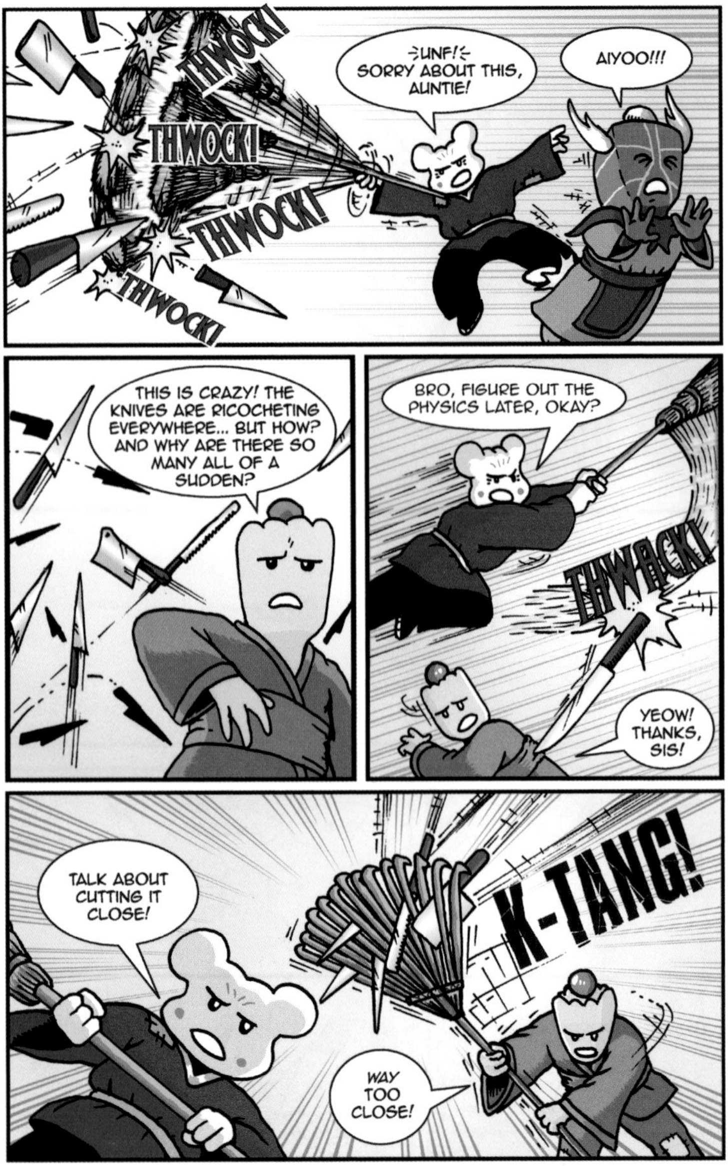
THWOCK!
THWOCK!
THWOCK!
THWOCK!
UNF! SORRY ABOUT THIS, AUNTIE!
AIYOO!!!
THIS IS CRAZY! THE KNIVES ARE RICOCHETING EVERYWHERE... BUT HOW? AND WHY ARE THERE SO MANY ALL OF A SUDDEN?
BRO, FIGURE OUT THE PHYSICS LATER, OKAY?
THWACK!
YEOW! THANKS, SIS!
TALK ABOUT CUTTING IT CLOSE!
K-TANG!
WAY TOO CLOSE!

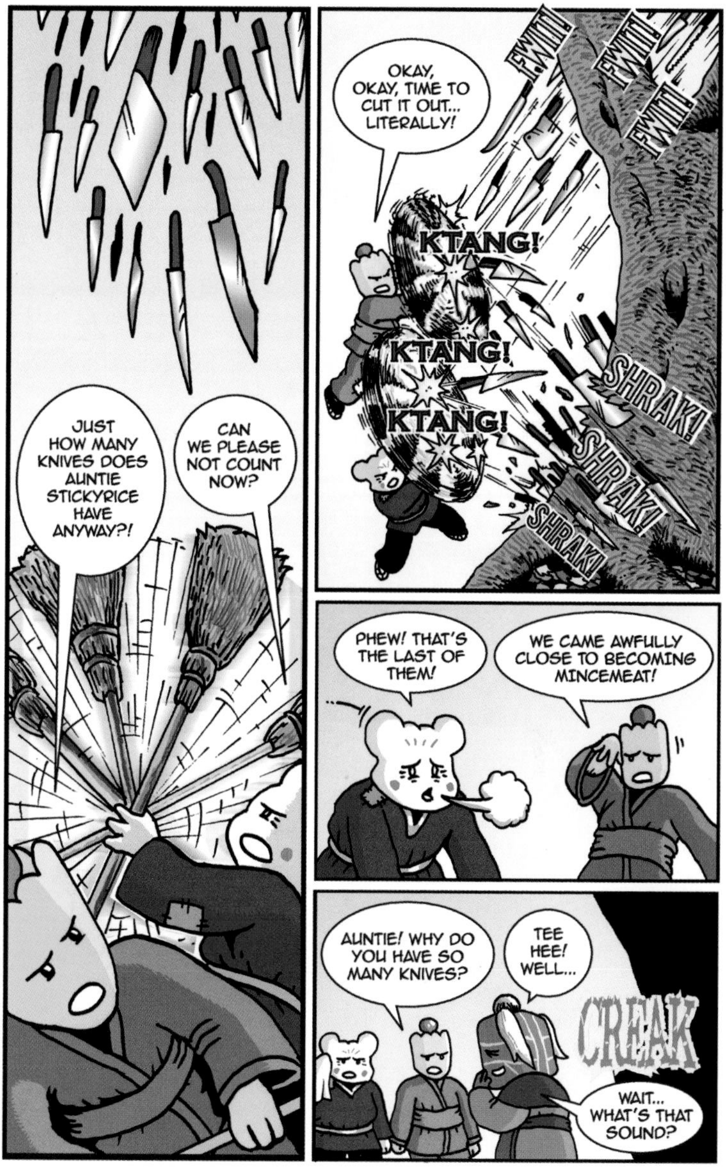
JUST HOW MANY KNIVES DOES AUNTIE STICKYRICE HAVE ANYWAY?!
CAN WE PLEASE NOT COUNT NOW?
OKAY, OKAY, TIME TO CUT IT OUT... LITERALLY!
FWIT!
FWIT!
FWIT!
KTANG!
KTANG!
KTANG!
SHRAK!
SHRAK!
SHRAK!
PHEW! THAT'S THE LAST OF THEM!
WE CAME AWFULLY CLOSE TO BECOMING MINCEMEAT!
AUNTIE! WHY DO YOU HAVE SO MANY KNIVES?
TEE HEE! WELL...
CREAK
WAIT... WHAT'S THAT SOUND?

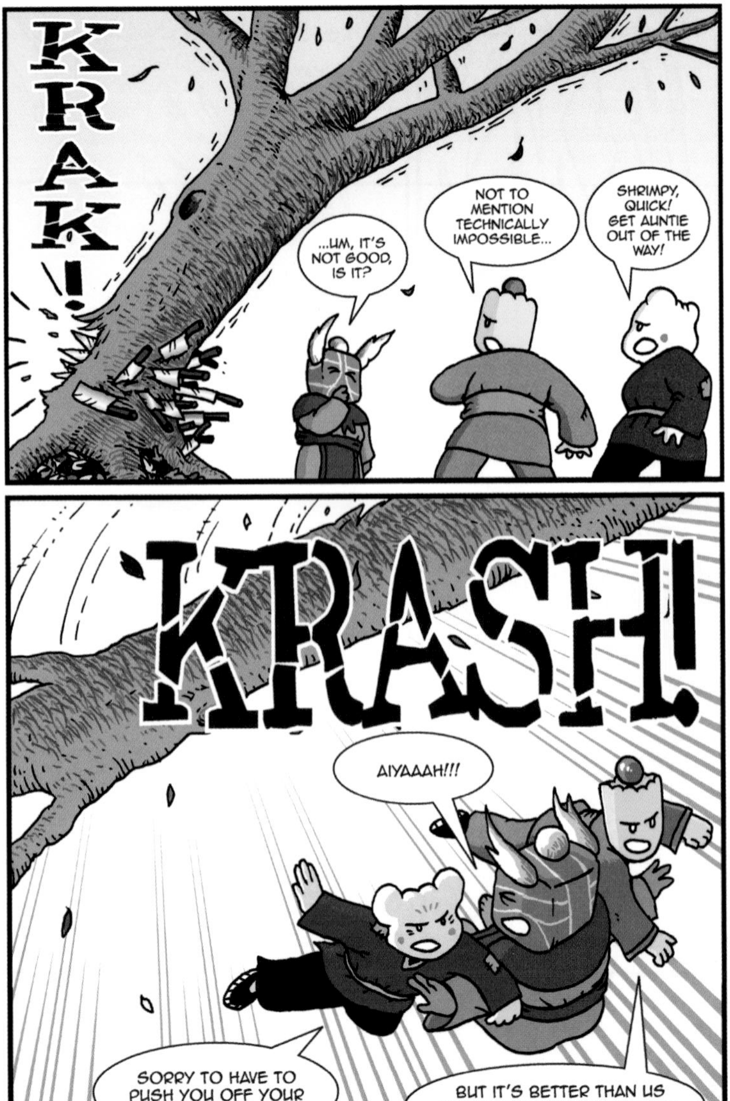
KRAKK!
...UM, IT'S NOT GOOD, IS IT?
NOT TO MENTION TECHNICALLY IMPOSSIBLE...
SHRIMPY, QUICK! GET AUNTIE OUT OF THE WAY!
KRASH!
AIYAAAH!!!
SORRY TO HAVE TO PUSH YOU OFF YOUR FEET, AUNTIE!
BUT IT'S BETTER THAN US HAVING TO SCRAPE YOU OFF THE GROUND!

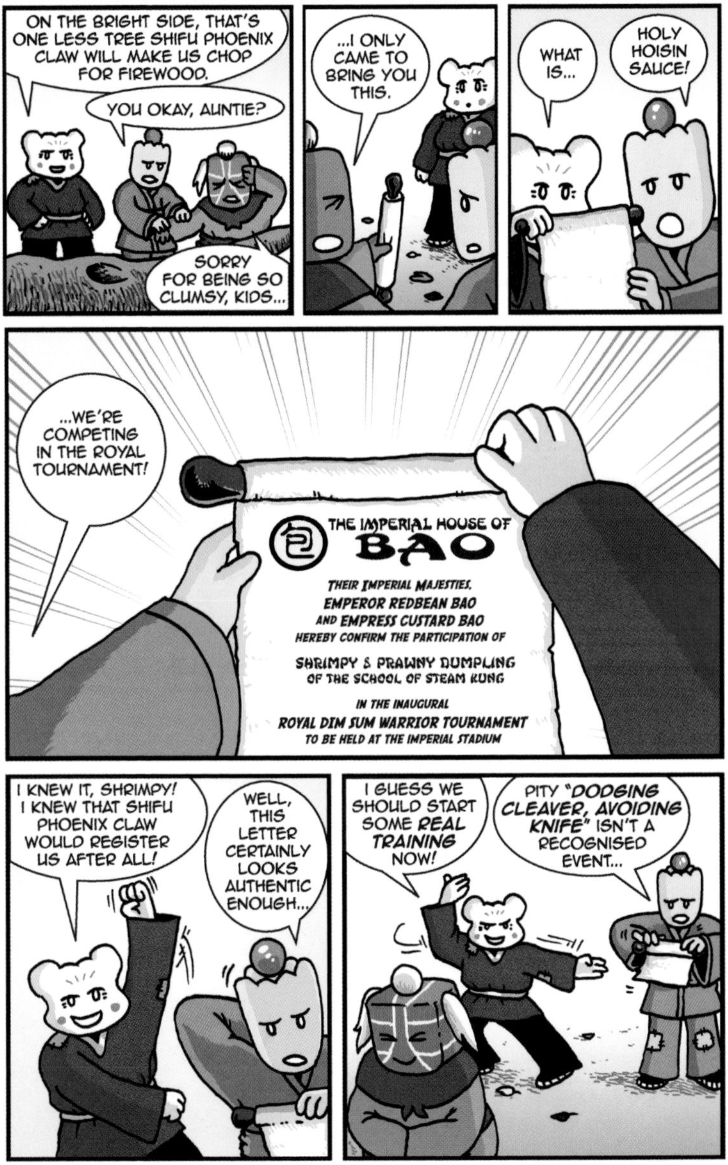
ON THE BRIGHT SIDE, THAT'S ONE LESS TREE SHIFU PHOENIX CLAW WILL MAKE US CHOP FOR FIREWOOD.
YOU OKAY, AUNTIE?
SORRY FOR BEING SO CLUMSY, KIDS...
...I ONLY CAME TO BRING YOU THIS.
WHAT IS...
HOLY HOISIN SAUCE!
...WE'RE COMPETING IN THE ROYAL TOURNAMENT!
THE IMPERIAL HOUSE OF
BAO
THEIR IMPERIAL MAJESTIES,
EMPEROR REDBEAN BAO
AND EMPRESS CUSTARD BAO
HEREBY CONFIRM THE PARTICIPATION OF
SHRIMPY & PRAWNY DUMPLING
OF THE SCHOOL OF STEAM KUNG
IN THE INAUGURAL
ROYAL DIM SUM WARRIOR TOURNAMENT
TO BE HELD AT THE IMPERIAL STADIUM
I KNEW IT, SHRIMPY! I KNEW THAT SHIFU PHOENIX CLAW WOULD REGISTER US AFTER ALL!
WELL, THIS LETTER CERTAINLY LOOKS AUTHENTIC ENOUGH...
I GUESS WE SHOULD START SOME REAL TRAINING NOW!
PITY "DODGING CLEAVER, AVOIDING KNIFE" ISN'T A RECOGNISED EVENT...

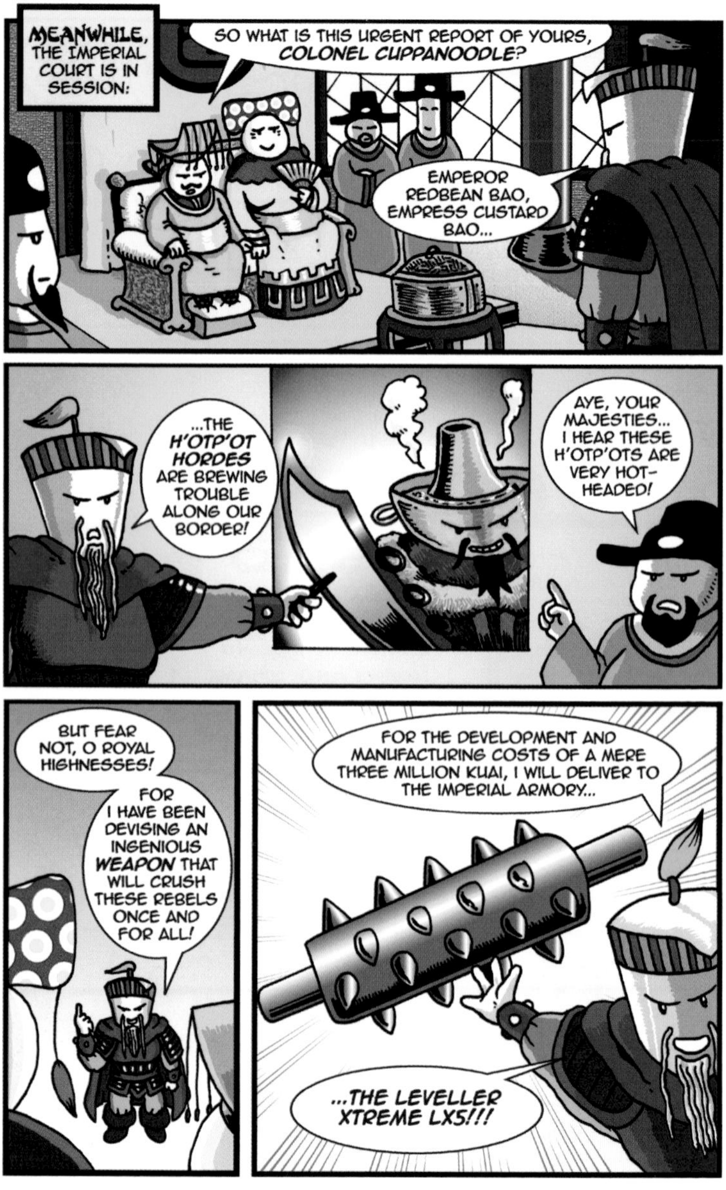
MEANWHILE, THE IMPERIAL COURT IS IN SESSION:
SO WHAT IS THIS URGENT REPORT OF YOURS, COLONEL CUPPANOODLE?
EMPEROR REDBEAN BAO, EMPRESS CUSTARD BAO...
...THE H'OTP'OT HORDES ARE BREWING TROUBLE ALONG OUR BORDER!
AYE, YOUR MAJESTIES... I HEAR THESE H'OTP'OTS ARE VERY HOT-HEADED!
BUT FEAR NOT, O ROYAL HIGHNESSES!
FOR I HAVE BEEN DEVISING AN INGENIOUS WEAPON THAT WILL CRUSH THESE REBELS ONCE AND FOR ALL!
FOR THE DEVELOPMENT AND MANUFACTURING COSTS OF A MERE THREE MILLION KUAI, I WILL DELIVER TO THE IMPERIAL ARMORY...
...THE LEVELLER XTREME LX5!!!

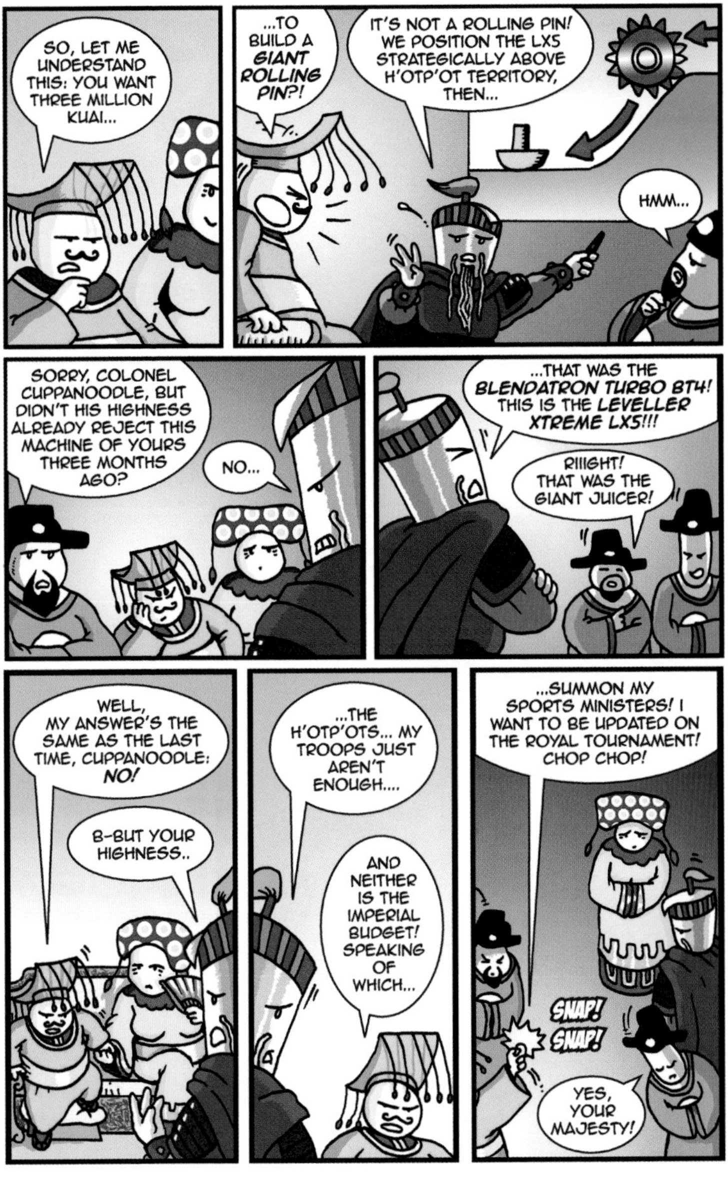
SO, LET ME UNDERSTAND THIS: YOU WANT THREE MILLION KUAI...
...TO BUILD A GIANT ROLLING PIN?!
IT'S NOT A ROLLING PIN! WE POSITION THE LX5 STRATEGICALLY ABOVE H'OTP'OT TERRITORY, THEN...
HMM...
SORRY, COLONEL CUPPANOODLE, BUT DIDN'T HIS HIGHNESS ALREADY REJECT THIS MACHINE OF YOURS THREE MONTHS AGO?
NO...
...THAT WAS THE BLENDATRON TURBO BT4! THIS IS THE LEVELLER XTREME LX5!!!
RIIIGHT! THAT WAS THE GIANT JUICER!
WELL, MY ANSWER'S THE SAME AS THE LAST TIME, CUPPANOODLE: NO!
B-BUT YOUR HIGHNESS..
...THE H'OTP'OTS... MY TROOPS JUST AREN'T ENOUGH....
AND NEITHER IS THE IMPERIAL BUDGET! SPEAKING OF WHICH...
...SUMMON MY SPORTS MINISTERS! I WANT TO BE UPDATED ON THE ROYAL TOURNAMENT! CHOP CHOP!
SNAP! SNAP!
YES, YOUR MAJESTY!

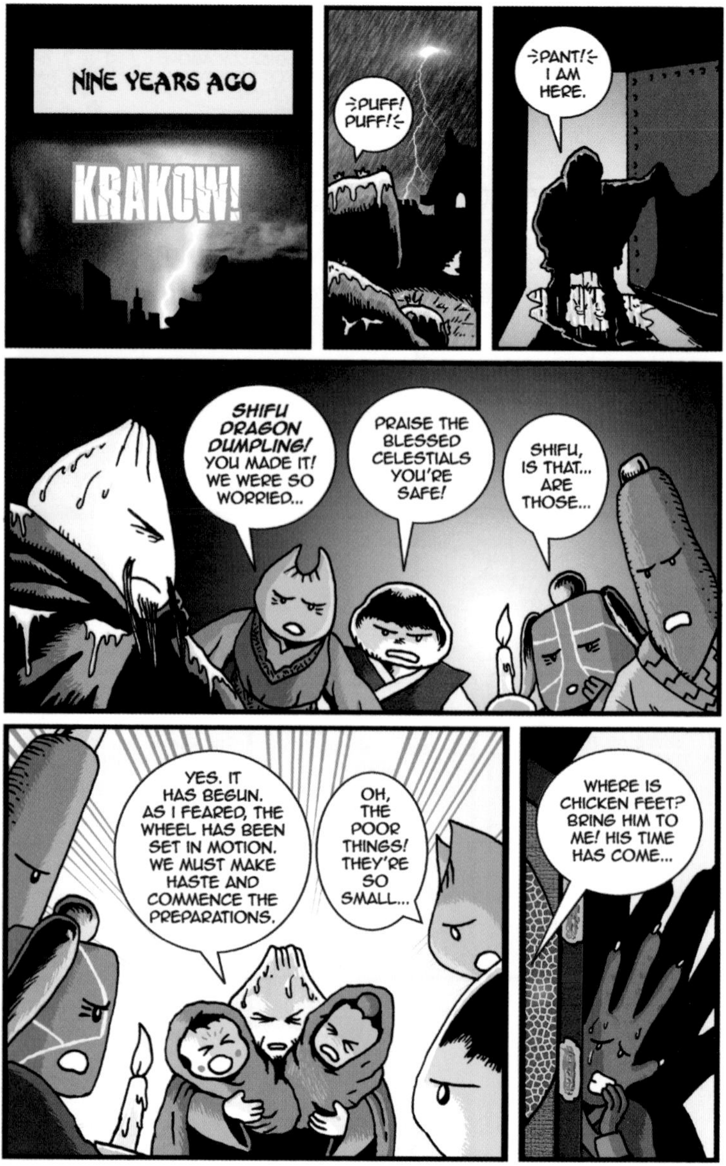
NINE YEARS AGO
KRAKOW!
PUFF! PUFF!
PANT! I AM HERE.
SHIFU DRAGON DUMPLING! YOU MADE IT! WE WERE SO WORRIED...
PRAISE THE BLESSED CELESTIALS YOU'RE SAFE!
SHIFU, IS THAT... ARE THOSE...
YES. IT HAS BEGUN. AS I FEARED, THE WHEEL HAS BEEN SET IN MOTION. WE MUST MAKE HASTE AND COMMENCE THE PREPARATIONS.
OH, THE POOR THINGS! THEY'RE SO SMALL...
WHERE IS CHICKEN FEET? BRING HIM TO ME! HIS TIME HAS COME...

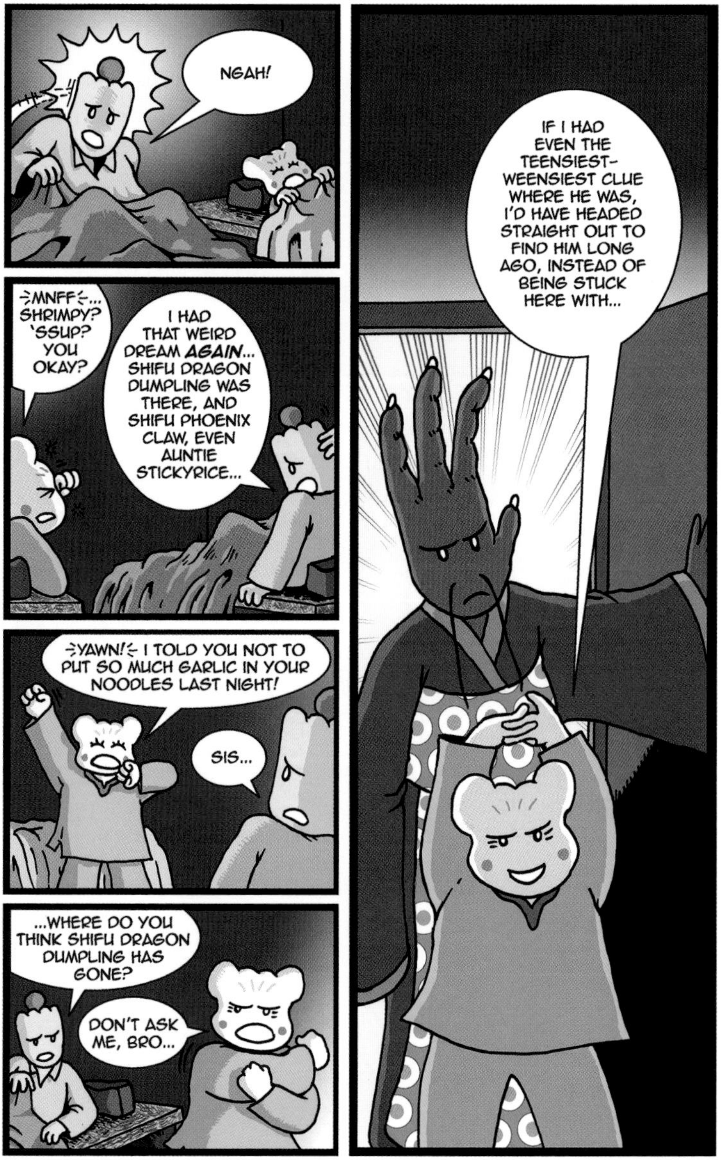
NGAH!
-MNFF-... SHRIMPY? 'SSUP? YOU OKAY?
I HAD THAT WEIRD DREAM AGAIN... SHIFU DRAGON DUMPLING WAS THERE, AND SHIFU PHOENIX CLAW, EVEN AUNTIE STICKYRICE...
-YAWN!- I TOLD YOU NOT TO PUT SO MUCH GARLIC IN YOUR NOODLES LAST NIGHT!
SIS...
...WHERE DO YOU THINK SHIFU DRAGON DUMPLING HAS GONE?
DON'T ASK ME, BRO...
IF I HAD EVEN THE TEENSIEST-WEENSIEST CLUE WHERE HE WAS, I'D HAVE HEADED STRAIGHT OUT TO FIND HIM LONG AGO, INSTEAD OF BEING STUCK HERE WITH...

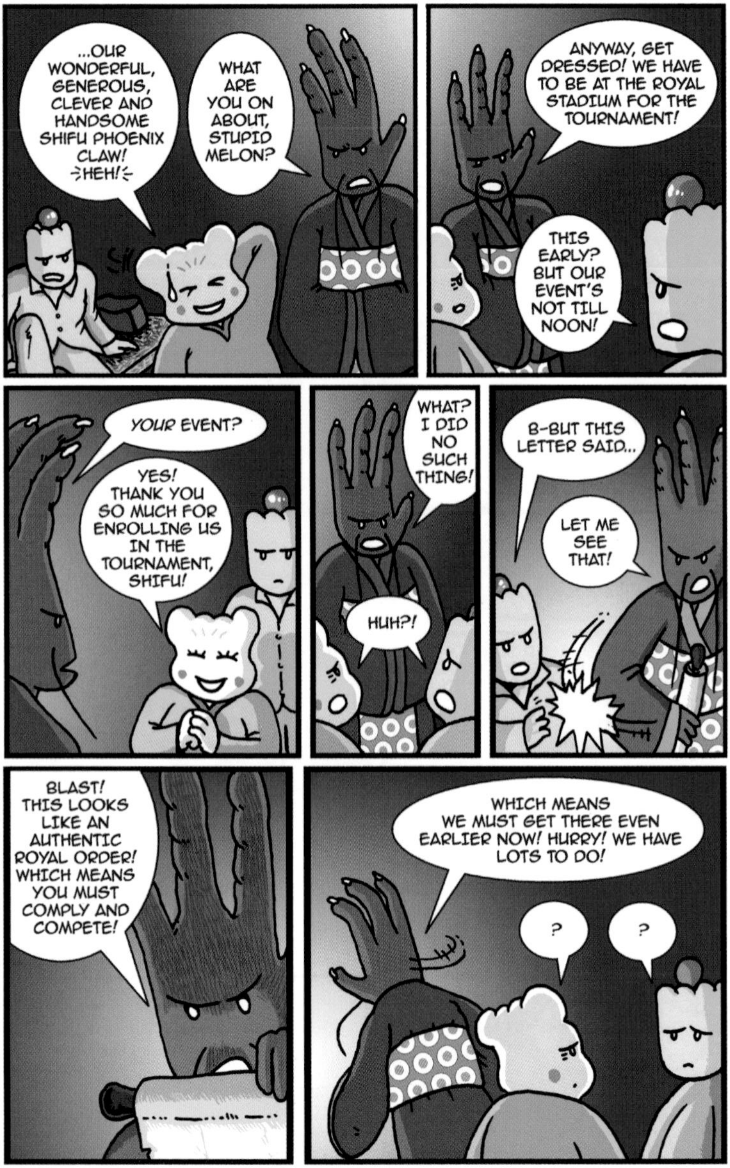
...OUR WONDERFUL, GENEROUS, CLEVER AND HANDSOME SHIFU PHOENIX CLAW! HEH!
WHAT ARE YOU ON ABOUT, STUPID MELON?
ANYWAY, GET DRESSED! WE HAVE TO BE AT THE ROYAL STADIUM FOR THE TOURNAMENT!
THIS EARLY? BUT OUR EVENT'S NOT TILL NOON!
YOUR EVENT?
YES! THANK YOU SO MUCH FOR ENROLLING US IN THE TOURNAMENT, SHIFU!
WHAT? I DID NO SUCH THING!
HUH?!
B-BUT THIS LETTER SAID...
LET ME SEE THAT!
BLAST! THIS LOOKS LIKE AN AUTHENTIC ROYAL ORDER! WHICH MEANS YOU MUST COMPLY AND COMPETE!
WHICH MEANS WE MUST GET THERE EVEN EARLIER NOW! HURRY! WE HAVE LOTS TO DO!
?
?

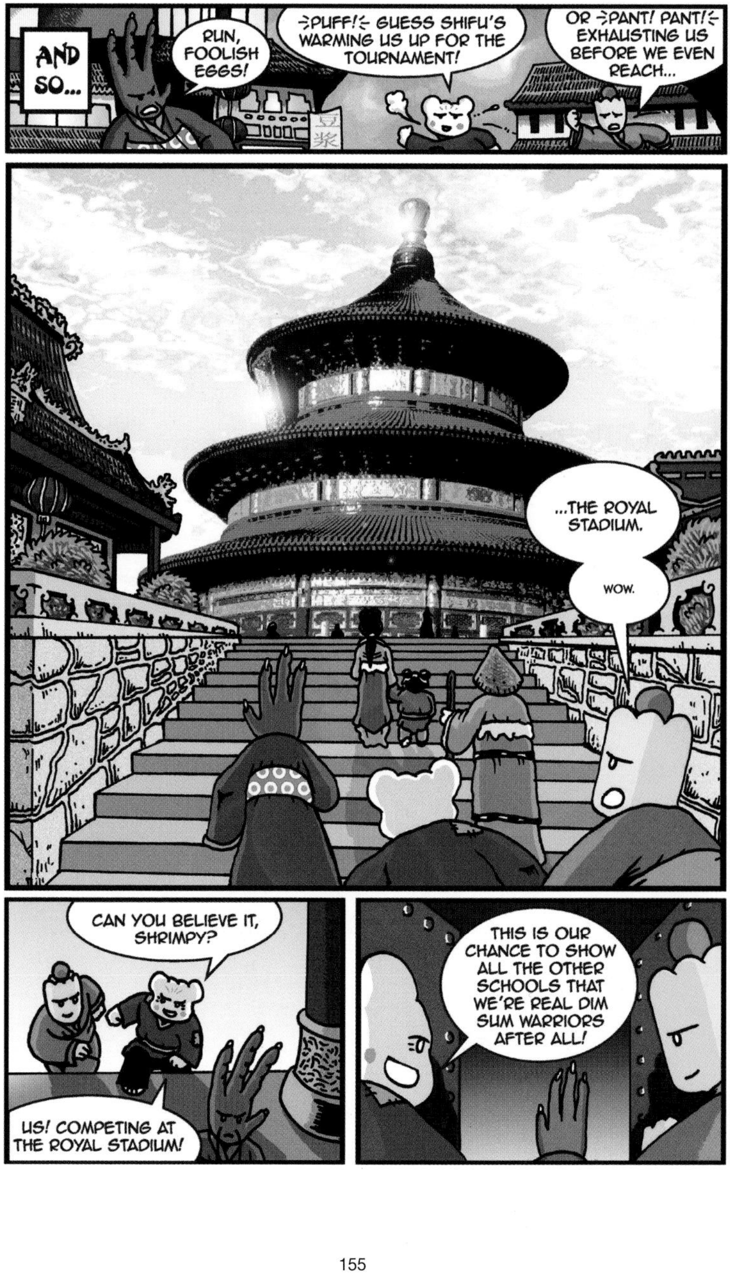
AND SO...
RUN, FOOLISH EGGS!
PUFF! GUESS SHIFU'S WARMING US UP FOR THE TOURNAMENT!
OR PANT! PANT! EXHAUSTING US BEFORE WE EVEN REACH...
...THE ROYAL STADIUM.
WOW.
CAN YOU BELIEVE IT, SHRIMPY?
US! COMPETING AT THE ROYAL STADIUM!
THIS IS OUR CHANCE TO SHOW ALL THE OTHER SCHOOLS THAT WE'RE REAL DIM SUM WARRIORS AFTER ALL!

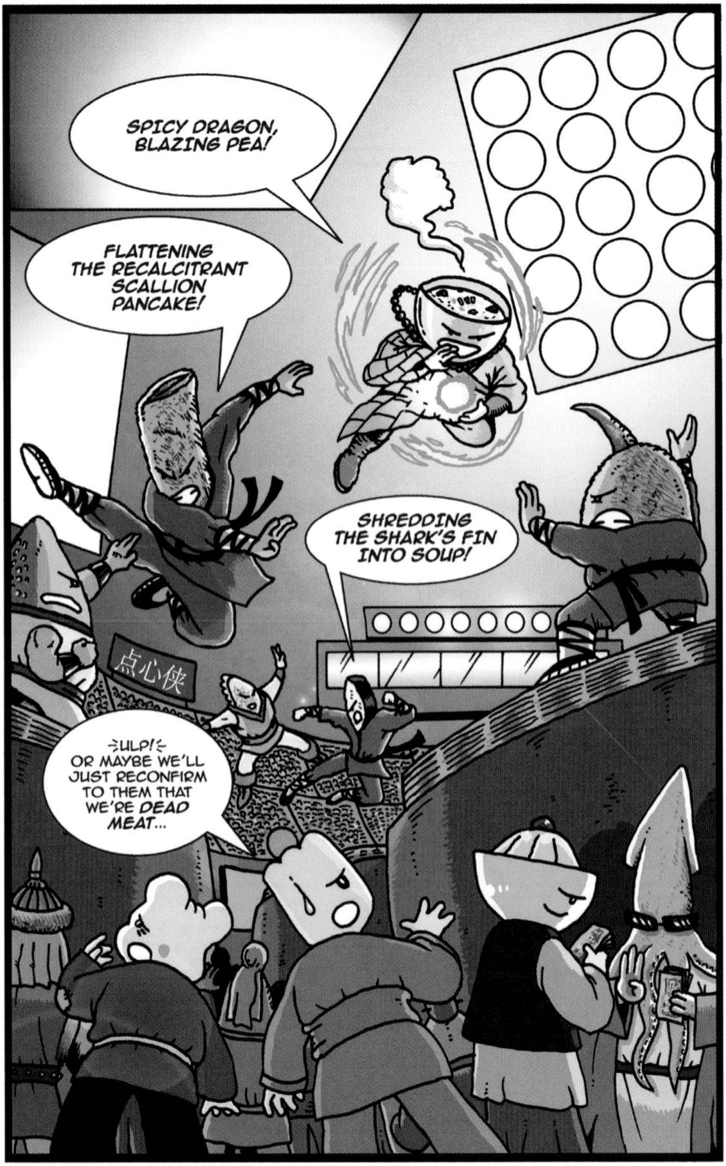
SPICY DRAGON, BLAZING PEA!
FLATTENING THE RECALCITRANT SCALLION PANCAKE!
SHREDDING THE SHARK'S FIN INTO SOUP!
点心侠
ULP!
OR MAYBE WE'LL JUST RECONFIRM TO THEM THAT WE'RE *DEAD MEAT*...

# TAKE
# A LOOK
# AT US
# NOW!

# “That rares… iumphs: an educational comic that's actually fun to read.”

*- Fast Company, Top 10 Coolest Original Digital Comics of 2012*

DIM SUM WARRIORS
点心侠
ENTER THE DUMPLING

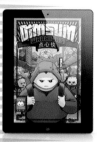

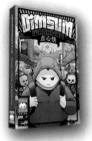

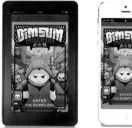

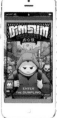

**INTERACTIVE BILINGUAL iPAD APP that supports the learning of both Chinese and English**

**DELUXE PRINTED GRAPHIC NOVEL with high grade paper and library quality archival binding**

**DIGITAL GRAPHIC NOVEL (with panel-by-panel guided view) Available in multiple formats, including Kindle (all devices as well as app), iBooks, Nook and Kobo)**

**"With Lee's delightful illustrations and Goh and Woo's engaging narrative, the characters could have been ingredients in a Waldorf salad and still been interesting."**
- Honorable Mention, Publishers Weekly
Critics Poll of Best Graphic Novels of 2012

**“What a great app! My kids and I loved tapping the interactive word balloons and switching back and forth between the languages!”**
**- Gene Luen Yang**, Eisner Award-winning writer, *American Born Chinese*

**“Fun and witty... a fully functional and brilliantly designed interactive language learning app for the iPad.”**
- Rob Salkowitz, digital media expert and author, *Comic-Con and the Business of Pop Culture*

**“A boon to parents who've got their kids studying Mandarin”**
- Motherlode, the parenting blog of The New York Times

For more reviews and features about Dim Sum Warriors by Time, the BBC, Public Radio International and other media, please visit us at

# www.dimsumwarriors.com

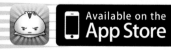

Available on the App Store

amazon.com

*And all good book and comic retailers*

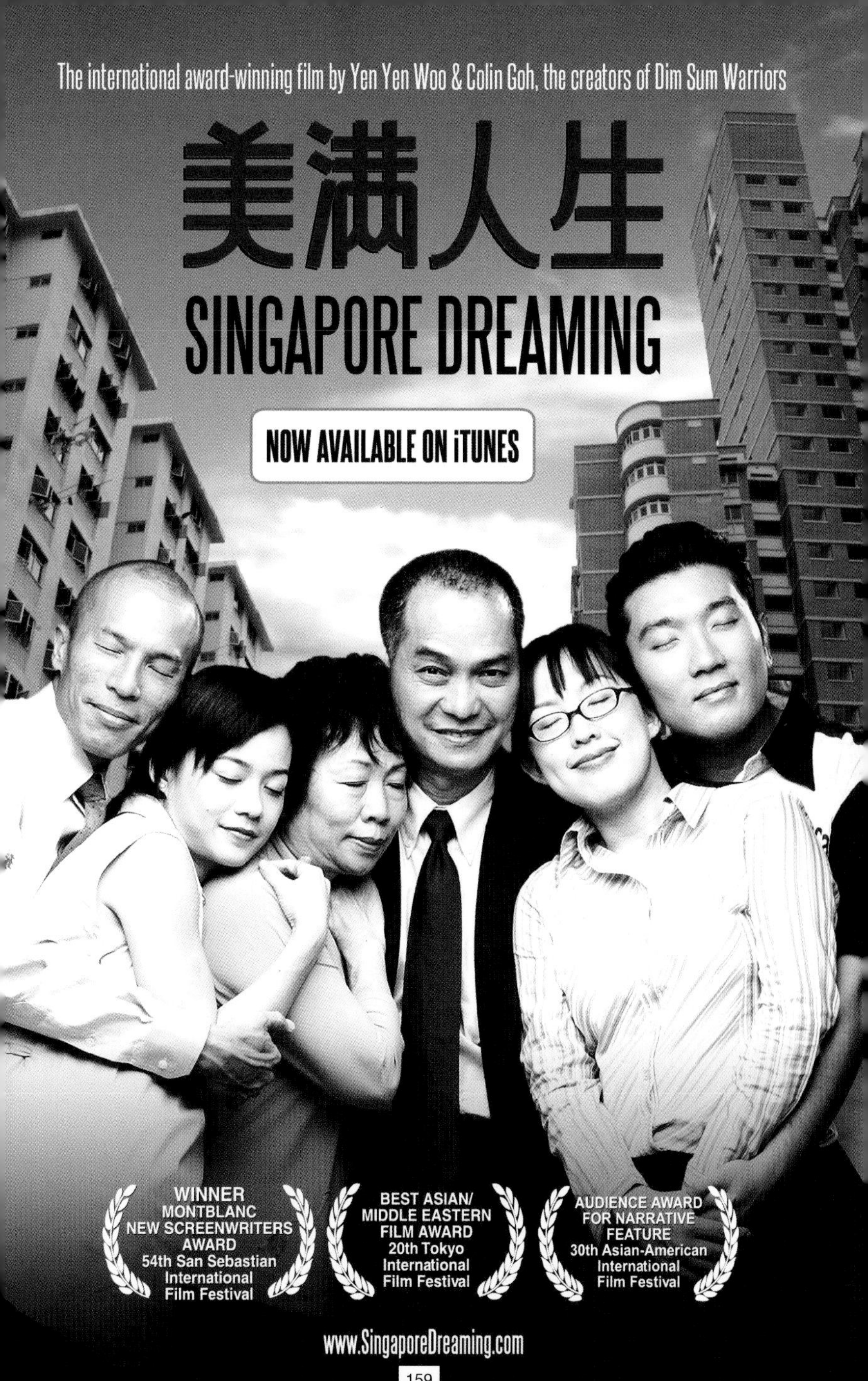
The international award-winning film by Yen Yen Woo & Colin Goh, the creators of Dim Sum Warriors
美满人生
SINGAPORE DREAMING
NOW AVAILABLE ON iTUNES
WINNER MONTBLANC NEW SCREENWRITERS AWARD 54th San Sebastian International Film Festival
BEST ASIAN/ MIDDLE EASTERN FILM AWARD 20th Tokyo International Film Festival
AUDIENCE AWARD FOR NARRATIVE FEATURE 30th Asian-American International Film Festival
www.SingaporeDreaming.com

# Get to Know Us Better!

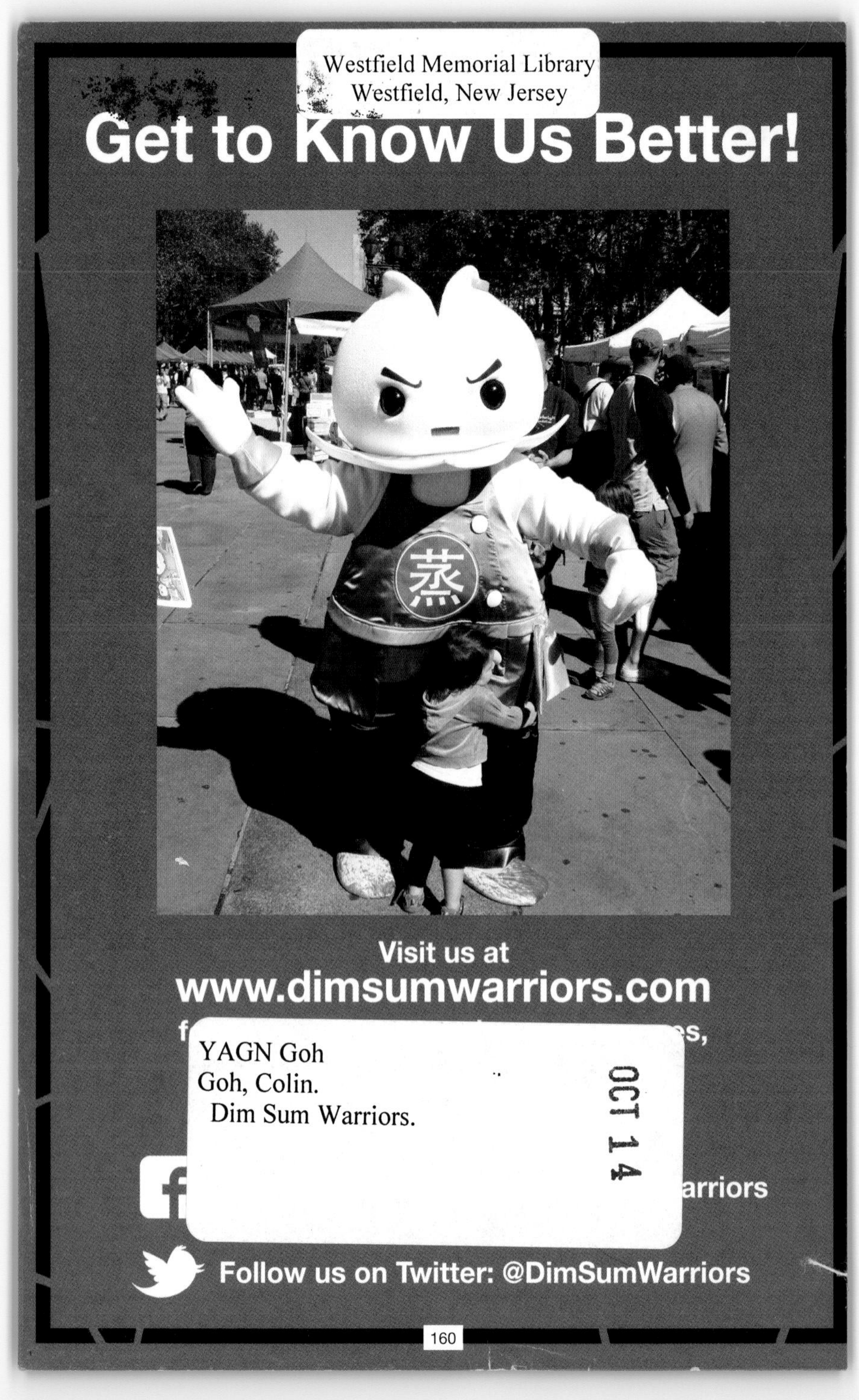
蒸

Visit us at
**www.dimsumwarriors.com**
f es,



arriors

Follow us on Twitter: @DimSumWarriors